D1825479

A STORM OF LIES

A FATHER'S FIGHT
TO RAISE HIS CHLDREN

Randy Zinn

SOR Press
GAITHERSBURG, MARYLAND

Randy Zinn/SOR Press
Gaithersburg, Maryland
www.randy-zinn.com

Publisher's Note: Any names, characters, or places have
been changed to protect anonymity. Any resemblance to
actual people, living or dead, or to businesses, companies,
events, institutions, or locales is coincidental.

A Storm of Lies / Randy Zinn. -- 1st ed.
ISBN 978-1-9536430-8-7 (paperback)
ISBN 978-1-9536431-0-0 (hardcover)

Contents

ACKNOWLEDGEMENTS

Special Thanks to Claire Joseph, Logan Russel, and Daniela Zorrilla

Edited by Kathy Macfarlane

Cover design by JD&J Design

Preface

Thank you for opening my memoir! I have a few notes before we get started.

Men are not known for keeping a diary, but I have since 1990 due to the terrible turmoil that marked my teens and twenties. I've kept doing it ever since, chronicling my life even when I didn't need to work out my distress in its pages. The events recounted herein are a combination of my memory and the sometimes minute detail of my biweekly diary. I often write up to 30,000 words (half a novel) a month. It has allowed me to render this story with a high degree of accuracy.

This memoir is the story of my tumultuous divorce and custody battle, which lasted from early 2016 into 2020. The well-being of my children was at stake, for their mother had a hidden problem that had been slowly destroying our relationship without me knowing the cause. And that secret led to behavior that was harmful to myself and which was starting to impact our children. That impact threatened to become more severe if my ex-wife succeeded in taking the kids away from me and preventing me from seeing them anymore, a desire that was itself destructive. Her chief method to achieve this was deceit, such an extraordinary abundance of seemingly every kind of lie that it led to the title of this book – *A Storm of Lies*.

With one exception, there are no composite characters because the cast is relatively small anyway. That composite is my main attorney, Michelle, and the cheaper, junior one who was often the one I dealt with, but I replaced him with her for ease of reference. Both were physically present and on most phone calls; however, he did the leg work and was often the one updating me or getting details from me, whereas in these pages, I have it being her.

No scenes are combined, with the possible exception of visits to one professional's office or another, whether it be a lawyer or therapist, when these happened in quick succession. Sometimes I couldn't remember which visit featured which subjects, but it's largely immaterial; the tone and substance of conversations are all here. It is, of course, the nature of memoirs to re-create dialogue, and in my case, there is the occasional exact sentence when it was memorable and I wrote it down. In my diary, I often noted the major subjects, sometimes in order, and the lines of logic (particularly when they were absurd), and this made it infinitely easier to recreate the conversations.

All names have been changed for privacy.

CHAPTER ONE

A Kiss for Your Thoughts

She said it mildly, even pleasantly. "Not only am I not kissing you now, but I'm never kissing you again."

I stood very still, my breath trapped in my chest. I wasn't ready to process my pregnant wife's response to me wanting to kiss her. We stood facing the same direction, my left arm still around her shoulder. She'd hardly favored me with a sideways glance during her announcement. Now she turned back to munching on the half-eaten wheat cracker, the remaining portion poised before her lips that had just said something deeply hurtful like her words were no more important than her snack. Leaning on the dark Corian kitchen island, the early afternoon sun streaming in, she paid me no mind as I pulled my arm away, stepped back, and exited the room. My heart clenched.

What the fuck? I thought. I felt confused, hurt, and in turmoil. Where did she get off saying something like that to me? I was too outraged, too disbelieving, too unguarded to speak. Like I always did when upset, I withdrew, not speaking, needing to work it out by myself despite feeling that a rational explanation would not be found in the suddenly dark shadows of my mind.

I stepped from the kitchen at the rear of our three-level townhouse into the mocha-painted dining room with its golden ceiling. Our three-and-a-half-year-old son Dave happily and obliviously played with a train set on the brown carpet. We'd never bothered with a dining room set and the room had become his playroom. No wall separated it from the pale green living room beyond, where a dark green, upholstered couch awaited me. I thought back to the reason there'd been no traditional kiss to ring in the new year two days earlier. I'd intended to make up for that just now and had told Sophia so, only to hear that response.

We'd been at her friend Kate's new house in Northern Virginia, it's hardwood floors and open plan turning the first level into an echo chamber. Kate's pasty white skin was a striking contrast against her naturally red hair, which was cut in a long bob. She was tall, thin, and devoid of body curves except her breasts that seemed larger than their average size precisely because they were the only curve on her. I didn't like her. She was nice enough when she bothered to talk to me, which wasn't often, and she never spoke to me except in a group conversation. It was as if I didn't possess some qualification for having a conversation with directly.

Was I insecure? Not really. I just felt the indifference for what it was: *you're not my friend. You're Sophia's husband. And Sophia's not really my friend. She's Amanda's friend, and Amanda is my friend. I tolerate you, but I wouldn't even notice if I never saw you again. If you happen to say something of interest, maybe I'll acknowledge it with my own comment, but otherwise I'd actually prefer you not be here in my house. Never mind that I've known you for fifteen years.*

I suppose I couldn't blame her. I had come to feel the same.

The rest of the clique was similar, including the husbands and boyfriends and stray brothers and sisters. Sophia was barely their friend anymore because we lived forty-five minutes away, causing them to mostly ditch us years ago. They had complained about the distance if they came to us, likely never noticing that we did not complain when we went to them. They stopped coming to our parties. Then they stopped inviting us to theirs, which had always been at Amanda's house. Some people live such sheltered lives that even a short journey like the one to our house seems crazy to them, and Sophia learned that she wasn't important enough for them to go outside this comfort zone. We had both been offended, a friendship of nearly a decade ending. And then they'd invited us, out of the blue in 2012 when they learned we were expecting our first child, as were several of them, and suddenly they were friends again. I was not, still. I learned that I was just as ignored as I'd always been, and so I never went, but this was New Year's Eve to ring in 2016, and so there I was.

The only nice one among them was Amanda, who had the same body style, hair (albeit it black), and pasty skin as Kate. But Amanda was the opposite of her. She was friendly, genuine and down-to-earth. Her husband and I had held one conversation in fifteen years, and when I'd told Sophia we'd talked for once, she had laughed and said that all the women always complained about how anti-social their husbands were. Sophia was the lucky one, they'd say, in having me. Part of me had been a little flattered, but I had mostly been surprised. If they thought I was so social, why did most of them avoid talking to me?

I was usually crazy bored at these parties and only came to keep an eye on Dave because I knew Sophia wouldn't. Sometimes I drank too much wine to help pass the time and because I was trying to make myself feel better about spending four hours with people I'd known for fifteen years but only having four conversations by night's end. But for this New Year's Eve, I drank little to make sure I'd drive home sober and avoid a ticket or worse. My son was old enough now to opt for playing with the other kids his age instead of me. I was left alone, feigning contentment with my isolation despite thirty people being all around me. I would have preferred to be anywhere else.

I watched Sophia, no baby bump showing yet. For some reason, she had insisted on not telling them she was two months pregnant with our second child. Since she hadn't tried to lose the baby weight from Dave, her voluptuous hips were wider, her butt and thighs larger, and at 5'2" to my 6'3", the weight affected her appearance more than it might have for someone taller. She wore light makeup, but she put it on thick when we went somewhere formal, and I had often wondered if this was influenced by her being Russian. A few streaks of grey were visible in her straight black hair, which hung past her shoulders. Her jaw was square, her cheekbones low. Her dark brown eyes had long since lost whatever warmth I'd once found in them, some crooked teeth seldom seen because she didn't smile often anymore. Or at least, not with me. She was laughing now, chatting it up with her friends as I sat eyeing the clock and thinking it was nearly time to go.

I turned to see Dave playing ten feet from me, shoeless like everyone at the party. His round head accentuated his happy cherub personality. He had Sophia's thick hair with my dirty blond coloring, but unlike either of us, his was a little curly. He shared our brown eyes, always twinkling with delight when he looked at me. He already had my height and Sophia's big bones, a professional football player in waiting. He was a gentle giant, sweet, pleasant, and cooperative unless you were hoping to make him try food. I adored him. As I watched, he suddenly slipped and fell forward fast and hard, slamming his mouth on the edge of a coffee table.

Oh shit! I thought, leaping to my feet.

When kids really hurt themselves, there's a moment of silence as the pain slowly builds. In that stillness, they're in shock, not sure if they really hurt themselves as their little body briefly numbs the pain. I picked him up as the gasping shrieks and tears began. Everyone in the room stopped and turned their attention to us as I sat him down on my leg, trying to comfort him. To my horror, blood dripped from his mouth! Sophia arrived and we tried to survey the damage, which didn't look too bad despite all the blood. We agreed that it was time to go home, being nearly 11 pm, which was well past his bedtime. Only now did I realize that in the chaos of arriving, we had forgotten to remove our son's socks, which weren't the kind with little sticky pads to improve traction on the wood floors. The inevitable had finally happened and I felt horrible for it. My empathy for his physical and emotional pain had me assuring him it would fade, he'd be alright, and there was no lasting damage. This wasn't forever, just a minute and he'd be okay again.

"Why don't I take him upstairs and start changing him," I began, dabbing a now red tissue against his mouth. "Can you find the diaper bag and bring it up?" We had already planned to change him for the night before leaving, knowing he'd fall asleep in the car.

"Okay," she agreed.

"I wanna go home!" Dave wailed through uncontrollable sobs and not for the first time.

"It's okay, buddy," I said in a soothing voice, rubbing his back. "We're gonna go." As I carried him upstairs, I repeated the plan to him, adding details about how soon the pain would fade, how he'd be asleep before he knew it, and he'd wake up in the morning feeling better. In a bedroom, I laid him on the bed and undressed him. He was calming but still crying to go home. I had thought Sophia would be here by now, but there was no sign of her. The room was cold, so I piled the clothes I had just removed back on him.

What is she doing? I wondered. It doesn't take this long.

Several minutes passed and I grew increasingly irritated. Sophia was forever telling me that she was going to do something and then ended up not doing it. I hated it. Lying. That's what it was. It had been eroding my trust in her for years. This was worse. Our injured son needed her and the sight of him still crying so hard upset me. I didn't even have tissues to wipe his tears or nose with and had to use part of the clothes I'd removed from him. The next step in making him feel better depended on his mother arriving and she was failing to do so. What was more important than her hurt son?

"Dave, listen, I'll be right back."

"Daddy! Don't leave!" he cried from the bed.

"I'm just going to the top of the stairs to call down for mommy, okay?"

"No!"

"Just stay here. I'll be right back."

"I wanna go home!"

I knew he wouldn't stay. He was too attached to me, especially when he was distressed.

I rose, ran to the stairs, and hollered down into the noisy party. No response. I returned to find a naked Dave almost at the doorway. I picked him up and put him back on the bed, piling the clothes on again. His mother didn't arrive. I went to the staircase to call for Sophia twice more and each time Dave followed me. He was calmer now. I silently grew progressively agitated because I knew from experience what his mother was doing. Knowing it was pointless, I told Dave to stay put. This time I ran down the hardwood stairs as fast as I dared in slippery socks, gripping the handrail. I reached the bottom and turned.

And there she stood, the black diaper bag slung over one shoulder as she leaned against a pillar with the other. She had a wine glass in one hand. She stood gaily chatting with Amanda, oblivious to our son's distress, just as I'd expected. I approached her from behind and yanked the bag off her shoulder without a word before turning and running up the stairs. Once again, I found Dave nearing the steps. In my haste, I'd neglected to close the baby safety gate to keep him from tumbling down. I changed his clothes and he eventually stopped crying as I carried him down the stairs, the bag over a shoulder. At the bottom, I looked over to Sophia. She hadn't moved. Kate had now joined the conversation and they were all laughing.

"We're leaving!" I announced, raising my voice over distance and noise. I didn't wait for a response. Both Dave and I soon had on our shoes and coats. I picked him and the bag up and headed for the door, glancing back as I opened it. Sophia still hadn't moved.

"We're leaving," I yelled once more, "with or without you." This time, Amanda made eye contact with me just before I walked out the door. My breath was visible in the frosty winter night air. I had no qualms about leaving Sophia there. She was a grown woman at the house of friends, so it wasn't like I was leaving her penniless on a street corner. And my son was my priority. His mother had once again shown her true colors.

I soon had Dave in the backseat of my beige, Acura MDX, where it was parked on the street. I had just buckled myself in, turned the car on, and put in gear when a knock came at my window. There stood Amanda without a coat, arms folded against the cold. I rolled the window down.

"Hey," she said, "she's coming. I'm sorry. We didn't have a chance to say goodbye."

I frowned in resignation and nodded. "Yeah, sorry, I have to get him home."

"Sure. How is he doing?"

"He's better. Fat lip but the bleeding has stopped. Guess I'll be starting the new year at the emergency clinic tomorrow."

"Yeah. I'm sorry. Here she comes."

Amanda left and Sophia got in the back seat beside Dave. We rode in icy silence all the way home, forty-five minutes of it, Dave lulled to sleep within minutes from the car's motion. Once I'd parked inside the double garage that took up half of the first floor, Sophia went inside without a word, leaving me to take both the diaper bag and a sleeping Dave. Despite the tendonitis in both of my arms making it unpleasant, I carried him up to the third floor of our townhouse and laid him on a low, inflatable mattress. I carefully removed the jacket to avoid waking him. Sophia and I didn't speak. She soon went into his room to sleep beside him, as she had been doing for more than a month now, because he'd been having trouble sleeping, and I went to bed alone, again.

On New Year's Day, I took Dave to an emergency clinic alone. I was relieved to learn he had no permanent damage. The incident the night before was the reason his mother and I hadn't kissed on New Year's Eve, a fact I hadn't noticed until January 2nd, and that's when I entered the kitchen and approached Sophia.

"You know, we didn't do a New Year's Eve kiss." I put my left arm around her shoulders. That I was intending to kiss her was obvious.

"Not only am I not kissing you now," she began serenely, "but I'm never kissing you again."

I now sat on the couch in silence, hurt, angry, and in turmoil. She had crossed a line. You can't say that to your spouse and expect to remain married to them. It doesn't matter if you're upset, though she hadn't sounded the least bit troubled. The clash between the hate-filled words and the pleasant way in which she'd uttered them was a weapon of quiet aggression. An invisible intrusion on my psyche, like some phantom of rage lurking in the corner of my mind but never really showing itself. I questioned myself. Was it really there? Did I hear wrong? Did she say what I think she just said? I struggled to reconcile the hurtful words with the nonchalant demeanor as she said them, a near total mismatch so odd that it messed with my head and heart. I couldn't trust it. Couldn't trust *her*. I felt conflicted. Which was I to believe, the words or the delivery? The doubts she created in me were part of the hostility, the line of attack. I wondered if she had done it that way on purpose.

As the week continued, we pretended the remark hadn't been made. It was the elephant in the room. We hadn't been speaking much anyway since early December when she had announced she was experiencing some depression and wanting space. As with her previous episodes, she didn't specify the cause. Our conversations about it had never allowed either of us to uncover the underlying reasons, leaving us unable to resolve it. It appeared to come and go on its own. As a result, I didn't ask about it much this time, having learned there appeared to be no answer.

Wanting space was a red flag of the impending death of our relationship, but I didn't see it. We had just agreed to have another child in October and she was now pregnant. It never occurred to me that she'd swing from agreeing to expand our family to obliterating it. We'd been married for fifteen years, together for sixteen, so maybe I was off my game.

Whether divorce was on her mind or not, I didn't know, but it had increasingly been on mine since Dave's birth in August of 2012. She had increasingly pulled away without explanation, our relationship becoming more like roommates, all passion gone. We didn't talk about our lives much either, as she wasn't interested in anything I wanted to talk about anymore. She would do things like agree to spend time together when Dave napped and then find an excuse not to be present when the time came. My attempts to resolve this were rebuffed as she acted like it was a co-incidence, despite it happening with few exceptions. I had felt alone in my marriage for a long time and felt certain there was no recovery, and that I would live a loveless life unless I divorced her and moved on with someone new.

But no one in my family had gone through a divorce despite marital problems, all of them somehow staying the course. For someone as laid back and forgiving as I was, the idea of being the first seemed peculiar. I'd never heard anything good about the effect divorce had on children. I didn't want to put Dave through that. His mother and I seldom fought, because we both wanted to walk away if we'd lost our cool. And yet, before the week was over, I changed my mind about divorce and I wanted out. She did it again and I couldn't take it any longer.

I came down the stairs, having just carried a sleeping Dave to his inflatable bed. Sophia wouldn't need to sleep with him this time. "Well," I began, seeing her nearing me as she moved to the kitchen, "I guess you can sleep in our room tonight."

"I'm never sleeping in the same bed with you again," she calmly informed me, continuing past me without a glance.

My heart slammed in my chest as if it were trying to fight against being ripped out by the sudden unexpected pain inflicted on it. I literally felt it, the door closing in my heart, sealing it off from her, never to be opened again. I was in shock and I was confused. Resentment building quickly. It all vanished as swiftly as it had come. It was remarkable really, the suddenness of my emotionless state, as I made a long overdue life changing decision, one I had been in denial about for the longest of time. And maybe that was the reason for the speed. I'd held out for so long, all while she was snipping away at the threads of our life, of our love, like Atropos, the oldest of the Three Fates. Sophia had finally snipped one too many – apart from Dave there was nothing left between us. Nothing held us together anymore. I was frozen to the spot, holding my breath and trapped in the moment of awfulness. Sophia had given me so many of these awful moments. It was a harbinger of what was to come. I accepted that she meant it without hesitation because of the cold distance that had been creeping over us like a new Ice Age.

Then I took in a slow breath through my nose. Calm. Clear. Resolute.

I want a divorce, I thought. I'm done.

That she was pregnant presented issues, ones I'd worry about later, but for the moment, I felt invigorated. Free. There was a way out of this cold, awful marriage, which reminded me of an idea – if you drop a frog in a boiling pot of water, it will jump out, but put it in cold water, then turn up the heat, it will stay there until boiled alive. It was time to jump out.

That was the day we stopped talking. We have rarely spoken since. Not about anything important at least and never for long when we did need to speak about the little things such as childcare or schedule changes. Almost all communication went via texts. I was the primary reason for this. If I could say something as innocent as telling her that I was going to kiss her and getting an icy response in return, then open season had been declared on me. It's not like I'd called her a bitch and could predict nastiness in return. The only way to ward off another awful remark was by not talking to her. I began looking up divorce and custody issues.

It was around this time that she began saying, "I can't talk because he's here" when she answered her phone. She'd then climb the stairs to Dave's room, and close the door. One day when I walked into the master bedroom, she was nude from a shower and hastily covered herself with a towel, like I was a stranger. I scowled, baffled, but I said nothing as I grabbed what I had come for and left the room. I knew every inch of her body, and she mine, going back sixteen years. We'd given each other erotic massages, washed each other in the shower or bath, and certainly been intimate in all the ways married people with children are. For what reason could she possibly cover herself?

One afternoon, as she sat working on her laptop on the couch, I walked past her feet and she lowered the lid most of the way. Once I'd stepped farther beyond, she opened it up again. The impression was that she didn't want me to see what she was doing, even though I was in front of her and couldn't see anyway. It happened again within the hour and when she left the room, she closed the lid all the way, effectively locking it. Suspicion swirling, I walked over to her phone and pressed the keypad. It wanted a six-digit code to access it and I went cold. We'd both had the same four-digit code for years because the goal was to keep out strangers, not each other. She had changed it, as I'd half expected.

Sophia was hiding something. I knew that she wouldn't tell me if I asked and she might just say something cruel again. If I knew what it was, would it explain the suddenly odd behavior? As I pondered on this though, it dawned on me that I almost didn't care. It wouldn't save our marriage. The wall around my heart had just been reinforced. But no one likes wondering, especially when the possibilities can rip your heart wide open.

My suspicions were about to soar.

CHAPTER TWO

A Final Agreement

Sophia may not have noticed that I seldom spoke to her anymore – and if she did, she certainly hadn't shown it. She had wanted her space. I now wanted mine, but I said nothing. We adopted the sort of behavior strangers exhibit in a large city's teeming streets, walking past each other without acknowledgment. The tension was thick, silent, menacing, hidden but naked all the same. A mutual awareness existed between us, a silent agreement that allowed us to avoid being in the same room overlong and risk interaction, but that was all. We weren't on a crowded metropolis street, but inside a townhouse empty of all life except us, our son, and the cat.

I would wait until after the baby was born, I decided, before filing for divorce. No sense in putting stress on Sophia while she was carrying my child. I wasn't an asshole, regardless of how hurt and angry I was. Divorcing her while she was pregnant would be cruel and it was not the example I wanted to set for Dave. Looking back, it seems funny that I had wanted to spare her this, given what she was planning for me.

Her offer to have a second kid had come as a surprise. I was twenty-nine when we met in 2000, she was twenty-

15

four. Our romance had been swift and passionate. She had invited me to spend the night on our first date but she wanted to wait before having sex or any fooling around. I promised that I wouldn't try anything and I didn't. My word mattered to me. That night we crammed into her little bed in the apartment she shared with a guy. She'd later told me how desperately lonely she'd been and how she'd often cried herself to sleep, dreaming of someone to just sleep beside her and hold her. And then there I was.

We initially bonded over my extracurricular activities, as she didn't seem to have them and mine interested her. Horseback riding had been the first, as I was taking lessons and she'd also had some before. We did it on that first date and it became a monthly experience for years. We loved doing something we'd only done alone before, sharing tips, frustrations, and achievements. In time, we also rode bicycles in a nearby park after I bought myself one with her input. I was even able to get her on the back of my motorcycle, despite the passenger position on a sport bike being a tough one, but I got her a helmet and she clung to my back as we hugged corners on local outings. I'd always ridden alone before, so I was finally sharing another hobby.

I had been a season ticket holder to the Baltimore Symphony Orchestra (BSO) years before we met and wanted to return, so we began regularly going after stopping in Little Italy for fine candlelight dining. I wore slacks and a sport coat, Sophia looked lovely in an evening dress, heels, and new jewelry I'd gotten her. We later took up Latin dancing after weekly lessons, going to local events where we could show our moves and try to meet other couples. We both became wine drinkers, often going to local wineries or festivals together, even traveling to Charlottesville, Virginia to spend a weekend with my sister and her family, in the middle of wine country. Our anniversaries often included winery visits, horseback riding, and a bed and breakfast.

I got her into skiing, being her teacher, and we did day trips together, splitting the driving duties. When we met, I was working as a tour assistant (TA) on random weekends for a ski company and she took the training, joined, too, and we worked the same weekends together, getting free lift tickets and room and board in exchange for a little work. We started taking cruises to Bermuda, the Bahamas, and various Caribbean locations, catching shows onboard, taking part in group games, and going on excursions that ranged from jet skiing to snorkeling (we bought our own gear), swimming with sharks, a dolphin encounter, city tours, and more. I had wanted to move to California but hadn't decided where and she went with me on a ten-day scouting trip while enjoying Yosemite, the Redwoods, and the Mt. Shasta area as I had done once before. But we decided the job market was too good back home.

All of this was in addition to the typical date nights with dinner and a movie. We liked the same types of films and shows and for the same reasons of adventure, humor, and style. And we seldom had to convince the other about doing any of these things. We almost always wanted the same thing, got excited about the same possibilities. It even happened with food, as we not only cooked together, but wanted the exact same meals – the same type of noodles/rice/potatoes with the meat, the same kind of vegetables. We'd finish each other's sentence about it, both laughing. And I had thought many times that if I couldn't make it work with her, I couldn't make it work with anyone. I'd had fewer than a handful of things in common with anyone I'd known before, and with her there were over a hundred.

One of the earliest things that had brought us together was my music and fiction. I had always been alone with them, hardly anyone willing to listen to one of my songs or read one of my books. I was a good enough author to eventually hit the best sellers lists in my categories on Amazon. As a musician, I had a Bachelor of Music in classical guitar but was really a composer first, and rock/acoustic guitarist second. Many called me a virtuoso and during our marriage, I would record and release multiple albums on my own record label, earning endorsements from Alvarez Guitars, Morley Pedals, and Peavey, and performing locally with my band. Sophia not only encouraged all of this, but would read and listen to my work, even letting me show her how I wrote and recorded music. This was my life's passion and I finally had someone to share it with.

She commented back then that she loved that I was artistic and yet highly technical, being a software developer like her. I had critical thinking and yet was passionate and romantic. I was philosophical, educated, and paid attention to world events. She didn't have to drag me to the symphony, ballet, or opera, as I took her. I was equally comfortable there as at a rock concert, but I was no drug user or alcoholic. I could spend all day reading (or writing) a book but could also get on my sport bike and take her for a ride. She seemed to think I was everything.

And I had found her to be smart, mentally quick, thoughtful, and able to hold an intellectual conversation. Our earliest ones had lasted for hours as we couldn't get off the phone with each other. She had cared what was happening in my life. She hadn't really seemed to have one outside of work until meeting me, but it didn't matter to me. She was pleasant to spend time with, wonderful to talk to, and in the early days, as physically passionate as I was. She wasn't funny, but she thought I was, and she both sought and took my advice, as I did hers. She learned about many troubling experiences I had gone through growing up, from bullying to dealing with disabilities, and things I had never told anyone, and through it all she was a compassionate, insightful, and comforting listener. Sophia became far and away the best friend I'd ever had, and I was the same to her.

And I loved her.

We never spent a weekend apart after the night of our first date – most of the things I just mentioned hadn't started yet. Within months she was moving into my two-bedroom apartment in the same county where I'd grown up. We'd been reckless during that time. We made love late one night, and while caught up in the heat of the moment, we hadn't used any protection. Realizing it afterward, we stopped worrying about it, and the inevitable happened. She became pregnant.

A flurry of conversations happened, and somewhere along the way, I was the first to admit to wanting kids. I had seen so many sitcom moments where a woman said it first and the guy hesitated before reluctantly agreeing that he wanted the same even though he was lying, afraid of losing the girl. I didn't want to be that guy, not from fear of losing her, but because I wanted her to know that it was something I really wanted and that I would be there for her. There would be no hesitation from me, no half-assed involvement as a parent. I was all in, even if the timing was bad since we'd only been dating for two months.

And so I said it first. It was Sophia who hesitated before saying she wanted kids one day, too. I hadn't seen that coming, the woman pausing. Had I believed a stereotype, that all women wanted kids?

We only told one friend, Alexa, a Greek woman who had introduced us. She was a year or two older than Sophia, tall, big-boned, a little hippy and ungainly, with droopy eyes and frizzy blonde hair past her shoulders. She was somehow both down-to-earth and flighty, like she had common sense but too vivid an imagination. She openly admitted to having ADHD and boy did it show. Alexa talked non-stop and was more than a little pushy with her opinions. She scared most people into not wanting to talk to her because a conversation with her was like being run over by an out-of-control car that mowed down everything in its path without ever losing speed. She had enough self-awareness to know that she was annoying and she would be the first to admit it, as if that mitigated this or gave you permission to also poke fun at her for it, like she did. I don't think she really granted *me* permission, of course, but I took it anyway. I had initially hated her – there was only so much exasperation I could take. She knew that she annoyed me, and somehow our mutual ribbing of her con-siderable personality quirks had turned us into friends.

I had worked with Alexa at my software development job and could never get her out of my office if she entered. We commiserated over coworkers and their quirks. She took breaks at my desk, commenting that I was the only non-full-of-shit person around, and she enjoyed my di-rectness. She had her own honesty, though "direct" didn't apply to her because of the way her mind ran all over the place, but it was there. Underneath our outwardly different styles was a similar down-to-earth quality that, if I'd been attracted to her, might have led to romantic interest from me. But we stuck to friendship and had fun doing things like spiking the holiday eggnog with a little too much vod-ka so that no one drank it except us. And with so much leftover, we kept sneaking down every day at lunch to raid it for a bit.

One day I'd taught her the basics of Microsoft Access, a database program, where you can develop screens, reports, and more by using the interface. And that's what I'd shown her, not code. She was no programmer like me, but then she got laid off and took a job at Verizon...as a software developer, making five figures more than me. I was being underpaid that much and with my job having become dissatisfactory in other ways, this became the last straw. I soon quit for greener pastures.

Around that time, Alexa invited me to lunch with her new coworkers, which included an old school friend – Amanda – and a new friend – Sophia. I was the only guy and I couldn't keep up with the chatter. Alexa noticed and tried to interest me in Sophia, but I demurred, having not spoken with Sophia before. Six months later, Alexa invited me to another hang out with them and their boyfriends, plus Sophia, at a pool hall. This time I rolled out my particular brand of flirting. My opportunity came when there weren't enough pool cues to go around and I joked that I would "only let Sophia play with my stick." After pool, Alexa made us sit together in a booth and more chemistry followed, so before long I had Sophia's number and a date.

When Sophia fell pregnant two months later, it was Alexa who helped us work through the emotions and consequences of any decision we would take. After much debate, Sophia and I agreed that we weren't ready to have kids yet. It was too soon, though Sophia admitted that the pregnancy made her happy. So was I, but once we decided to have an abortion, we both knew we had made the right decision. I went with her and we told no one else. To this day, even my parents don't know.

Six months into our relationship and Sophia was all moved into my two-bedroom apartment and we were engaged shortly thereafter. We were married six months later in October 2001, at the nearest courthouse, neither of us being religious. Only a few friends attended, including Amanda and my best friend, who before long moved halfway around the world. We had a small reception at my parent's house that afternoon and then the big reception the next day.

After getting hitched, we agreed to wait five years before having kids, so we could enjoy life and our time together without those responsibilities. But as 2006 rolled around, she suggested we put it off and I agreed. We still had time. Again and again we postponed it, the joke being that we were six, then seven, then eight years into the five-year plan. Being the youngest of three kids, with an older brother and sister, I had said I wanted three kids – boy, girl, and a "spare" like me – and Sophia had responded with wanting just one and "let's see how it goes!"

But as the years had passed, her resistance to having kids rose even as my desire increased. She exclusively expressed negative sentiments to me about the prospect, usually citing how much work they were. There wasn't a romantic thought in her head about having kids, as far as I could tell. But by then I'd picked up on one of her personality quirks–she thought both good and bad things about something, but only said one or the other, usually the bad. This may have been like oppositional disorder, because my positive remarks were always met with a negative one from her. Then again, perhaps she really didn't want kids and I was just missing the sign.

I had definitely missed a more obvious one. In the early 2000s, my sister married a man with three young boys, and for ten years, we visited them in Charlottesville. On one visit, we suddenly realized Sophia had vanished in the big house, so I went looking for her and found her locked in an upstairs bathroom.

"Are you okay?" I asked through the door.

"Yeah," her tired tone belying her words.

"Are you sure? Do you need anything?"

"Yeah, to be left alone."

So then she was not okay. I assumed something physical as the cause, since she was presumably sitting on the toilet. Otherwise why have the door closed? "Why? What's the matter?"

She let out a big sigh. "I just can't take the kids anymore. I need some quiet time."

That struck me as odd. The boys were a little rowdy, but I never saw anything more than boys being boys. My concern vanished because I didn't take this seriously, to be honest. In fact, when I told my sister and her husband Sophia's remark, we all laughed, thinking Sophia was a bit of a lightweight.

As her stalling to have kids dragged on, I began to despair. I began wondering if she had lied about wanting them? Or had she changed her mind? I asked but she wouldn't say. Was I going to be faced with the decision to stay with the woman I loved or divorce her and find someone else? Because I was growing certain that not having kids was a dealbreaker for me.

I increasingly fantasized about teaching my kids one thing or another and it wasn't the stereotypical dad stuff like throwing a baseball or riding a bike. It was more about being fair-minded, dealing with bullies, how to view challenges. Some of my daydreams were for when they were older, like how to cook, or get a good deal on a car, and how to decide what you wanted out of life. I wanted to give them the kind of guidance I never got from anyone. My kids wouldn't learn things the hard way like I did. As a child, I had learned from my parents and older siblings that if I asked a question about anything in life, they would mock my ignorance, even call me stupid, and so I'd stopped asking. The result had been floundering into all sorts of personal problems that likely could have been avoided had I just known a thing or two. I had long since let go of the resentment (mostly), and I couldn't bear the idea of my kids feeling that way about me or going through anything I could spare them.

I sometimes wondered if being able to do good things for my wife and I had strengthened my paternal instincts, bringing out the desire to provide and care for someone. Even taking care of our various cats over the years might have. I had a lot to give but sometimes it seemed like Sophia just had a lot she wanted to take. As we both entered our 30s, her biological clock was ticking and in the end that was why she finally agreed in 2011, to have a child at the age of thirty-four. We did all the usual things to get ready, from baby-proofing to parenting classes at the hospital. Despite my eagerness to be a dad, preparations were all I could think of when someone asked me if I was excited, because it dominated my mind and activities. Sophia always ducked the question, but at least she never said no.

David was born twenty-five days early in August 2012, in the middle of the Olympics. Sophia's water broke after I helped her to bed, but she remained in denial about that all the way to the ER until they checked her in. Dave was facing the wrong way and had to be delivered by C-section. I was brought into the delivery room moments before they pulled him out around 2am, Sophia's lower half-obscured by a blue sheet, the doctors all in blue scrubs. Sedated but awake, she smiled about not feeling a thing.

The nurse cleaned Dave up and brought him to me, not Sophia, who was too sedated to hold him. He was quiet, eyes closed, a bundle of uncertainty in my arms. I'm not going to lie and pretend tears of joy poured down my face. I felt relief more than anything else, for there was so much worry about becoming a first-time parent that it overshadowed everything else. Was I the only new parent who felt that way about their first? Maybe I was more practical for all my dreams of that moment. Well, I had dreamed of later moments, really, so maybe it came as no surprise that my joy was a bit muted. It wouldn't be until Dave's personality began to emerge in the days ahead that I began to feel the joy of being a dad.

As for Sophia, she seemed more resigned to being a mother than anything. She took care of his physical needs, like diapering and feeding, and buying him clothes. She used the breast pump for over a year, both at home and at work, both of us cleaning the bottles and equipment regularly. And yet during all of it, she was distant from our son, not wanting to read to him or play with him. She did not try to make him smile or laugh. She never made baby sounds to him. She seemed to have no interest beyond his physical body, and while she took great care there, it seemed like a duty. Granted, some of it isn't exactly fun, but something like a bath can be a time for play. While I tried to make it fun for us, she just got it over with and did the bare minimum.

In the years that followed, we sometimes talked about having more kids. Sophia's stance was always the same – she wasn't sure that she could handle more kids, it was too much work and that having brothers and sisters hadn't exactly worked out in my family. Maybe Dave was better off alone. She had a point, but I had a better one: having seen what could go wrong, I would twist myself into a pretzel to make sure my kids got along with each other.

My brother was almost four-and-a-half years older than me. My sister about two years older. They hated each other and hadn't spoken since the year 2000. Their seemingly constant fighting over perceived and actual insults had largely ruined my family, with me caught in the middle or as collateral damage. My brother had always ignored me unless he wanted something. My sister wasn't much better, often insulting and bossy, but that was due to her personal demons. Her normal personality could be fun, but you never knew when she'd go a little nuts with anger, false accusations, and inciting hostility. My relationship with her, and hers with our parents, had ended for good in 2010 after one such incident.

The troubles between my siblings had as much to do with parental mismanagement as the bad attitudes of my brother and sister. I would listen to my kids, not silence and ignore them. I would help them get along, not let them fight until they were screaming and cursing at each other. I would be involved in their lives, not too interested in myself to care.

Sophia was an only child. At age three, her parents divorced and her father abandoned her. She never saw him again except for one time in her late teens, when she learned that he'd remarried and had had other kids – her half brothers and sisters – and had stayed with them while acting like she didn't exist. I knew he was an asshole the moment I heard this, and I hated him. She'd had zero contact with those half-siblings and didn't know their names. She acted indifferent toward her father, but in an unguarded moment, could admit to hating him. She'd partly lost her mother and home, too. Forced to get a job as a teacher in Moscow, Nina gave Sophia to her parents to raise in the Russian countryside during the week. Sophia and her mother were not close. Sophia acted like all of this was no big deal, but I think it left a mark that might've turned her into a ticking bomb that would eventually destroy our marriage.

In her teens, Sophia moved alone to North Carolina for one college first and then another, leaving her old life behind – not there had been much of a life to leave behind. She didn't have much of a life in the U.S. either. Sophia had few friends, no boyfriends before me, just a few uninspiring fumblings in the dark. Eventually she moved to Northern Virginia for a job at Verizon, where she met Amanda. It was Amanda who then welcomed an old friend Alexa to the company and Alexa then introduced me to them. Two years after marrying, we bought the house in 2003, and before long, all those friends drifted away. It wasn't until learning she was pregnant with Dave in 2011, and that most of them were, too, that they all suddenly became best friends again, bonding over being pregnant together.

While I was soon thrilled to have Dave, Sophia seldom said anything good about being a mother. I had to settle for catching her smiling at him. I lobbied on Dave's behalf many times, saying he deserved a brother or sister. He was such a great little kid. He was always happy, smiling, and easy going. Even Sophia had to admit we'd gotten lucky. I slowly began to accept that I might not have another kid, not to mention two, and it filled me with a deep sadness that would send me into a depressive state. We didn't talk about it often, and when we did, it was seldom for long, because Sophia always said something negative about being a parent. It hurt me deeply to hear it. It sounded like she regretted having Dave and that was a stab in my heart. Our talks became short because I did my best to avoid hearing that from her. Did she *know* she could make me drop the subject that way?

So it came as quite the surprise in the late summer of 2015 when she changed her mind without us having talked about it for months.

"I might be willing to have another kid," she ruefully said, sitting down next to me on the couch.

I turned away from my laptop with a mock look of concern that she'd gone insane. "What?"

She laughed. "I know. I know. I must be crazy. But there's one condition, and it's a big one."

"Okay, what is it?" I put one hand on hers.

"That I don't work for two years after the baby is born."

"Two? That's a long time."

"I know, but I can't handle working and having two kids. It's too much for me."

I cocked an eyebrow. We both worked 40 hours a week, with a similar commute, but I was the primary caregiver to Dave. I did almost everything around the house, and I had written and published three novels during 2014-2015 after his birth. She mostly sat on the couch when home. Understandably, being pregnant and giving birth were difficult, but she wasn't suggesting not working during that, but for long after. Once she'd recovered from maternity leave, she'd presumably go back to being a couch potato. I didn't understand what was "too much" for her about it and she didn't explain. I didn't push it either – I couldn't let the offer of another kid slip away and I didn't care much what condition it came with. That said, I talked her into one year and "we'll see how it goes!"

It was true that she was often tired. We had never figured out why and it had been going on since before Dave's birth. One explanation was Lyme disease, which she'd gotten from a tick bite. Some people never fully recover. She had often been depressed, too, and unable to find a reason. We'd occasionally talk about it. She would say that she *should* be happy because she had a great job, a great husband, a great kid, a house, a car, etc., and yet she wasn't. We'd joked that maybe she was having an early midlife crisis. We had this talk for years.

A part of me didn't take her claim of fatigue too seriously – she always claimed to have no energy to help around the house, and yet she'd drive an hour to the barn where she kept her horse, saddle him, and ride for an hour or two before giving him a thorough shower and cleaning. She would bring home all of her leather of saddles, tack, and more, spending two hours conditioning them. She was like the female version of the stereotype of the man who claimed to be too tired to help his wife but then had the energy to work on his car. Honestly, I felt taken advantage of. It was the cause of many arguments and much resentment for me. It was the first lethal injection into our relationship. She hadn't ridden much since Dave had been born, and yet she refused to sell the horse that cost hundreds a month to stable.

She stopped taking the pill when she made her offer of another kid and I accepted. We were in the middle of a frequent and particularly upsetting routine of hers – withholding sex for months. She always started this by saying she was having "feminine problems" like a urinary tract infection (UTI). She would insist on no physical contact at all – no kissing, no hugging, and no hand holding. Even sitting next to each other was off limits. Her excuse was a slap across the face – that if any of that happens, guys assume you want to have sex and since that was out, so was everything else. I was offended, hurt, and a little mad. It made me bitter. I wasn't just some guy. I was her husband! We seldom argued about it anymore because I already knew nothing would change. Even reminding her of our first platonic night together didn't change anything.

"That was an exception."

I replied, "No, it wasn't. How many times have I kissed you and made no attempt at having sex?"

"Whatever."

This was something she'd taken to saying years earlier. The thoughtful, compassionate conversationalist I had wanted to spend the rest of my life with had slowly vanished and I still didn't know why.

"Don't say 'whatever' to me."

"Whatever."

"Damnit Sophia, stop dismissing what I say. And stop telling me that I want sex when I don't. Who are you to tell me what my intentions or desires are? It's arrogant. I'm the authority on that, not you."

"Whatever."

"Jerk."

There is a natural progression in a romantic relationship, from no physical contact to intercourse, when intimacy becomes normal. She would artificially kill our intimacy then leave it dead for months. There would finally come a day when she'd make an announcement.

"I'm ready for you to woo me now," she said, putting down a glass of wine as we stood in the kitchen, me cleaning up after the dinner I'd made as she stood idly by, not helping. Those days had passed.

I scowled in irritation. "You're *what*?"

"I'm ready for you to woo me."

"What does *that* mean?"

"I'm ready for you to take me on dates. Maybe you'll get lucky."

I frowned as I put cutlery and plates into the dishwasher. "So what, you expect me to do all the work to revive the intimacy of our relationship again, when you're the one who killed it? Is that it?"

"Yes."

"Why is it my job alone?" I said incredulously, turning to a dirty pot in the sink and starting the water.

"It just is." She said coolly.

"Then I'll take a hard pass. Why don't you take yourself on a date? If I had my wallet on me, I'd give you twenty bucks and tell you to have a nice time." Of course, it would take more than a $20 bill, but it was my turn to be rude.

"Why can't you take me somewhere nice?"

"Because your behavior toward me hasn't made me *want* to."

"Well, if you want to have sex, you're gonna have to take me out."

Giving conditions that have to be met before sex can happen is messed up, especially when those conditions are put forward by your spouse. I felt devalued, rejected, and unwanted. She killed my ability to express my affection for her, made that affection go away, and then wanted me to still feel it anyway and get her to feel it again, too. And she wasn't going to participate in recovering this part of our relationship. I imagined filling out paperwork for date ideas, submitting them to her, and having her stamp "Rejected" on them in red letters and give them back to me, with "-10" on them for each rejected proposal. My overall desirability score would drop each time, so I had to get it right ASAP.

She was proving she didn't love me while expecting me to prove that I still loved her.

Weeks would pass before my resentment faded enough that I actually felt like taking her somewhere. She initiated nothing, not even offering suggestions for activities. She had a funny way of pushing me away as if curious to see if I'd come back. By 2015, our relationship had been deteriorating for years, and each time she pushed me away, I was already farther away to start, and it seemed only a matter of time before the distance became insurmountable.

But I wasn't thinking about that in the summer of 2015. She'd finally agreed to have another kid, and I was thrilled. We came off this latest period of forced lack of intimacy and I got to have sex with my wife exactly two times before she got a UTI and cut me off. By the time it cleared, she thought that she was pregnant and said that another infection might risk the baby. I certainly didn't want to put our baby at risk, so no more sex for me. Or kissing. Or hand holding. Or...you get the idea. As it turns out, we never had sex again..

CHAPTER THREE

Happiness

Sophia got lucky. She'd long since left Verizon for another company, where she wrote software that was greatly admired by the government agency for whom she ultimately worked. As we tried conceiving child number two, a woman wanted to hire Sophia to build similar software as a product for her company. She offered a $30,000 raise. I normally made $15,000 more than Sophia, but she would leap over me by $15,000. Sophia had concerns about the position, but we were nine months away from her quitting her job anyway, so we could pocket the extra money first. She accepted the position in October 2015, when we celebrated her birthday and our fourteenth wedding anniversary.

Her new job was 45 minutes away from the house and two blocks away from my current client. But my contract with them was ending. I worked as a consultant through a one-person LLC company I owned, and I had for years. Since that had started, we always used Sophia's employer's health insurance rather than trying to arrange it via my LLC. But now I took a new job as someone's employee. The reason was that Sophia would be quitting her new job in nine months, leaving us with no health insurance...unless I worked for an employer, not myself.

In December, Sophia had a surprise for me.

"I volunteered to help my boss set up for her Christmas party," she began, as we sat on opposite sides of the living room couch, using our laptops, as we often did. The couch had a recliner on each end, and we had long since made the decision that having our feet up mattered more to each of us than being beside each other. I suppose that said something, in retrospect. "I'm going to help all day, do the party, and then stay in a hotel that night."

"What?" I asked in disbelief, looking over. "Since when does one of us get to commit to something like that without talking to the other one first?" Her tone made it clear I was not invited and it wasn't open for discussion.

"I don't need your permission," she said, sipping her tea.

I snorted and watched my words. Our three-year-old son was in the room. "That's a messed up thing to say. You're going away for the weekend and you don't need to tell your husband before planning it and committing to it?"

"I *am* telling you."

"Yeah, after the fact. And I already have golf booked for Sunday."

"Cancel it."

I glared at her for the indifferent dismissiveness, a frequent tactic of hers. Was she *trying* to make me feel unimportant, especially when compared to her employer? Whatever happened to compromise and making plans together? She certainly knew how to make me feel bad, taken for granted, and unloved. I missed the woman I had married, wondering what had happened to her.

"Why the hell should I cancel it? You knew about it because I asked you if you can watch Dave before booking. You're the one making unilateral plans."

"Whatever."

Asshole, I thought, growing hot. I wondered if the laptop on my legs was causing that or if it came from within. "Dave has a high fever, too, so now is not a good time."

"You can handle it. He'll be fine."

So much concern for our son's health, so little time. Was she trying to make *him* feel unloved? I'd never let that happen. But I changed the subject. "And why do you need a hotel? It can't be more than 45 minutes away."

"I'll be too tired."

"Yeah, that's exactly why you shouldn't be doing it. You're pregnant and fatigued already. Why put this strain on yourself?"

"I didn't know that when I volunteered weeks ago."

"Weeks ago?" I stopped myself from swearing. She had kept this from me that long? I wondered if it was on purpose. If she'd told me at once, I would have had the same reaction and cancelling might not have looked as bad to her boss, but weeks later, her boss was likely counting on her. Had she known that and manipulated the timing of informing me?

I added, "Well, you know it now. Your boss is a woman with kids, so it's not like she wouldn't understand. You need to cancel, Sophia. You have the ultimate excuse."

"I'm not doing that. This is important. I can make a good impression on her."

"For the job you're quitting in nine months when you give birth!?" She seldom had good priorities, from my point of view.

"Maybe I won't do that." She sipped her tea.

That brought me up short. I had just put my consulting business of eight years on hold for this, and now she was once again making a decision, this one having a significant impact on me, without bothering to say anything. Some partnership we had here. "Since when? Anything else you want to inform me of, Your Majesty?"

"Whatever." She moved her laptop off and rose with tea mug in hand, heading for the kitchen.

"Stop saying that to me. Look, I'm all for you keeping the job. You were the one who wanted to quit, and whatever happened to being too tired for it? Speaking of which, how is it that you have no energy to help around here but you have it to help someone else? While pregnant."

She stopped at the kitchen and deigned to look back at me as she informed me, "Look, I'm the breadwinner now, so I get to do what I want."

I scowled. "What did you just say to me? I made more money than you for fifteen years and you're making more now for what, a month, and you're throwing it in my face, like this entitles you to something?"

She didn't bother to answer as she walked out of the room.

Sophia left early on Saturday morning, prioritizing her new job that she intended to quit over her health, her son, and her husband. She would attend a holiday party while I took care of our sick son, whose high fever made it more challenging. I nebulized him several times, cleared out his stuffed-up nose, and gave him medicines to help break his fever. Overnight, he restlessly slept next to me, waking up often. I barely slept as I needed to check his temperature often in case we needed to go to the ER.

By Sunday, his fever finally broke. Sophia texted that she was going to be another hour or two later than she'd claimed. She repeatedly pushed the time back, effectively cancelling my plans without an apology or acknowledgment. At least she didn't type "whatever" when I expressed my opinion about it. She still wasn't home by 3pm, when I collapsed on my recliner, utterly exhausted. Dave sat on the floor, our calico cat Minx watching him. He looked at me hopefully.

"Daddy, can you play with me?"

I stifled a sigh of exasperation so he didn't take it personally. He'd only asked once where his mother was, being used to her absences. I glanced at the clock. "Well, I'm pretty tired. Mommy should be here in thirty minutes. Maybe she'll play with you."

He looked away sadly and said with a resigned sadness no three-year-old should be capable of, "Mommy never plays with me." Then he perked up, mentioning his nanny with hope in his voice "Maybe Emy will play with me *tomorrow*."

My mouth fell open. Sophia never played with him. She knew it. I knew it. But I didn't realize Dave knew it until he said it. I felt demoralized. So often, I'd sit on the floor with him, playing actual games or just making ones up, purposely teaching my son to be silly, imaginative, and fun.

One of his favorite games was Squish, which started with him standing on the couch and me sitting on the middle seat, at the edge. From the corner of my eye, I saw him trying to walk from one side of me to the other, so when he passed behind me, I leaned back and gently pinned him to the couch, saying, "Squiiiisssh."

He giggled. "Again!"

And so we invented Squish, a timing game, where I rhythmically leaned forward and back, always saying "squish" when my back touched the couch. He had to get from one side to the other without getting pinned. Sometimes I got all of him, but sometimes just a part.

"Oh! I got a foot!" I pretended I wasn't giving it back, but he often pulled it out as I feigned disappointment. There were moments when I was just sitting there, not intending to play the game and he'd come running over, climb up, and shout, "Squish me!"

Our best game was the Monster Game. Every kid loves chicken nuggets, but Dave was picky and wouldn't try the dinosaur-shaped ones. He ran out of the kitchen and up the stairs, which doubled back halfway up. He stood on the landing, peeking around the corner. I pretended a nugget was walking in the air, adding narration.

"Doh dee-doh dee-doh. Here I am at the park, just minding my own business. Such a nice day for a walk. I wonder if there's anyone around here who could play with me..."

Dave stuck his head around the corner, realizing he was missing my latest goofing around.

I pretended that the dinosaur had seen him. "Oh, hello! If you don't mind my saying so, your mouth is awfully big. How many teeth do you have in there anyway?"

"A lot," he said, coming down a stair or two, grinning.

"Can I see? Come closer and open up."

"Okay."

I put half of it into his mouth. "Now, whatever you do, don't bite down, okay?"

Grinning hugely, he bit down all the way through it.

"Oh my God! He bit me! That really hurts. What kind of monster are you? That's no way to play with your friends!"

Dave giggled as he chewed and swallowed, then ran back up the stairs and around the corner, peeking out and laughing as I continued narrating the half-eaten nugget's thoughts.

"Oh, I need to get some help. Maybe I can limp back to town. Hey, are you sorry? Maybe you can make it up to me by helping me. A kiss would make it all better. Come on over here."

"Okay." Dave came back.

"Now, no funny business. Just give me a kiss." Dave slowly opened his mouth as I put the nugget in. "Oops! I fell in. Hold on. Don't close. Wait! Wait!" He bit down. "And I'm dead."

Dave ran back up the stairs and I grabbed another nugget.

"Doh dee-doh dee-doh. Hmm. Where is my brother? He said he'd be here at the playground. Maybe there's someone I can ask. Excuse me, sir? Have you seen my brother? He's about so big, looks kind of like me, actually."

"He's in my mouth," replied Dave, laughing.

"What? He's in your mouth? How did he get in there? Do you mind if I go in and say hello?"

"No." He came closer and opened his mouth, as I put the nugget halfway in.

"Hmm, I don't see him. Oh wait. There's his leg!" Now I changed to a suspicious tone. "Hey. Hey wait a minute..."

Dave bit the nugget in half.

"Oh my God! He bit me! You monster! How could you do that?"

Laughing, Dave ran back up around the corner.

"I need to tell the sheriff! You won't get away with this! Well, maybe I should investigate first. The monster doesn't seem to be here anymore. No sense in scaring the town unnecessarily. Let me circle back around."

Dave crept down the stairs toward me as I pretended the dinosaur nugget didn't see him. He then gobbled down the rest, so I grabbed another.

"Hmm, I wonder where my kids went. They were supposed to be here. It's time for dinner. Oh, excuse me, sir? Have you seen two little nuggets around here?"

"Uh-huh. I ate them."

"What? You ate them?"

"Yeah."

"Well, I don't believe that for a second. Your mouth isn't that big."

"Yeah it is."

"Oh yeah? Okay, well let me see for myself."

"Okay."

I started putting the nugget into his grinning mouth. "Well, looks like I owe you an apology. It is quite roomy in here. Could even get a big screen TV in here. Getting a little smaller and darker. Wait, you're not closing your mouth, are you?"

"Uh-huh."

"Wait. Wait! No! Oh my God! He bit me! Ow! That really hurts!"

In no time, the nugget was gone. I grabbed another and adopted a formal tone as Dave disappeared around the corner again, hiding.

"Alright, this is the sheriff of Nuggetville. We're investigating some missing persons reports. Sir, have you seen anything suspicious? No? Mind if I ask you a few questions? Come on over here."

"Okay."

"Listen, there are reports of a dangerous monster. I'm a little hard of hearing so I need you to get real close to my ear and tell me anything you know." I put the nugget near his mouth and he promptly bit it in half.

"Oh my God! He bit me! You're the monster! I should've known. You looked suspicious. I need to trust my instincts better. Come over here so I can arrest you. No, wait, don't open your mouth. No! No! Aiiiiiiee-eeeeeeee!!!!!"

Dave laughed and ran back up the stairs as I grabbed another.

"Freeze! Hold it right there! Aw shucks, I didn't mean to scare ya. That's just something they teach us at the academy. Come on over here! Listen, I'm the deputy of Nuggetville and we've had some trouble in these here parts. You look like a nice enough fella. If I can just get a DNA sample, I can send you on your merry way, with a mighty thanks from the folks of Nuggetville! I just need to climb up there and get a sample from your mouth."

"Okay."

"Alright. Let me see here. Might have to climb a little further into the back there, and...Oh my God! He bit me!"

The first few times we played the Monster Game, Dave was laughing so hard I thought he might inhale a nugget. I had to keep telling him to calm down. Every time I made them, he ran from the room and up the stairs, yelling, "Monster Game!" As usual, his mother didn't think it was the least bit entertaining when I told her about it.

"Cool," Sophia said, insincere as always in response to our stories of fun together. That was her way of saying, "I'm glad you find that interesting, but I couldn't care less."

Back when he was a toddler, when it was her turn to watch our son, she'd put Dave in a pile of toys and return to the couch, watching her iPad with ear buds in.

"What are you doing?" I would ask from where I sat.

"What?" she'd reply, as if surprised by my question.

"Would you play with your son, please?"

She dismissively waved an arm in his direction. "He knows how to play with his toys."

Did that sentence really just come out of her mouth? "That's not the point."

"If you want to play with him, play with him."

"I just did for an hour. We take turns, remember, so each of us has some balance in our lives?"

"I am watching him."

I sighed, eyes on Dave, who sat picking at his toys as if unsure what to do next. "Not just making sure he doesn't wander off and hurt himself, but interacting with him. Ever think of that?"

"Whatever." This was how Sophia always took the easy way out of tough conversations.

One of two things usually happened next. If Dave seemed content to play by himself, I let him. But as toddler, he had often looked excited as she put him down among the toys, but then she'd walk away and he sometimes looked back at her as she left, as if confused and wondering what was happening. Was she not going to play with him after all? The disappointed, questioning look on his face killed me. And so I'd say something to her about it, leading to this argument. It never changed until I gave up on her. I'd usually return to playing with him to replace that bewildered expression with a happy one. This had been happening since he'd been born. And the weekend Sophia spent helping her boss for a Christmas party, when he was three, he finally said it himself and it replayed in my mind.

Figure 1 Our Son with Some Toys

"Mommy never plays with me. Maybe Emy will play with me tomorrow."

After I put my heart back in my chest, I ignored my exhaustion and got down on the floor and played with him until she came home from her weekend of toiling for her new boss. Dave and I deserved better, and I frowned as she cheerfully told me how much fun she'd had at the holiday party without us, and how charming and handsome her boss's adult sons were; how much she loved her job and the people there, which included those handsome, charming sons. She was oblivious to how obnoxious she sounded. Worse still was that she didn't seem to care at all that our son had been very sick or that she should stop doing something for her boss to help her family instead.

Soon after, she said she was depressed and needed space.

On Christmas Day, I'd made dinner without her assistance, as usual for many years now. She refused to eat with me and our son. I shrugged it off and brought a plate over for her, not getting a word of thanks. I wondered how much hormones from a possible pregnancy were behind whatever was going on with her. She refused to unwrap the presents I'd gotten her, which our son eagerly did for her; she effectively rejected all of them. For weeks I tried to ignore the sight of the unopened gift boxes until I finally did something with them. It was painful.

A few days after Christmas, at a sonogram appointment I attended, we confirmed that she was two months pregnant and Sophia actually suggested we celebrate, but she also asked me not to tell anyone in case something went wrong. Then New Year's Eve happened, with Dave getting hurt. She refused to eat with us again on New Year's Day and I once again brought her a plate to where she sat on the couch. The next day she told me she was never kissing me again. Then came the locked phone, the attempt at hiding her laptop screen, and the phone calls that she took in another room behind a closed door. And the comment that she was never sleeping in the same bed with me again.

I always did all the laundry because she wouldn't anymore, but after that comment, when my heart slammed shut and I settled on divorcing her, I stopped doing her laundry. I stopped telling her where I was going when I left the house. She stopped eating the leftovers from meals I made and I stopped asking for her opinion on what to cook for us; I also stopped making enough for both of us. I removed my wedding ring. I knew I didn't love her anymore and I hadn't in a long time. I didn't even like her. Or respect her for that matter. My attitude had become undeniable. I had changed and I had had enough. I stopped referring to her as my wife, either out loud or in my head. I had stayed in this marriage in hopes of salvaging it and to have kids, then to not make Dave be the child of divorce, but now I was done.

Days later, she sent me an email, announcing that she was having emotional issues and that she was seeing a therapist and that she didn't want to talk about it. The tone of it said, "mind your own business." I wasn't sure how to react. I questioned her motive for telling me if she did not want to talk about it. I had suggested marriage counseling several times over the years and she always refused, saying she didn't want her employer to know.

"How are they going to find out?" I once asked as we ate homemade chicken fajitas for dinner, sitting side-by-side in the kitchen as usual. Together we'd figured out a recipe of sour cream, fajita sauce, guacamole, shredded cheese, tomato, and salsa to go with the chopped chicken cooked and seasoned with fajita spices, all bundled in a tortilla wrap.

"It's part of health insurance," she replied.

"They don't see that."

"They can find out."

"I really don't think so, and who cares anyway?"

"I do."

"Why?" I frowned as my homemade fajita dripped sauce onto the plate, but also down my hand and forearm. She was better at wrapping it than me and seldom suffered the same degree of problems.

"It's private."

"So? Why is that more important than our marriage?"

"I don't want to talk about it," she said, taking a bite.

"Yeah, you never want to talk about anything. Just avoid. You care more about what people you hardly know think of us for getting marriage counseling than you do about our marriage."

We had this talk more than once with the same justification from her, and while I never said it, I always thought, *What are people going to think when I divorce you? Ever think about how that is going to look?*

She was so concerned with appearances on this, or so she claimed. Pretty much no one would know if we went for marriage counseling, but if we got divorced, everyone we knew would find out. Family, friends, employers. Our kid's friends and their parents. Neighbors. Literally everyone. Even people we hadn't met, for the rest of our lives, would find out we got divorced. Someone had a perspective problem and I was pretty sure it wasn't me.

Like all arguments, it pretty much went the same way every time because she never budged. Every request I ever made for change was met with the same answer: "no." And so the arguments eventually died. The wounds festered until one day our marriage would be nothing more than a giant, oozing, puss-filled sore. And that day had come. I didn't know what had changed her yet, but I knew part of what had changed my heart about her – always getting that answer. It was death by a thousand cuts. Indifference toward me made the love I'd once felt for her slowly die with every repetition.

But here she was finally going to a therapist. It raised so many questions for me. What was so serious that she finally "broke" and sought help? How long had she been seeing this therapist? Part of me didn't care because I'd closed my heart to her. She was out. It was only a matter of time before the baby was born and we got divorced. I just had to figure out the timing.

A week later, she sent me an email with the ironic subject line, "Happiness." Part of me was relieved that she didn't do it in person so that any wrath in it might be easier to deflect, and part of me saw it as a sign of just how bad she'd become at communicating with me. She said she wanted to separate because she had baggage and resentment from our relationship and needed to work through it, and it would be better to do it alone. She had reached a point of no return, she wrote. So had I.

But nothing had happened since she'd gotten pregnant by agreement. Nothing that I knew about, and that was the question. I wondered how long she'd been feeling this way. She had been distant for so long, for years, emotionally and physically. We hadn't been having sex. Then suddenly she suggested having another kid despite twelve years of stalling the first time, then again for three years, and refusal to do much with our son. Why had she suddenly wanted another kid? She got pregnant almost immediately, so much so that I'd joked at the time that maybe she was already pregnant. She had laughed.

But I wasn't laughing anymore. When she'd returned from helping at that Christmas work party, she had kept saying she thought her boss's sons were so young, so handsome and so charming and had spent the weekend with them, then the night in a hotel room. Those phone calls she always took in another room. The laptop screen hiding.

Changing the code on her phone. She was never kissing me again. She was never sleeping with me again. She needed space, wouldn't accept my gifts, wouldn't spend holidays with me and our son. She was instigating a separation. I looked up private investigators but didn't hire one. Not yet at least. Part of me felt sick with paranoia, suspicion, outrage, and looming hurt of the most desperate kind.

And part of me also didn't give a crap.

Just get out of my life, and our son's life, and when you have that baby, assuming it's mine, give him or her to me and go. Just go. We don't want you here any more than you want to be here.

I remembered a conversation years earlier when, in an unguarded moment, she'd said, "I don't want to be anyone's mother! I don't want to be anyone's wife!" At the time I'd thought she was just blowing off steam. I would soon think it was a rare moment of honesty from the most deceptive person I've ever known.

Early in our marriage and for several years, when we had petty arguments, she used to end them by snapping, "Why don't we just get a divorce?" It always brought me up short. "You cannot say that," I would quietly respond. She would never apologize and it finally took me quietly threatening to divorce her if she said it again to make her stop. We'd still been in love then and the stunt had always been deeply painful to me.

Now, to her email announcement that we were getting separated, I only responded, "I assume you're the one moving out."

She replied yes. I sure as hell wasn't. I was the primary caregiver to not only Dave, but to our cat Minx.

We lived in a three-bedroom townhouse bought when it was a patch of dirt in 2002. We moved in in January 2003 right after it was built to our specifications. We'd chosen everything that you can think of: appliances, window treatments, flooring, cabinet materials, countertops, extra wall sockets and wiring, the garage door opener, a whirlpool tub. We added a front door peephole, kick plates to doors, an extra bathroom, two decks, a kitchen backsplash, an alarm system, a programmable thermostat, and a humidifier. We landscaped the garden. I had personally painted rooms without her help (because she wouldn't). We added shelves in the garage, laundry room, and the master bedroom closet. I had almost exclusively taken care of everything besides the cleaning, be it air filter changes, fixing damaged walls, deck and hot tub maintenance, you name it. I wasn't moving out of the house I'd maintained mostly by myself.

The sharing of adult responsibilities had been a war of attrition, with Sophia steadily backing off so that it became lopsided. I either had to do it or it never got done. Her modus operandi was to say she was going to take care of something, but she never did, and this had been one of the growing wedges between us. While she was pregnant with Dave, she announced she was never cleaning again. Never mind our 50-50 agreement. To avoid resentment and arguments, I hired a maid service. Yes, she was the one moving out of *my* house. It hadn't felt like ours in a very long time and I couldn't wait for her to leave.

Her statement that she resented me was mystifying. What did she have to be resentful about? How I cooked almost every meal because she wouldn't? How I paid all the bills because she wouldn't, to the point that collection agencies had repeatedly come after us until I took it over in vexation? How I collected all of her laundry from wherever she'd thrown it, washed it all, and laid it out in a big, flat pile that was usually still there the next week when I did laundry again? How I did most of the grocery shopping, including the monthly trip to Sam's Club? How I took out the trash and did the recycling? How I got the mail and dealt with it? How I paid the nanny, did payroll and benefits for her, and arranged all of our taxes with my CPA? I could go on. I found myself married to the Ultimate Do-Nothing Spouse, and it had been killing our relationship for a long time.

Figure 2 The House

What do I have to do? I wondered on learning she was leaving. *She* was leaving *me*? Not the other way around? Were we in Opposite Land? I'd thought for years that it would end when I'd had it with her shit and threw her out.

She'd given me a choice – doormat or nag. Which did I want to be? If she didn't take care of something, either I'd just do it, in which case I was a doormat, letting her walk all over me. Or, I was a nag because I said something about it. Well, I wasn't a doormat. I wasn't a nag either, really, but that's what a partner calls it when they refuse to do their part and you say something about it. It's almost a compliment, because it's better than having no spine and being walked all over. Or is it? I hate to admit that I'd become both. If she refused to do something ten times. I'd say something every tenth time and let it go the other nine because saying something got me nowhere. I was apparently nine parts doormat to one-part nag.

And now I was all parts furious and eager to be rid of her.

She'd need an apartment we couldn't afford, especially if she quit, but when I asked her about it, she admitted that she intended to keep her job. She invited me to join her at her therapist's office, which was five minutes from my new job, to learn about her "emotional issues." Indifferent but curious, I agreed, and so I met her there around lunchtime on a Thursday in January. The therapist, Pam, was in her fifties, plain in appearance and manner, and sat across from us as we sat on opposite sides of an ironically named loveseat. After some introductions, it started.

CHAPTER FOUR

The First Trap

The small room had a door to one side, a window opposite through which I could see my car from the first
floor of the two-story building, and a loveseat with an arm-
chair across from it, where Pam sat with a notepad on her
lap. I felt calm. After all the weird behaviors and remarks
from Sophia, I was hoping to find out what was going on,
but I had no idea what was in store for me.

As if she didn't already know the answer, Pam asked
my wife, "Sophia, what did you want to come talk to me
about?"

I thought this was an odd question, given that Sophia
had seen Pam on at least two previous occasions. Shouldn't
the therapist already know why Sophia was coming to her?

Sophia replied, "Well, I've been having some emotional
issues and I wanted to work them out."

"What are you hoping to do?" Pam asked, and I began
to feel suspicious, hardly listening to Sophia's answer, a
protective wall rising within me. I sensed they had rehearsed this, like a lawyer interviewing their own client on
the witness stand, having coached them on what the questions will be and how to answer. That impression continued with Pam's next question.

"And what would you like Randy to know?" Pam asked. They were definitely following a script. The wall flew upward. It's not every day that you realize something against you has been planned and it is now being revealed.

Sophia said, "I'm going to move to Virginia and I'm taking Dave with me, having custody Monday through Friday, and Randy can visit on the weekends."

Shock. Wait. What? The woman who avoided having kids for years or doing anything with our son for several years more was the one that Dave would live with? I had assumed she would leave Dave with me and sometimes come to visit, which I didn't even think would be that often, indifferent as she was to him. She knew I adored my son and hung out with him all the time, and that neither applied to her. I was confused and bothered by the sudden threat to my time with Dave. Was she just trying to upset me? Because it worked.

Stifling my emotions, I said, "There's no way that's happening. He should be with me. In fact, I don't know why you aren't thanking me for taking him off your hands."

"He'd be better off with me."

I scowled. "You gotta be kidding. You didn't even *want* kids."

"That doesn't matter," interjected Pam.

Sophia said, "Yes, I did. You were the one who didn't want them."

Sometimes a lie is so egregious that you're beyond speechless. This was a bold attack on the truth and our history, and an attempt at characterizing me as an unresponsive parent, which was mind-blowing in its hypocrisy.

"What?" I asked in disbelief. "You agreed to five years and then you made me wait twelve years. *Twelve.* And another four for this one. I don't want to hear any bullshit like this."

"It's not bullshit."

"Yes, it is. I'm not having a conversation like this. If that's what we're here for, I'm leaving right now."

I meant it. I already felt like I'd been lured there under false pretenses. She'd written that I was there to find out what was going on with her. Instead, it appeared that they had made plans to inform me of unilateral decisions she was trying to make about my access to my children. I felt very threatened and suspicious of what else was going to come out of her mouth, aggression to ward off more attacks already building in me.

"I'm much better at taking care of Dave than you and do most of it already."

I laughed without humor at the absurdity of it. "Give me a break. That's perfectly backward. I do almost everything because you're always too tired. And your condition for having another kid was that you quit your job because you couldn't handle it even though I'm Dave's primary caregiver and do almost everything around the house. Now you're saying that you're going to keep your job, double the number of kids and therefore work involved in parenting, and move out, meaning you'll have to do everything by yourself when you hardly do a thing now. How does that make any sense when you can't handle it with one kid?"

"My mother has agreed to move from Russia to help me."

I was shocked and threatened anew by her having a solution. I hadn't actually expected one, having asked a rhetorical question. Or so I'd thought. She hadn't seen her mother since 2001 when her mother's husband had a business trip to the Midwest and they got a hotel near my apartment, which Sophia had just moved into. We had an engagement party they attended, but they didn't even come to our wedding six months later. Aside from that,

Sophia hadn't seen her mother since around 1994 when she'd moved to the U.S. There weren't even remotely close, seldom talking on the phone, but now Nina was moving away from her husband in Russia, to help the daughter she never saw? Indefinitely? That was a huge deal. Something didn't add up. Why would she give up so much? What in the world was Sophia telling her mother was going on here? Suspicion and paranoia grew along with simmering turmoil.

I observed, "Your mother hardly speaks any English. How is she supposed to watch Dave and communicate with him?"

"She speaks it very well and Dave can learn Russian."

I couldn't know how well Nina spoke English, but unless it had changed dramatically from the time she'd been here, this was bullshit. And our son learning Russian was such a trivial, *potential* bonus that it couldn't make up for the negative impacts of living with a mother who didn't want him and a grandmother he didn't know, and losing the only home he'd known. And me, his primary caregiver. It showed lack of judgment about what mattered, which was not tearing his life apart.

I said, "That's not exactly practical, and how long is him learning Russian going to take before it helps anything? And if her English is so good, why would Dave need to learn Russian?" That seemed like a pretty good point to me, but as usual, Sophia dodged instead of answered.

"Kids learn languages very quickly."

Pam calmly interjected from across the room, "Randy, will you agree to let Sophia have the children with her? We can start immediately if you agree today."

I scowled at her. She was trying to pressure me into an agreement. Is that why I was really here? The wall grew thicker. "Forget it. It's not happening."

"It would be better for everyone," said Sophia, "especially Dave."

"No, that would be the worst thing that's ever happened to him."

Pam interrupted, her words suggesting once again that everything happening now was rehearsed. "Sophia, why don't you explain why you plan to move to Virginia so Randy will agree with you?"

I shot her another look of annoyance. Manipulate me into agreeing, was that it? They were going to try *reason*? On *me*? Sophia was the least reasonable, least honest person I knew. This ought to be good. I expected lies. The wall grew more.

"I'm going to move to be near my job," Sophia announced as if it was a done deal, not something under discussion. Any impression we were here to talk about her emotional issues was dead. She had lied and I felt like they had sprung a trap on me, one for which I was not prepared. I eyed the door. "The commute is too far with a baby."

More surprise. I couldn't even look at her opposite me on the upholstery. "With a baby? What, you're taking the baby to work?" That was ridiculous. I'd seen a mother bring a newborn to the office before, but that was always for a short visit. She seemed to be implying she would have the baby there all day, five days a week.

"Yes. My boss has said I can bring it in."

I shook my head. "Really? First of all, I am not okay with the baby going into work with you. That is no place for an infant. It isn't babyproofed and – "

Sophia interrupted, "I don't really care what you think is okay. You're no – "

"Watch it," I snapped, and she went silent. "How are you going to work with a baby in the office all day? Where are you going to put it?"

"My boss has an old crib she's offered to bring in, and a bed that she'll put in my office."

I did a doubletake. Why was her boss being that nice about this? Especially to a new employee? This was beyond extraordinary. There had to be...

I went cold. The obvious answer was that the baby was her grandson or granddaughter. Because one of her charming, handsome sons was the father. Sophia had started the job in October, met them and suddenly suggested we have another baby in November – and had instantly gotten pregnant. Supposedly by me. The pregnancy was considered two months old in late December because it's dated to the woman's last period, which would have been right before we had sex all of two times and she claimed to know she was pregnant that fast. I had joked that maybe she was already pregnant even though we hadn't been having sex. She had laughed. A slow horror crept over me. "I can't talk, he's here."

Oh my God... Fear. Betrayal. Ignorance. Suspicion. Confusion. Anger. Emotion surged, but the possibilities were so awful that I was almost quiet inside, the way the beach gets calmer as the water recedes, unsuspecting people not knowing a tsunami fast approaches.

"I can't spend an hour and a half each way with a baby in the car," Sophia said, interrupting my thoughts. "Going back and forth like that, it's too much."

I scowled. "It's a 45-minute commute."

"No, it's not."

"Yes, it is. And you know it is because that's how long it's taking you right now."

"It takes an hour-and-a-half, almost two hours."

Frustration. "Stop it. I worked two blocks from there for months last fall, the same amount of time you've been working there now. I know for a fact that it takes 45 minutes, not twice that or more."

"If anything happens, like an accident, it takes twice as long."

I spread my hands in incomprehension. "You're acting like an accident happens every day."

"They do."

"They do *not*. Stop lying." This was ridiculous and insulting to my intelligence. Sophia had done gaslighting to me before and I was tired of it. This whole conversation was turning into gaslighting on steroids as she questioned reality, erasing the truth with what she wanted it to be. I felt increasingly agitated and bothered by the assault on my knowledge, experience, and memory.

"I'm not lying," she denied.

"Well, if this isn't lying, then the word has no meaning. You're acting like the worst-case scenario is the everyday default."

"Well, I have to assume the worst and plan for it. You've never been in a car with a baby and you don't know what it's like."

I snorted at the outrageous lie. "What? You can't be serious. *Of course* I've been in the car with him. For Christ's sake, the only car seat we own is in my car outside *right now*!" I couldn't believe her nerve. The car seat had two bases, which I'd installed in both cars, but her Infiniti G35 coupe sports car was difficult to use with the seat and I did most of the driving Dave around. The whole reason I'd wanted to buy a one-year-old SUV in 2009 was in anticipation of having kids. The SUV was mine, not hers. Technically we both owned each, but you know how it goes.

Sophia said, "I drove Dave out to Leesburg one time so everyone at work could meet him, and it was a nightmare. He kept crying, and I had to keep pulling over. It took me hours to get there and hours to get home again. I am not doing that every day!"

"No one is asking you to. You don't have to take the baby to work even once."

"Yes, I do."

I'd say I scowled again but I don't think I had actually stopped. "What the hell for? You'll be on maternity leave and when you go back, we can use daycare."

"I have to breastfeed him."

"No, you don't."

"The milk has to come from the breast, not a bottle."

This was a new one and utter bullshit. "Since when? First of all, breastmilk is optional because formula exists, and secondly, you can use the breast pump like you did last time." That would allow her to store milk in bottles, even freeze the milk. We'd done it for over a year with Dave, so this sudden insistence on direct breastfeeding seemed like a fake restriction to justify moving to Virginia.

"I am *not* doing that!" she yelled. This was the only time she'd gotten animated so far. "It's too much work. I have to clean everything multiple times a day. You never cleaned any of it, so you don't know what it's like."

"Bullshit. I cleaned them all the time when the parts were at home."

"Now who is lying? The baby is going to work with me every day. You have no say in this. And I'm not doing a 90-minute commute with one, so I'm getting an apartment in Virginia near my job. And Dave is going to live with me, too. You can visit on the weekends."

"It's 45 minutes!" I almost yelled, latching onto the least complicated lie coming out of her mouth. I noticed she only said I could visit my kids, not that I would have any custody. She was serious about taking them away from me and appeared determined to use deceit to achieve it. She was threatening me, which only worsened when Pam opened her mouth.

Pam interrupted. "Randy, can you agree to let Sophia have custody of the children?"

I glared at her. "No. Drop it."

"You've never been in a car with a baby," Sophia repeated, opening her mouth to say more, but I cut her off.

"Oh really? Who drove you and him home from the hospital?"

"Okay so one time."

"No. Not one time. I'm the one who took him to daycare and picked him up almost every time for the four months he was going there, before we hired the nanny."

"That was me."

I looked at her in shock. "Are you kidding me with this?"

After her two-month maternity leave had ended, we'd enrolled Dave in a daycare just outside the neighborhood. They were open 6:30 am to 6:30 pm. I left for work at 6:15 am anyway, so I exclusively dropped him off on the way, Sophia having gotten him ready while I did the same for myself. Then she went back to bed and eventually went to work by 9 or 10. In the afternoon, I almost always got him because she only came home early enough once every two weeks. I typically got him on the way home because I felt guilty leaving him there, even though a couple of hours to do errands or exercise without him was easier. Occasionally I had asked Sophia to pick Dave up when I knew she was coming home early. It was the only reason she ever set foot in the place.

I was the one who pulled the plug on daycare because I saw what was going on. The biggest offense had been repeatedly discovering Dave with someone else's pacifier in his mouth, despite names being written on them. This was unsanitary and grossly negligent. Parents were supposed to remove their shoes before entering the two baby rooms, donning slippers, and this was especially important in winter with road salt on shoes. Yet parents didn't and the caregivers didn't make them either. Other problems existed, so despite the expense, Sophia and I had agreed to find and hire a nanny, which led to Emy working for us for three years to this point.

I said to Sophia, "You realize I had to sign my name on a paper every time I dropped him off and again when I picked him up. It wasn't even a code that either of us could've been punching in."

"No, you didn't."

Seriously? "Yes. I. did. My signature is the one on the paperwork, not yours. There is literal proof."

"No, there isn't."

I threw up my hands in exasperation, feeling assaulted yet again, the truth shredded. I would later confirm the daycare center had the records, but they wouldn't turn them over without a subpoena I could get later if needed. And ending up in court was seeming painfully obvious. My wife was badly threatening me and my surging emotions were getting closer to the surface with each lie.

Pam interrupted. "Sophia, why don't you explain why Dave would be better off in your custody so Randy will agree to it?"

I wanted to tell Pam to shut up. My impression was that if I didn't agree, they would just roll out another set of lies about my parenting, or anything else, and then try to get me to give up my kids again. No? Here are more lies we'll say in court. How about now? No? Rinse and repeat.

Sophia said, "Well, I'm the primary caregiver and – "

"Oh, give me a break," I interrupted.

"What? I *am* the primary."

"Bullshit. I watch him every weekday from 4 pm until 8, 9, or 10 when he goes to bed. You watch him for one hour, maybe two in the morning. And we're both there on the weekend. This schedule alone makes me the primary caregiver."

Dave usually woke around 6:30 or 7 am and the nanny worked from 8 am to 4 pm. That meant that Sophia watched him for 90 minutes at most and she didn't do anything with him, either. I knew because Emy was required to fill out a Daily Sheet I'd created, indicating when she fed, changed, and played with him, amongst other things, so I knew what had happened when I took over in the afternoon. The notes had led me to ask Emy to confirm something, and she did: every morning, Emy changed Dave's bedtime diaper and clothes. She'd feed him breakfast, because in the 60-90 minutes that Sophia was up with him, she'd done neither. This had led to several arguments with Sophia, mostly about the pee-filled diaper. There was no improvement in her negligent mothering. I had three years of these Daily Sheets to use as proof of her deceit in court, which was where I was increasingly certain we were headed.

Sophia added to her lie. "I'm the one who's home at 4 pm every day."

I guffawed, shocked at her audacity, and with good reason. "No, you're not. The nanny works from 8 am to 4 pm. You're claiming that you're there in the morning when she arrives and when she leaves in the afternoon?"

"Yes."

"So then how are you doing an 8-hour workday? She gets there at 8, you take a shower and change and get to work by 9 at the earliest, and that's being generous, because you do everything slowly. You'd have to be there until 5 pm to get 8 hours in. To be home by 4pm means you're leaving by 3pm, or even earlier, because according to you, it takes 90 minutes or more."

"Yes."

"That means you're working at most from 9 am to 3 pm, 6 hours or less every day. How are you being paid full time wages and benefits for part time hours?"

Without missing a beat, she replied, "I work from home when I get there."

I shook my head. "So you're supposedly watching him and working at the same time?"

"Yes."

"Well, then what am I doing?" I asked, playing along.

She waved her hand dismissively and unconvincingly said, "You're doing...whatever it is that you do."

I snorted. "You might want to improve that lie. You do realize that the nanny is going to contradict you."

"No, she's not."

"Really? How are you going to get Emy to lie for you? She knows perfectly well which one of us is there in the morning and who arrives by 4 pm so she can leave. For three years now. She's never going to say you're there at 4 pm instead of me."

Without hesitation, she calmly said, "Well, 4:05 then."

"Oh, well *that's* convenient."

I imagined Emy being on a witness stand, being grilled by Sophia's attorney, forced to confess that when she left at 4 pm, yes, I was there and Sophia was not. But that Emy wasn't there at 4:05 pm and therefore could not dispute Sophia's supposed arrival then. For three years, Emy had not once seen Sophia arrive in the afternoon, but she also couldn't say Sophia had never arrived just after Emy left. Sophia was not being contradicted and the assumption was that she must therefore be telling the truth? Clever, appalling, even obscene, it just might have worked. But you'd have to be a moron to believe it.

"So let me get this straight," I began, feeling like a logic bloodhound if ever one existed, "you're saying that I lived my life around the need to be home by 4 pm for three years, five days a week. Awake at 5:30, out the door by 6:15, at work by 7, leaving by 3 pm, home by 4. And during all that time, I somehow never noticed that you were *also* home at 4. And I therefore did not need to be? When I'm living my life around this schedule? How dumb do you think I am? How dumb do you think a *judge* would have to be to believe that load of crap?"

"Well, it's the truth."

"You do realize I have countless texts, probably two or three a week, of me asking you when you're going to be home, and you replying 8, 9, or 10 pm?"

Sophia was lucky to leave by 6 pm, because she often went for lunch or coffee with coworkers, and for years she'd also worked four ten-hour days, taking Monday off. I put Dave to bed most of the week. That meant 2-6 hours of him in my care on weekdays. The math wasn't hard. I was indisputably Dave's primary caregiver.

On those Mondays, her extra day off, she was supposed to relieve Emy at 4 pm so that I could have one day where I didn't need to rush home. But many times, at 2:45 pm, she'd text that she was at the barn, an hour from the house, about to mount her horse for a ride. I would have to cancel my plans, just as she had planned. She could've gone horseback riding all day but consistently waited to pull this stunt, like I was too dumb to realize that she was doing it on purpose. "The one who cares the least wins," someone once said. Sophia knew I'd take responsibility for Dave. The selfishness caused arguments, but no apologies came nor a change in behavior, until I eventually gave up. Now she had the gall to say she was the one who was there every day at 4 pm, adding insult to injury.

Sophia denied that I had these texts that proved her late arrivals after 8pm.

"Yes, I do have them. Going back three years."

"That's not true."

He said, she said. That's what she wanted to create.

Sophia said, "My friends and I have all agreed on what's best for Dave."

"Excuse me? I don't give a *shit* what your friends think." I had a sudden impression that I had been summarily picked up and removed from my family, deposited somewhere else. Now my wife, her therapist, her friends and even her employer, were making unilateral decisions about what was going to happen in my family. My input was not considered necessary or even relevant. Some of these people had never even met me – and even the ones who had hardly knew a thing about either my marriage or parenting because they only saw me a handful of times a year and ignored me when they did.

Sophia countered, "Well, you *should* care what my friends think, because they're going to testify for me."

"Testify about *what*?" I snapped. "The alternate reality you're spinning?"

She dodged the question. "You never spend any time with Dave, especially on the weekends."

My jaw hit the floor. "What!? You're the one who never spends time with him."

"No, that's you."

"What the fuck? Yeah, you know, good luck getting Dave to lie about that. He just said it out loud the other day that you never play with him."

"He never said that."

"How the hell would you know? You weren't there!"

"Yes, I was."

Another doubletake. "So wait, you were there when he did *not* say something? That makes a lot of sense." You would need to be around someone 24/7 to know that they had never uttered something.

"You never take care of him. You hardly know how to change a diaper."

I was speechless. I had literally changed thousands of diapers. The lie was so outrageous that I almost wanted her to say it in front of a judge. Due to our schedules, I'd changed him far more than her, especially given that she didn't do it in the mornings before Emy arrived. I was increasingly reeling from the relentless lying, like my world was being deeply questioned, my fatherhood attacked, raped, and pillaged for plunder. Everything was backwards. I had been hurled unsuspecting into Opposite Land and it was worse than Hell.

Sophia continued, "The baby has to stay with me, and the kids should be together, so that means Dave, too. I'm sure you'll miss him, but you would get to visit on the weekends."

"Oh, I *get* to visit my son. How kind of you. Any other big favors you're willing to do for me today?"

"You should be happy I'd let you see them at all."

"What did you just say to me? Who the hell do you think you are?"

"You get frustrated with him too easily. You can't handle parenting."

My mind once again violently yanked into another distortion of the truth. I was reeling. "Jesus. *Every* parent gets frustrated with their kids at times," I said.

"I don't," Sophia piously stated.

I laughed without humor. Let her make that claim on the witness stand. But in a way, she was right. She rarely got frustrated with Dave, but the reason was that she seldom watched him for more than an hour by herself. On the weekends, we were both usually there. It was a direct result of how little solo parenting she did. Sometimes a child doesn't listen, or repeats a behavior you've asked them not to one too many times. Or they make yet another mess. Or you can't calm their crying no matter what you try –

changing them, feeding them, talking and singing to them, walking around with them, cuddling them, and more.

Pam said, "Randy, we really feel it would be in Dave's best interest to live with – "

"Excuse me," I coldly interrupted, "I don't give a *damn* what you think about anything. You know *nothing*. How dare you participate in this? This is unprofessional."

"You're being rude," said Sophia.

I was losing it. "Oh, *I'm* being rude. That's a good one. Anyone want to apologize? Why don't you go first, show me how it's done, since you're so saintly and all."

"This is the kind of behavior that makes people uncomfortable around you. Our son is afraid of you and he'd be better off if he didn't see you anymore."

Silence. I was in utter shock, offended to my core. Telling me other people were uncomfortable around me added the weight of consensus to her jaw-dropping accusation, a kind of bullying. It implied countless people had felt that way about me, I didn't know it, she did, and some of them would be testifying about how awful a person I was. My son being afraid of me was a deeply offensive characterization, far beyond appalling. And the idea that he'd be better off never seeing me again was the most heavy-handed assault on me yet, an over-the-top threat to my ability to see and raise my son, who I adored. I could not overstate how protective of him I was, like every parent should be, and the idea he needed to be protected from *me* caused a deep shock.

After I pulled my jaw off the floor, I turned to Sophia and snarled, "*Fuck* you."

Serenely, she continued, "You abuse him the same way you abuse me, and I can't let that happen," she concluded piously.

"Oh, shut the hell up. That is insulting and completely fucked up." I was dimly aware that my responses might start to sound like she was right, but I finally couldn't take it anymore. This was too much and I was knew that she had launched an all-out attack on me as a father, but she was apparently just warming up for the big finale.

"You hit Dave and – "

"I have never laid a *finger* on him!" I yelled, furious. Accusing me of child abuse was an outrage I would not tolerate. He had never even been spanked – by anyone. The tsunami of emotions in me was reaching the shore.

"You refuse to comfort him when he's crying."

"Oh *that's* rich, coming from *you*! You don't know the first thing about comforting someone. You stand there telling me my emotions aren't real and I need a psychologist every time I'm upset about something."

"You *do* need one. You're proving it right now with your inappropriate emotions. There is something wrong with you."

"Fuck off."

"I come home hours after Emy left to find Dave hasn't been changed and he's crying."

"*I thought you were there at 4 o'clock!*" I yelled. "No! 4:05. Isn't that the lie you were telling?"

"Randy," began Pam calmly, and I glared at her, "if you really care about your children – "

"Don't you *dare* start a sentence like that to me," I snapped.

Pam continued, "We're just trying to prevent you from ending up in court and – "

"Really? Because based on what I'm hearing, that's exactly where this is headed, and fast."

"Well you would lose," said Sophia, pleasantly. I got the impression she was amused that she'd finally gotten a rise out of me. "Everyone thinks so."

"Well then I'll see your lying ass in court!" I yelled and got up, walking out the door before anyone could say another word.

CHAPTER FIVE

The Storm

Moments later, I slammed my car door shut, then I said out loud, "You fucking bitch." I started the car. "You fucking *bitch*." I put it in reverse, pulling away from the low building. "You *fucking bitch*!" I started forward to exit the parking lot. "You fucking bitch."

I just kept saying it over and over as I drove the few minutes back to work. Again as I parked. As I walked across the parking garage. "You fucking bitch." Down the hall. "You fucking bitch." I got in the elevator. "You fucking bitch." I rode my way up. "You fucking bitch."

My employer had the entire sixth floor, and as the elevators opened to let me out, I said it again. "You fucking bitch."

I slapped my hand over my mouth, suddenly realizing a coworker could've been standing there on the polished floors, the glass walls all around. But they weren't. I walked through a cube farm to my desk, choosing a path to minimize interaction, and sat down. I couldn't have been there more than five seconds when I bolted from the chair and marched into the nearby HR Director's office.

I blurted out, "Something just happened and I have to leave." I then added, "And I'm not coming in tomorrow." A big snowstorm was coming.

She asked if I wanted to talk, so I closed the door and said too much because I was too upset to censor myself. I opened up about the separation, pregnancy, and may have said I wasn't sure the baby was mine, her startled look bringing me back to my senses too late. I soon went home, work laptop with me, and surprised Emy with my early arrival.

Nearly as tall as me, she'd come from Guinea and had a strong accent, but she was easier to understand than any of the other nanny's we'd interviewed, all from West Africa, too, for some reason. Her son was the oldest, and her daughters seemed less like twins now because one hardly ate and was inches shorter than the other. Emy typically wore a wig of medium length, black, straight hair. She was down-to-earth, sensible, and quick to laugh, and a little simple so that I had to explain something one step at a time rather than all at once. But we all liked her, Sophia being the only one a little cold in her interactions.

"I need to tell you something," I began, walking into our kitchen, where Dave wrapped himself around my legs in a hug and I patted his back. "I wanted to let you know that Sophia and I are getting separated and – "

"Oh, I know, she told me weeks ago. I'm so sorry."

That brought me up short. She had told Emy before telling me? Emy was our employee, one whom I dealt with the most. Any time Emy needed something, whether it was supplies, advice on dealing with Dave, or time off, she called me. I printed, reviewed, and saved the Daily Sheets and time sheets I'd created for her, managed her payroll and vacation balances, approved time off, and wrote her checks. I filled in when she wasn't there. Basically, I did everything because Sophia just wouldn't.

But the one thing Sophia would do was tell our employee she was leaving before telling me. Had she told Emy not to say anything to me, making it clear to Emy that our nanny knew something I did not? Or had she been willing to take the risk of Emy being the one to inadvertently tell me, her boss, such as by offering me sympathy...

"I'm sorry to hear Sophia's leaving you," I imagined her revealing.

Shock. "Wait. What?"

Horror. "Oh my God. You didn't know? I'm so sorry."

Either way it was wrong to both me and Emy. Was Sophia trying to humiliate me? From my expression, Emy realized Sophia had told her before telling me, answering that question. She felt embarrassed and apologized awkwardly as I waved her off. I didn't say much more to Emy other than assuring her no pending change to her employment was imminent. But it was likely coming to end even before this. We intended Dave to start pre-school that summer.

It was okay for Sophia to tell Emy, her mother, friends, and her boss this and that I was abusing her and our son, and that she wanted their help in taking Dave away from me, but it had not been okay to tell friends and family she was pregnant? These were related, I now knew. Had she avoided telling them the good news about the pregnancy because she would next tell them she was leaving me? If so, she'd decided this before Christmas. That explained her refusal to accept my gifts or eat holiday meals with me and Dave, a cruel letting on.

I still didn't know why this was happening. She made it clear something absolutely massive was going on. I had only one idea about why she still wasn't telling me the reason, despite this supposedly being the reason for her seeing Pam: Sophia was having an affair and the kids, both of them, weren't mine, and she'd had it with the charade.

How much was she planning? Who was in on it? How many people were keeping me in the dark about actions taken against me? Is it paranoia when it's really happening?

I had the overwhelming impression that Sophia wanted to kidnap Dave and disappear. It was the first thing I googled when Emy left, learning that parental kidnapping is illegal and would backfire and when it does – Sophia would lose all custody. Despite this, for months, at every traffic light, I checked the nanny cams on my way to work. Would I see Sophia with a suitcase, leading Dave away? I spent the first hour of my workday eyeing the video feed via my phone until Emy arrived at 8 am. The strain was awful.

I kept thinking that there was an alternate reality where my personality was totally different, as was hers, and so was our life. And that Sophia had replaced mine. She'd spewed the most astonishing series of lies I'd ever heard, with a straight face and mild tone. Yet the underlying sentiment was *"FUCK YOU!!!!"* The cognitive dissonance had me gob smacked. Stunned. Floored. Speechless. Aghast. Reeling. I had been carpet bombed by the nuclear version of passive aggressiveness.

Clearly, the goal of those lies was to take my kids away from me and prevent me from ever seeing them again. I'd been lured there with a lie, to find out about her emotional issues. It had been a trap, an ambush, a conspiracy of women both present and absent, to inflict the most personal and painful attacks on me that I had ever endured. The relentless minutes of pressure to give up my kids had been accompanied by the lies I would be subjected to if I refused. Sophia had planned it in advance, with help. How many people thought that what she had just done to me would be a good idea? A just and deserved one? A righteous act of goodness to save innocent children and their saintly mother from the monster I was suddenly being made out to be? I wondered what lies she had told them to make them believe that I was the monster that they now believed me to be.

The fact that she was pregnant sickened me to my core, even more so because there was nothing I could do about her having full custody of the unborn baby. I had no doubt she wanted to use that to take Dave away, too. I was horribly vulnerable, acutely aware of it. Sophia knew it, I was sure of it. She had the ultimate card to play. An implied threat of me *never* having custody hung over me.

Had she gotten pregnant on purpose to spring this on me? A shotgun wedding, when a man is forced at gunpoint to marry a woman he's gotten pregnant, is accepted reality. But we also seem to accept that a woman would trap a man on purpose this way. Was it so far-fetched that she'd used a pregnancy to end a marriage on her terms? Had the second child I had dreamed of only become a reality to take the first one away from me? A method of control? Of extracting pain and turmoil as a bargaining chip? Give them up or watch what I'll say about you, and do to you, with help from as many people as I can enlist.

She had just obliterated every last shred of my trust in a storm of lies. She had mentally raped me. With help from a psychologist. It was the most emotionally and psychologically violent hour of my life. I looked up ethics for mental health practitioners, hoping to lodge a formal complaint, but I came up empty. Sophia had questioned everything and I now found myself doing the same, back to our beginnings. Had she ever loved me at all? Who was this person I was now married to? She'd gotten her U.S. citizenship through marrying me. Was that all she'd been after, the rest a marriage of convenience? Until it ceased to be. She now had a job making more than me and was kicking me to the curb, my usefulness over.

The question plaguing my mind was paternity. Some people had joked that Dave looked so much like his mother and not like me – "Are you sure you're the father?" Before the day was over, I ordered a paternity test for Dave and me. The most reliable ones required a visit to a facility, but others were almost as good, cheaper, and didn't require a visit. If the results were a positive match, I would accept that, and if the results were negative, I would do the more accurate one at a facility. I felt nauseous and deflated. I couldn't believe that I was doing this, but I needed to know. I loved Dave desperately anyway, but legally, I might have no standing if he wasn't my biological son. I read that you can acquire parental rights by acting like one, but of course, Sophia was disputing that I did anything at all. The perfectly backwards lie was just one of many that deeply offended me and had me reeling in pain.

If I had to pin the end of our marriage on a single day, a single hour, that was the one. There was no going back. The shock was so deep that it wouldn't fully hit me until four days later.

That Thursday night, after Dave was asleep, I removed every family photo from the walls and tabletops. My mother had embroidered something about our two hearts being together forever, and I shoved it in a closet face down. When Sophia came home, I sat working on my lap-top in the room next to Dave's, the door closed; avoidance ramped up that day, lasting until she moved out. I couldn't stand the sight of her and didn't want to hear another fucked-up lie.

I'd avoided her a little before, but now I never entered the room she was in and instantly exited one if she entered and I was blatant about it. I preemptively ceded her a space she'd need to enter, like the first floor on her arrival. If Dave was asleep in his room then, I was in the next – my music studio, a converted bedroom, the door closed. If he was awake, I was on the second floor with him until Sophia ascended the stairs to there. I would leave for another floor, taking my laptop and drink. There was no mistaking that I was not returning.

By silent agreement, each of us suddenly had our own spaces. She had Dave's room and the entire second floor – kitchen, living room, and dining/playroom. I had the master bedroom, my music studio up there, and the first floor. That second floor was Dave's, which meant she mostly had him on the weekends much to my resentment. I often asked her to go upstairs so that I could spend time with him, and she either agreed or sent him down to the kid-unfriendly first floor with me.

I wouldn't make eye contact with her for more than six months. We think those avoiding eye contact are lying, but it was her. I didn't want my mind to come into contact with the mind that was behind those eyes ever again. That mind that had raped mine.

If I accidentally looked her in the eye, that window to the soul, I felt repulsed and reflexively looked away. I would turn sideways, too, literally unable to face her. If she talked to me, I walked away, responding verbally as little and as politely as possible. We stopped talking – largely due to me. Virtually all communication was via texts that were rare and short.

The day after the meeting with Pam, a record setting blizzard kept us home (Emy didn't come), trapping me in the house with Sophia, who I desperately wanted to get away from. My neighbor helped me clear the driveway of three feet of snow. I didn't want Sophia to do it since she was pregnant – not that she would have anyway, even if she weren't pregnant.

I didn't understand why she was doing any of this. She was keeping me ignorant, a weapon of passive aggressiveness, one all the more sinister for the intent (take my kids) and method (excessive deceit, ganging up on me, serious false accusations behind my back and finally to my face) while pregnant (and giving so many signs that the baby wasn't mine), all for an unknown, purposely hidden reason. Suspicion roared in me. My heart was black with fear. Hate and paranoia coursed through me like a poison. My confused, and desperate mind twisted down dark pathways as I searched for understanding amid the rubble that was our marriage, future, and stability. All I could think of was why? And why handle it this way?

Was she having an affair? Who was the father of the baby she was carrying? When did it start? Did her friends know? What lies had she told her friends about me? Any or all of this? Did they actually believe it? Did they also agree I should never see my kids again? What were her friends going to say when testifying against me? Had she told them I was abusing my son? Why did Sophia want custody? *Why was she lying about everything in the last part of our lives together?*

What the hell was going on?

I never knew just how desperately I loved Dave until that weekend, the thought of our bond being shredded did the same to any peace left within me. I thought of the games he only played with me. The silly things we did together. The way he rocked himself to sleep on the couch next to me, an act that drove Sophia crazy but which I loved because it was so him. The nights reading a book with him in my lap, however frustrating it could be when he wouldn't fall asleep. We had little routines that were just me and him, and I loved all of them.

I thought of all those moments when his mother wouldn't play with him, couldn't comfort him, refused to give him what he wanted. She was going to teach him that he did not matter in this world. That he was on his own. That no one loved him. There was no way I was letting a cold, uncaring, selfish person like her raise my son without me there to counter that and to show him what it was like to be adored by a parent. He already knew, but she could reverse it if she succeeded in keeping him away from me. As a cousin of mine said on learning of Sophia's intent to take the kids, "How can she do that to Dave? Randy is all he has." That cousin had only seen the three of us together twice for a few hours and had already picked up on this. Anyone watching me and him, and Sophia and him, could see it fast.

On Saturday, via email, she apologized for upsetting me and said that if there was another way, she would take it. I didn't believe her and shot down her suggestion that we both get apartments in Virginia and rent out the house. We fundamentally disagreed on what was a lot of work and what was nothing.

To her, easy was moving to another state, finding two apartments (much more expensive in Virginia at the location she wanted), emptying the house and moving twice (some of it to storage we'd acquire), renting out the house/becoming landlords, firing Emy and finding day care for Dave, terminating my Maryland business (it still technically existed even though I didn't have a client right now, on purpose) and possibly reforming it in Virginia, making her mother come from Russia to move in with her, bringing the baby and her mother to work, setting up a crib and bed in her office, and other stuff like registering both cars in Virginia. Never mind how disruptive this all was or that commuting patterns would eliminate D.C. and Maryland job markets from consideration. I considered all of this monumental as she tossed it off like I was unreasonable to not leap at the chance. It bears mentioning I'd do virtually all of the work because she seldom accomplished anything. So yeah, no work involved at all.

To me, easy was her moving near the house, putting the baby in day care or keeping Emy, and pumping breastmilk or using formula. She acted like using a breast pump was herculean and formula would destroy the baby's future, leaving it susceptible to sickness, poor growth, and death. Therefore, breastfeeding was mandatory, which meant the baby at work with her mother in tow, and since the forty-five minute commute could sometimes be two hours, we had to assume it always was and this was impossible (waiting for traffic to die back down was not an option despite having a *bed* in her office). I considered all of this to be deceitful and I wasn't about to destroy my life or Dave's over it.

Especially when I had no idea why *she* was even leaving the marriage right after agreeing to have another child and successfully getting pregnant. Or why she was lying and accusing me of abuse. Why would I go through all of this for a woman leaving our marriage? For a baby I wasn't sure was mine. Never mind that our agreement had been for her to quit that job. Or that trying to force me to move (with threats of abuse claims or taking my kids away) was altogether different from me doing it voluntarily. She was asking for colossal life changes and acting as if it were trivial, while what I was asking for was minor and she made it seem like a colossal sacrifice. Cognitive dissonance.

I still didn't know the cause of all of it, either. If she wanted to leave, why didn't she just leave – why did she have to turn this into a war zone.

She told me one friend had separated six months earlier and everything was great. Alexa was leaving her husband, too, taking her two kids. Sophia's best friend said it worked out for another friend. They were all encouraging her to blow our family to bits, obviously knowing something I did not. Enablers all, sowing destruction and likely agreeing that I be kept in the dark about the reason for it all. A conspiracy. What was Sophia hiding?

The shock of the meeting with Pam finally hit me Sunday night as I was watching my New England Patriots lose a game that would have sent them to the Superbowl with a victory, and I couldn't have cared less. I lay on the floor, nauseous, in turmoil, my thoughts black with desperation. I felt attacked, outnumbered a dozen to one. I felt snowed in and trapped in my prison of a basement, trapped by lies, trapped by depression, trapped by helplessness. I was trapped by ignorance, by wondering, by desperation to know what the fuck was going on. Why was any of this happening?

Going into a divorce, one of the greatest fears is to be falsely accused of abusing your spouse and children. Being investigated, viewed suspiciously, manipulated, bullied, and accosted. Made to defend every decision, word, and action. Being scrutinized for signs of you hurting others, of being a danger to them, of being evil. Sanctimonious reproach stalks you, judging eyes ready to damn you at the slightest provocation. You're a bug under a microscope, to be dissected by your holier-than-thou betters, no amount of damage done to you enough to inhibit the poking, prodding, and ripping you apart. You must live like an angel, walking on eggshells, for the slightest transgression will be taken out of context as proof you are a monster.

The scenes played out in my head, of sitting handcuffed to a table, grilled for hours, a cloud of grotesque suspicion over me, infecting my mood, my mind, my soul. Investigators examining my son for wounds, physical and otherwise. Trying to get him to incriminate me. To placate them. To say I was hurting him. Making him cry in protest because he loved me, but them pressuring him again and again. Are you sure he didn't hurt you? Really sure? Sometimes it seems like it's not a big deal, but it really is. He's hurting you, isn't he? Do you ever cry when he talks to you? Yes? See? He's hurting you.

Shame. Indignity. Humiliation. Slander. Injustice. Conspiracy. Outrage. Hatred. Fury. Vengeance.

I thought about all the times Dave and I giggled and grinned together. The rocking himself to sleep beside me. Reading him bedtime stories. All the games we played. Squish. The Monster Game. Tickle Monster. And how I would never get to play them again. My dreams of future fathering turned into a nightmare.

What if she got full legal custody? She could move away. Not even tell me. Legal kidnapping. She tells him I am dead. Or I don't exist. Or she doesn't know who I am. Or that I didn't care about him anymore, having abandoned him, but her father did that, too, and she'd turned out great and so would he. Or that I was abusing him. He was safe now. She would protect him. He needn't be afraid of me anymore. I'd never find them. He had nothing to worry about. She'd tell them that if anyone claiming to be their father ever showed up, they should run in fear to the nearest adult and tell them. I wondered if he would remember me, our games, our fun. That he loved me and that I adored him. I imagined never meeting the baby, that Sophia's lover would raise them both. That the kids would think he was their dad. And maybe he was. I didn't know and had to wait what felt like an eternity to find out.

I imagined myself finding them. Finding my boy, but him running screaming away from me until I picked him up and put him in the car, driving off, tires screeching. I would calm him down. I would remind him about The Monster Game. About Squish. And he would begin to remember. He would begin to smile. We would start to laugh. Maybe we would invent another game right then. He would remember that he loved me and that I adored him and had never hurt him. That he had never been afraid of me. I would take him places to have fun together again, knowing it was just a matter of time before the police would arrive with lights flashing, sirens blaring, as a cheap, out of the way motel we were staying in gave me up for a reward. Betrayed again.

Before it all caught up with us, I'd make videos. Lots of them. One for every year of his life, of me telling him the things he needed to know, the things I wanted to teach him, all those dreams of conversations about life I wanted to have, so he could watch them on his birthday and I could still be a father to him after I was gone. I'd send them to my parents for safekeeping.

He would know his mother was a fucking liar.

It would only be a matter of time. I would make him look at me, smile at him like the sun for all I was worth, one last time, and tell him to go with the officers in the distance. To not look back. That I would catch up with him in a minute. That it was okay. One last kiss. One last hug. One last goodbye. I'd wait until he walked away, looking back at me anyway until, at last, someone took his hand and led him away. And only then would it be time. I would pull out the gun as officers began shouting and running, but I'd be too fast, they're too slow, and the barrel would go in my mouth as I yank the trigger and blow my fucking brains all over the place.

I found myself on the floor, sobbing at the blackness Sophia had put into me, dreaming of escape. From this hell she wanted for me. From the lies. From the alternate reality. From life turned to death.

I sobbed quietly. I couldn't stop, the child's play mat beneath me wet with tears and drool as I lay on one side, rocking back and forth, the NFL game drowning out the few sounds I made.

Why was any of this happening?

I didn't eat dinner, my appetite gone. I hardly slept and when I did, it was torturous, as it had been since The Day. The day the storm of lies had begun like acid rain. I was hardly better the next morning, skipping breakfast. I again found myself lying on the floor in the same place, my head toward the silent TV, feet toward the recliners, my back to the stairs. This time I was quiet, unmoving, eyes closed, as if numb. The blizzard kept everyone home another day. Four days of being trapped in the house with her. I was supposed to be working from home but didn't care.

I was lying there when Sophia said from upstairs that she was sending Dave down. He wore pants made from a fabric similar to snow pants, the ones that make that swishing sound with every step. I heard him coming down behind me and stop at the stairs' bottom. After a pause, more swishing came around my feet and stopped in front of me. Another pause.

"Are you asleep?" Dave asked quietly.

"No," I replied, eyes still closed.

"Are you resting?"

"Yes." We'd had this conversation before, where he assumed that if my eyes were closed, I was asleep, so I had told him sometimes I'm just resting, not actually asleep.

I heard him moving and it sounded like he was getting down on the floor in front of me. Then I heard silence. Wondering what he was doing, because there were no toys to play with in front of me, just behind, I finally opened my eyes to find him face to face, so close our noses almost touched.

"Hi," he simply said. A dash of sunlight from my son right when I needed it, to chase away the blackness inside me. I smiled despite myself.

"Hi."

He got up and started walking away around my feet again, as if headed for the stairs to go.

Suddenly I sat up. "Don't leave!" I said, reaching for him, panic rising.

"Okay," he said, coming over to me. I grabbed him and sat him on my now crossed legs, his back to me, and within moments, we were playing with the soft blocks on the floor. We spent an hour with me building a tower and him knocking it over, my despair fading. At lunch, I asked Sophia to go upstairs so I could spend time with Dave because I needed him. She agreed and was gone in a few minutes. I escaped the dark basement for the exceptionally bright second floor, the white snow blasting even more sunlight into the level. I credit Dave from pulling me from my weekend of darkness, both literal and metaphorical. She'd take him away from me over my dead body, and she'd have to do the killing, not me.

CHAPTER SIX

The First Clues

I had heard of women experiencing post-partum depression so severe that they killed themselves and sometimes their children, a thought that filled me with terror. Every weekday morning, before leaving Dave in her care as I went to work, I discreetly assessed her mood, trying to tell myself that she was not so disturbed as this, that she'd never do such a thing. It was true of my normal Sophia, but that one was long gone and I just didn't know this one. I had read the news articles about these murdering mothers and a frequent remark from family was that they never thought the mother would do such a thing. It's a trust that is sometimes not warranted, with tragic consequences. Each day, leaving Sophia alone with Dave had me on edge until I saw, via the nanny cams, Emy arrive.

Sophia's erratic behavior and suppressed emotions strongly suggested she was capable of this. Her suppressed rage suggested she was capable of suddenly exploding and making a rash decision. She was clearly hiding something enormous. Could such thoughts and desires be among them? I would never know, as secretive and deceitful as she had become, until it was too late. I couldn't know how severe her depression was for the same reason.

I was also concerned that she would abort the pregnancy and not even tell me, or lie that it was a miscarriage. It could not have been more obvious that something had drastically changed since getting pregnant in October. Having changed her mind about another baby was certainly a possibility. It's not like she had ever expressed enjoyment of motherhood either in words or deeds.

I assumed her therapist knew of the depression. I wanted to ask if she'd been prescribed medication and if she was taking it, but I knew she wouldn't tell me the truth. I also suspected that medication would affect the baby, causing additional concern. I felt trapped. Medication might have helped Sophia, but it might affect the baby and not be prescribed, and yet if she didn't get the appropriate kind of help, she might kill herself and both of our kids. After Pam's performance, I didn't consider her qualified for much of anything, but a doctor who dealt with physical issues and not mental ones might be superior in this regard. I had to know if there were medications that might help and not impact the pregnancy. With a sonogram appointment approaching that Thursday, I asked Sophia to mention her depression to the doctor and she agreed to so do. But I suspected she wouldn't.

That Thursday, I attended her next sonogram appointment in Maryland, in a three-story office building, as more snow fell outside, the peaceful landscape at odds with my turmoil. As I'd suspected, she said nothing about the depression, even as the middle-aged doctor left. While the subject was hers to mention, the toll it was taking, and the severe risks I feared, made it mine, too. I had to get an answer and asked the doctor to return.

"There's something else we need to talk about," I began, as he closed the door. I stood to one side of the exam table that Sophia still sat on, a computer monitor in one corner of the ceiling. We had seen the sonogram on it.

"Okay," said the doctor.

"Sophia's been having a lot of depression and I was wondering if there's anything that can be done about it, something that won't affect the baby."

Sophia raised her voice, adjusting her shirt with her back to us now that the sonogram gel had been wiped off. "That's private. I'd rather talk about it later."

"You promised to address it and didn't."

"It's none of your business." She turned to the doctor and bluntly advised him, "I'm leaving him, so that's what this is about."

I scowled at the inappropriate remark. "So your pregnancy-related depression is not the doctor's business but us getting separated is?"

"The pregnancy has nothing to do with it!" she snapped, glaring at me.

"Well you were fine before you got pregnant and – "

"Everything in my life is great, except you!" she yelled. "I'm sick of you. *You're* the problem!"

Shock passed over at me. At the sudden hollering, at the idea that I was the problem despite being the one who did almost everything for her at home because she wouldn't. At the phrase "sick of you." That one both resonated deeply because it was exactly how I felt about her, and it was cognitively dissonant because she couldn't possibly have something to be sick of about me. How could she be tired of me doing everything I did for our family, unless she was sick of me trying to get her to help? It almost made me want to laugh, her wife privilege. But I flushed in humiliation and anger at her saying these awful things in front of someone, putting me on the defensive against yet another attack from her. And yeah, I was the problem.

"What the hell is – "

She cut me off, face contorted in rage as she screamed, "You caused me to have a panic attack!"

This time I stepped back, stunned by the hostility. Speechless. Disbelief. When did she have a panic attack? If I had caused one, how would I have not noticed, unless I wasn't around, in which case, how could I have caused it? Confused, I stood in silent chaos, my expression turning to hard stone as I tried to save face, to maintain some sense of dignity, which Sophia seemed quite eager to rob me of.

"I'll step outside," said a very uncomfortable looking doctor, hastily opening the door and trying to close it until I grabbed it. Beyond agitated, I followed him right out, closing the door behind me and seeing a few nurses in the hallway looking sideways at me, having overheard that, I assumed. I flushed again, unbearably hot all over, anger burning quietly and growing like a raging fire.

I asked him, "Is it possible to use the blood tests you're about to do to determine paternity?"

His sober expression revealed how awkward this was continuing to get and a fool could see he was doing his best to maintain professionalism. "No. I'm afraid you'll have to wait until the baby is born."

I frowned because that contradicted my research, but I let it go. I wasn't at all impressed with the doctor. I just walked away silently.

Sophia's claim of a panic attack was my first clue. Was this what had changed everything? I looked them up and learned they can cause extreme emotions and the "fight or flight" response, and that sometimes people respond with rash behavior. I didn't doubt she'd had one because of the rare passion with which she'd screamed it at me. It seemed I had accidentally goaded her into some honesty. Maybe I should've started doing that on purpose to get information. But I got more that weekend.

Alexa called, claiming she was concerned about me, but I suspected she was pumping me for information for Sophia, who'd admitted Alexa was helping her. I considered Alexa one of the enemy. Part of me wanted to hang up, but I didn't give a shit anymore. When asked, I admitted to not loving Sophia anymore and some reasons even before recent events, mostly about Sophia's refusal to participate in our relationship in numerous ways. I had only stayed with her for Dave. Alexa said she could hear the contempt in my voice and suggested the marriage was likely over.

I also admitted to ordering the paternity test, which produced a genuinely shocked response that might've given comfort, since it suggested Alexa didn't know of an affair. She didn't believe it. But Sophia was so adept at secrets and lying that this offered no peace. All she had to do was not tell Alexa, who admitted to thinking Sophia was being unreasonable and had trouble admitting to wrongdoing. "Stoic" was the word she used. Alexa revealed that the therapist was the one to suggest Sophia leave me. After how many sessions was this, I wondered. And after having met me zero times? My version of events didn't deserve consideration? I didn't recall Pam looking shocked at Sophia's remarks, so she'd likely heard them. I found her recommendation irresponsible. Was she some sort of man-hating, home-wrecking quack?

In the days ahead, the amount of Sophia's direct deposits into our joint checking account, from where all bills were paid, dropped as she funneled cash elsewhere behind my back. Did she think I wasn't going to notice? More secrets. I also learned of her opening new bank and credit accounts. Our "joint" credit cards were really mine and I'd long ago added her to have access, which I now quietly revoked. I also removed Sophia as a beneficiary on my retirement plans and insurance, my will, and altered power of attorney and related documents to exclude her. It was time to get serious about ending this relationship. We were still living together only because we couldn't reach an agreement on Dave's custody.

And then I received word about another relationship. Sophia sent a short text about the result from the blood test the doctor had taken – "It's a girl." That was all. No excitement, not that I'd expected any from her. Already having a son, I'd really wanted a daughter to have both experiences, so at least I'd gotten my wish. Assuming I ever got custody. Or that she was mine. I was about to set in motion learning Dave's paternity.

After his bath one night, I did the test. For years, his bath routine included laying him on the bed in the master bedroom while I put lotion, his diaper, and then clothes on him. The only way to get him to lie still for this was to turn on Mickey Mouse on the TV, which stood atop an armoire across from the bed's foot. A dresser with mirror and two nightstands completed the room, which was enormous partly from a sloped ceiling, where we'd added a light/fan combo, and a four-foot extension we'd added during the build. That could've been a sitting area, but Sophia's desk occupied it along with Dave's 4-in-1 crib. Beyond were three connected windows and pine trees that obscured a view of a suburban highway below and a lake, more trees, and another community past that. Two walls were painted cream and two mauve, a cross between deep pink and pale purple that matched the "white cherry" bedroom set. The curtains and bedspread were similar colors. As a guy, I would have preferred something else, but being married, I had accepted some femininity without objection. The walk-in closet and master bath with its shower and separate, triangular Jacuzzi and double sink completed the master suite.

I had finished with Dave and would have turned off Mickey Mouse and picked him up to go downstairs, but I needed to do the test. I had already done my part, rubbing two cotton swabs along the inside of my cheeks before placing them into a sealed and labeled envelope. Now it was his turn. I stood on one side of the bed, his feet at me, his head turned to my right as he watched the TV.

"Dave, open your mouth."

He complied, not looking at me until I put his pair of swabs in and swirled them around the same cheek. Without turning his head, he looked sideways back up at me, mouth agape. I smiled to reassure him, trying to ignore the juxtaposition of a cheerful Mickey Mouse blathering away and the awfulness of testing my son to see if he was mine. It could've brought me to tears if I'd let it, but I was getting practiced at steeling my heart and stifled my reaction to project normalcy for Dave's sake. He didn't need to know that was what I was doing carried colossal significance for both of us, both our lives potentially shattered by the results. Let him think it was nothing at all, the quiet despair in me stuffed deep down so that the cheerful banter of Mickey Mouse was all he'd know. I wore the most faked smile of my life.

When I pulled the swabs out, he asked me, "What's that, Daddy?"

"I'll tell ya later," I said casually, putting the swabs away. I suspected he'd forget all about it and he did. I sent them in the mail the next day. The experience is one that I will never forgive Sophia for giving me.

I began regular calls with my parents about what was happening, my mother doing all the talking for them, as she's a motormouth and my father's always been quiet. Sometimes I wasn't even sure he was listening to the call anymore. My brother has always been indifferent toward me, but even he expressed some sympathy about the situation, as did his more compassionate wife, with whom he had two kids. Like everyone who really knew us, they were shocked, disbelieving, and upset about my account of what Sophia was saying and doing. No one, including my neighbor Carrie and her husband, believed for a second that Dave was afraid of me. And he now began to say he wanted to sleep in "Daddy's room," having figured out his parents didn't sleep together anymore. If he was so afraid of me, why did he want to sleep with me? He'd voluntarily alternate between us going forward.

Everyone knew Sophia didn't play with him and had avoided having kids.

"I remember the one time you three visited, and Lena was here," my mother began, referring to my cousin, twenty years my senior and who had lived near them years earlier. "She came in with presents for Dave and immediately got down on the floor and played with him. Sophia said it made her realize that she had no idea how to play with her son. And I just thought how sad that was."

Others had noticed Sophia's inability, like our nanny Emy, who didn't believe a word of what Sophia was now saying about my relationships with Dave, especially the lie that he was afraid of me. For years she'd been telling me with a laugh that Dave would routinely announce, without prompting, that "Daddy's my best friend." Emy said that he would be better off with me and she did not approve of Sophia. In the looming custody fight, her words carried significant weight. I had her and the house on my side. Sophia only had 100% custody of the baby due to being pregnant. I began tracking the lies in a spreadsheet because I was losing track, there were so many. It had columns for the lie, the truth, and how I could prove it.

In February, via email, Sophia proposed a custody schedule that was wildly in her favor, an attempted flip of who was primary caregiver, which matters in custody fights. I used a spreadsheet to map out our time with Dave since birth, based partly on work schedules. It revealed the truth. She disputed it, and I told her I was not agreeing to anything on my attorney's advice. This is how she learned I had one, which prompted her to say she had hoped to do this without lawyers. I told her she should've thought of that before the lying, the rudeness, and the custody grabbing attempts, and that she'd need an attorney anyway because I was going to divorce her. She claimed she'd been very courteous and said nothing in anger to me. I laughed aloud. But I had to wonder about her stunning lack of self-awareness.

That night I sent her a long email describing what she'd put me through so far. That and her response might've been our last open communication. An apology from her was rare, but she gave several, not for her behavior, but for hurting me. She claimed that if she told me more, I'd be hurt far worse. "An affair" leapt into my head and I felt sick at the surging worry that the baby wasn't mine. What else could it be? She admitted that after Dave's birth, she closed her heart to me to protect herself from any negative energy from me. And then came the big reveal.

She didn't say when it happened, but sometime in November or December, she'd been sleeping in Dave's room when she'd woken up in a suffocating panic attack that caused an overwhelming desire to get away. Without me knowing, she had decided years earlier that we could not work on our relationship until he was in kindergarten. But now she was pregnant with a second child. Nine months plus at least five more years until that one entered kindergarten; she implied both kids had to be in school before marriage counseling could occur. Sophia had realized, supposedly in her sleep, that instead of only waiting two more years, she had nearly six to go and freaked out about having to endure our relationship troubles that much longer. Two more years she could handle, but six? The idea caused the panic attack.

What did the kids being in school have to do with us working on our marital problems? I still don't know and suspect it was an excuse for avoidance. By the time they entered school, she would have found another excuse, I am sure, but she may have genuinely believed she'd consent to marriage counseling after that. She admitted to being very good at ignoring both my feelings and hers, which she dealt with by suppressing them, but the panic attack caused a surge of suppressed emotions about our relationship to erupt like a volcano, which seemed an apt comparison. I was Pompeii to her Mt. Vesuvius. She admitted to feeling out of control and that it scared her into getting the therapist. She thought I deserved to be with someone better than her, a rare moment of humility instead of the arrogance I'd so often seen.

I felt much better on reading all of this. The panic attack was brought on by her own irrational plan of when to deal with our marital problems. Now I knew why she'd been pushing me away for years, a confirmation of my experiences with an admission of cause. I knew how I'd transitioned in her mind from being a wonderful husband to being a huge problem despite my behavior remaining consistent. The admission of ignoring my emotions was a huge blow, though we hadn't argued about that in years. If she had just told me these things, we could have separated with some chance of reconciliation, but it was too late. And someone who suppresses and avoids emotions cannot be helped until they reach their breaking point. And she had. I doubted her therapist, especially *that* one, could help her.

Sophia had repeatedly implied a temporary separation. I suspiciously imagined her thinking, "If he thinks it temporary, he won't insist on his rights and by the time he learns otherwise, it would be too late for him!" But maybe she meant it. Her actions all year were marriage-enders, but she appeared oblivious to the fact. Her greatest self-delusion was that after making me wait twelve years for Dave, and another four for a daughter, that I'd be okay with her taking the kids I'd dreamed of and she had never wanted.

Even if had I not adored Dave, I couldn't let his apathetic mother raise him alone. I often intervened when he was upset because only I knew how to calm him. It came with being primary caregiver. Dave knew it. Even Emy struggled. But Sophia hardly tried.

One afternoon he woke from a nap beside Sophia on the couch, while I was in the kitchen. He began crying and when I looked, Sophia sat absorbed in her iPad, earbuds on, ignoring him. I made suggestions to calm him and went downstairs, through the baby gate. Minutes later, the crying hadn't stopped and I went to help. I found him lying on the floor before the gate, which had stopped him from reaching me. The pitiful sight broke my heart. Sophia hadn't moved from the couch. How could I let her have my kids? I picked him up and took him with me. Sophia's accusation that I never comforted him had been shocking for a reason.

At the mailbox in March, I found an envelope with the paternity test results. Holding my breath, I stilled my emotions all the way into the house until I reached my desk, refusing to think or feel anything in case a wall of anguish was about to destroy me. No sense in letting it in a moment sooner than necessary. I took a deep breath and opened the envelope, eyes furiously scanning for a result. I found it at once.

Dave was mine.

I closed my eyes, letting out a sigh. I began to laugh, my eyes watering with relief and after a moment I flopped into the chair and put my forehead on the desk, the cool surface making me realize my face was hot with emotion. The laughter faded, giving way to a relieved smile. I thought,

One down, one to go I had legal rights to my beloved boy. I decided we'd celebrate that night without him realizing that's what I was doing. He wouldn't question an extra helping of ice cream and cookies. I grinned at him more broadly over the next few weeks than I had in months. He was mine!

I soon met my D.C. attorney, Joan. My first question was parental kidnapping. Joan confirmed that an Amber Alert would be issued, Sophia would get caught, land in jail and I'd end up with the kids, probably for good. I could not record the nanny cam footage to show how my relationship with Dave really was unless certain to not record Sophia, too. She said Sophia's mental state could be taken into consideration, and that she had admitted in writing that she couldn't handle two kids, and now had emotional and mental issues.

That month, I joined Meetup.com, getting in the dating mindset, updating my wardrobe and trying to lose weight. I hadn't dated in 16 years and I wasn't looking forward to it, but I wanted to be with someone who made me happy instead of miserable. But I didn't want a relationship and its baggage. I wanted to be free. Sophia was spending a lot of time out with friends or staying late at work, telling me via text of happy hours, billiards outings, and more. She acted really happy about it, like I was some sort of dead weight she was finally free of. Yes, I felt the same way, but at least I was gracious enough to not to let on about it.

I suspected why she felt that way. Our agreement had been to share housework 50-50, but after buying the house in 2003, she began backing off and I began objecting to having to do more and more. The arguments about it increased. So did her refusal to carry her weight. I'll admit to becoming bitter about it. She seemed to think she was getting away with it, but if your partner says something about your behavior, you haven't gotten away with it. If they lose respect for you, you haven't gotten away with it. If growing tension erodes affection, you also haven't.

"The one who cares the least wins." As the one who cared more, I resented the idea. I wanted bills paid on time, but she was okay with collection agencies coming after us. As a result, the finances became my responsibility. I wanted to eat meat, veggies, and rice/noodles at once, but she was fine with having each part separately, five or ten minutes apart when they were finally ready, so I had to cook. Wearing wrinkled clothes was okay to her, so she'd leave the finished laundry in the dryer all day. If I didn't want wrinkled clothes (and I didn't) I had to deal with the laundry. She enjoyed piles of paperwork on every conceivable surface, but I hated the clutter, so had to deal with it all. There was no compromise. I suspected she did it on purpose. "How can I repeatedly screw this up so that he takes over and I get away with doing nothing? Marital bliss shall surely follow."

These were simple tasks. I wasn't asking her to move across the planet, give up her friends, her job, her life. I asked her to do her share and her answer was no. I will not do that for you. For us. You will do everything for us. Fuck off if you don't like it. "The answer is no" became the dominant theme of our marriage. Every request was met with the same disregard for what I wanted, for my emotional upset, for my desire for a resolution.

I wasn't a neat freak. She was a slob. She'd claim an intention to deal with something but she seldom did. It eroded my trust. If she couldn't keep her word on the small things, how could she keep her word on bigger things? I believed her and felt angry when she once again claimed she'd do something for us. To her, the problem was my reaction. To me, the problem was her behavior. In a way, we wanted *almost* the same thing. I wanted her to stop this behavior. She wanted me to stop *saying* something to her about it.

On late night talk shows, a guy would sometimes put a plate on a stick and getting it spinning. When it stopped, it would fall and shatter, unless he gave it another whack. Keeping one spinning wasn't hard, but he'd start another and another, getting a dozen going. How many could he do until they all crashed? This was my marriage long before Sophia's panic attack. How many problems could she create before we shattered?

We never know why we attract someone. I genuinely loved that she was smart and capable, a partner in awesomeness. Then we got married and she admitted after an argument that once she had me, she felt she didn't need to be so strong anymore because I was strong. She could be a slacker. I'd just take care of everything. She could take advantage. I had sarcastically thought, "Yay for me." But you never know the things your partner loves you for. You may be killing one of those traits.

I felt disrespected. I think she felt entitled. And now we were getting separated.

Nag or doormat, Randy, which do you want to be?

I choose nag.

No, stupid. You were supposed to choose doormat. I wanted to marry a doormat.

Funny, I wanted to marry an equal partner and I did. And then you increasingly ceased to be that person. Goodbye.

The gender stereotype is that the woman has to do it all. She wants kids, is responsible, is an involved parent, deals with the nanny, runs the house, pays the bills, does the laundry, and cooks. He has no energy to help but does to work on his car. My marriage was reversed. In place of a car was her horse. When the relationship failed, the guy moved out, but Sophia was doing it.

I was proudly Mr. Mom. It mattered to me that my kids knew at least one of their parents adored them, had dreamed of their existence, had fantasized about the things we'd do together, had imagined explaining one thing or another, showing them this and that. It took me and Sophia to create them, but aside from that, I was the only reason they existed. If it had been up to her, they would not. I am the reason they are on this earth.

And she wanted to take them away from me.

Over. My. Dead. Body.

It's better to have loved and lost. And I would do everything to make sure my kids would never be the same when I died. That they would never get over it. It sounds wrong, but I wanted there to be no question in their hearts, minds, and souls that I loved them fiercely and with everything I had. I wanted them to know what being loved so strongly felt like. My son already knew. Dave looked at me with a sparkle in his eyes, especially those times when he'd done something with his toys and looked for my approval.

"Daddy," he would say, grinning in expectation of approval, "this is silly, right?" after he'd built a tower with things not meant to be one. Because I had taught him to repurpose toys. I encouraged him to be funny. To be silly. To be imaginative, to laugh, and giggle. To be full of glee and mirth. To turn the simplest things into something that made you smile. And it was the reason he cried if I became upset with him. It took nothing, like the time he walked up to me with his plastic golf club as I sat in a chair and, without warning, smacked me in the face with it.

"Ow!" I said, scowling and rubbing my forehead. "What do you think you're doing? You know better. Give me that." And I took the club from his hand.

The smile on his face fell. A moment of soberness. Then his lips curled, his eyes turned down, and he began to cry loudly. He put his arms out and stepped closer for a hug from me. I instantly calmed down and dropped the club, picking him up and putting him on my lap, squeezing him and patting his leg repeatedly.

"It's okay. I'm sorry. I didn't mean to get mad. You surprised me. You can't walk up to people and hit them with stuff, buddy. Especially in the face. It kind of hurt, you know? I only get upset with you for a few seconds, so it's not like I'm going to *stay* mad at you. Try not to get so upset yourself when it happens. I still love you. It's okay. You're not in trouble. Don't worry about it. It's okay."

He nodded but kept crying, slowly calming down, and within minutes, we were best friends again.

Sophia cited such moments as proof that I was abusing Dave. This is what she meant. I found that insulting and ridiculous. She failed to notice that when I was upset with him, he came to me for comfort, not her. This meant he loved me, not that he was afraid of me, and he wanted to know I still loved him and forgave him, that everything would be okay. If he had been afraid of me, he would have run to someone else and away from me – he wouldn't even want to play with me in the first place. Kids do not run to someone they are afraid of and try to get a hug from them, especially when that person is upset with them. It was a sign of how close he and I were. That Sophia couldn't or wouldn't see it was revealing.

Sophia had said on multiple occasions that no matter what happens to you, an emotional reaction was unacceptable. It caused arguments, as she was forever trying to tell me that there was something wrong with me if I became upset about something. Especially if she was the reason. It had been years since I'd heard such bullshit from her, but I increasingly began to suspect that this was playing a role in our separation.

And I brought up her disapproval of emotions to a professional before long

CHAPTER SEVEN

The Coleslaw Incident

Not far from the house we both still lived in, Sophia and I sat in a room with Marie, a child therapist who doubled as a collaborative divorce coach. The aim was to not be hostile towards each other – as if that ship hadn't already sailed, sunk, turned into a coral reef, and become a popular dive location. My lawyer had suggested this, and Sophia agreed for a professional's opinion on what was best for Dave. We'd interviewed several and settled on Marie. The small room had a window, a lone chair for Marie, a paper whiteboard, and a love seat, where I tried to sit as far from Sophia as possible.

Marie wanted to know what our objectives were, so I said my main one was continuity and stability for Dave. Marie agreed that it was crucial only to have Sophia say it wasn't important. She thought ripping Dave away from Emy and his home to one or two different homes and caregivers was fine. I thought it was callous. I wondered how much Sophia having been ripped away that same way at his age had influenced her opinion; she seemed to think she'd turned out fine – but I increasingly wondered whether this was the reason for her attitudes about human emotions and her inability to deal with them.

"Sophia," began Marie, "what is your first objective for Dave?"

"Creating a peaceful environment."

"Creating one?" I asked, confused and purposely not looking at her, to minimize direct interaction. "He has one now."

"No, he doesn't."

"Yes, he does."

"I don't think so."

I spread my hands. "What's not peaceful about the house?"

"It's just not."

Marie gestured with a pen in her hand. "Can you be specific?"

"I'd rather not," Sophia admitted.

I almost chuckled and shrugged my incomprehension at Marie. Sophia keeping secrets, again. What a shocker. "Maybe you can give us a hint," I suggested, a hint of sarcasm in my voice.

"I just think there are too many negative emotions there."

My face fell. *Oh my God,* I thought. *It's back. Holy shit.* It had been a long time since I'd heard Sophia imply or outright tell me that my emotions meant something was wrong with me. I'd actually forgotten about it. And I was appalled at its sudden return. Was this what was going on? I sat silently groaning at the possibility.

We'd had seemingly endless arguments about it. They all fit the same pattern – I became upset about something. She'd realize it on overhearing me curse, or my tone. Sometimes my upset had something to do with her, but if often didn't. Either way, she'd start in on me. Very often, my computer was the source. One particular incident many years earlier stood out.

We were sitting on opposite sides of the couch using our respective laptops. I tried to print a document from Microsoft Word, but after going through the File -> Print menu, Word crashed. I didn't outwardly react. When I launched it again, it kept crashing. I had no choice but to close all of the programs and files I had open and reboot the computer, which took several minutes because I had so much loaded on it. I finally relaunched Word and it told me another file I had been using was corrupted. I had just lost an unknown amount of work, probably hours if not days; auto-save won't help when the file is corrupt. I took a deep breath to keep my cool, fear of what I'd lost surging in me. Would I be able to recreate it? The document I wanted to print was still useable, so I tried to print it again. Now the computer showed that the printer was no longer "installed" on the computer. It had been there just a minute ago! No explanation, of course. I glared at the screen, trying not to curse. This can be an easy fix.

I tried to use the "find" feature of Windows to locate the printer "driver" and install it, but it couldn't locate the device on my network to determine the driver. There are multiple ways to do this. All failed. I grew more irritated with each one. I sighed heavily. Why was this such a pain in my ass? I knew what I had to do – go downstairs to the printer, get the model number, return, google it, and try to find the software driver to reinstall it. I couldn't help thinking that this was a lot of work to print a single sheet, when that should've taken ten seconds and now I was nearly ten minutes into this.

Armed with a model number, I googled for the driver. The manufacturer website proved to be another irritant, being slow, hard to navigate, and difficult to lead to what I needed, but after several more aggravating minutes, I finally downloaded the file and closed the browser. I was now silently angry, frustrated, and impatient. When I went to launch the installer file, I couldn't find it. It was mysteriously missing from the "downloads" folder, forcing me to repeat my online search for it and download it again, only to see it put into the same folder, and now when I looked, there were two of them! I muttered curse words under my breath and launched one of them.

No sooner did I do so then Windows crashed and gave me the dreaded "Blue Screen of Death." This is an operating system error so severe that all you can do is reboot and cross your fingers, hoping the damage is not irrevocable. I backed up my computer once a week but that's still a lot of stuff to lose, for me anyway. Holding my breath, I let the machine reboot only to have it give me the worst possible result – Windows was so utterly corrupted by the crash that all contents were unrecoverable. I tried another reboot. Same result. Another. Same result. I hadn't just lost the corrupted file now. I had lost the entire contents of my computer. Fear roared as I tried to remember what I'd worked on, what was gone forever.

And I knew my next steps – spending several days reinstalling and configuring Windows and all of my software, which was a *lot*. It was a huge amount of work and, in the meantime, I had no computer to use until I was done, my personal productivity clobbered to nothingness when I always had a mountain of stuff to do. All because I'd tried to print something. A ten-second task had failed and cost me dearly. I finally lost it.

"God damn it!" I yelled, picking up the laptop and indelicately putting it on the end table next to me. I stood up, fuming and starting to pace, wanting to cool off. I wasn't ready to accept it. Sometimes you need a minute, but Sophia would give me nothing.

"That's not appropriate," Sophia informed me, still reclining.

I scowled in disbelief and pain at the rejection of what I was experiencing. "Yes, it is."

"No, it's not."

"How would *you* know? You don't even know what happened."

"It's just not."

I jabbed a finger at my laptop. "Did you see the Blue Screen of Death?"

"So?"

"What do you mean, 'so'? I just lost everything on my computer, all because I tried to print something."

"That's no reason to be upset."

"What the hell are you talking about? *Of course*, it is." I stopped pacing, standing far from her in the room as if unconsciously trying to stay away from the sentiments coming from her.

"You can just reinstall."

"Yeah, I *will*, but that doesn't mean it's not upsetting. And there's no replacing things that are *gone*."

"You don't have to react that way," she advised me, looking at her laptop as if I hadn't warranted her full attention.

"Yeah, well, you don't have to say that to me, but there you go."

"Why can't you just be calm like it never happened?"

I laughed without humor, starting to pace again. "You know, just because it didn't happen to you, and you're not upset, doesn't mean that it didn't happen to someone else and they shouldn't be. You have no empathy whatsoever."

"I don't see what that has to do with it. I wouldn't be upset if it happened."

"Bullshit."

"You're the only one who gets upset about anything."

I gestured futilely. "What the hell are you talking about? *Anyone* would find it upsetting. You know what?

Never mind. Why don't I grab a glass of water and pour it all over your computer keyboard and see how you feel about the result?"

Dodging that, she went for condescension, typing a few keystrokes and still not looking at me. "You need to calm down."

"And you need to stop saying things that are only upsetting me more. Leave me alone."

"There's nothing upsetting about the things I'm saying."

I gave her a withering look she didn't see. "You have a rosy interpretation of your impact, I'll give you that. Is there something about my tone that gives the impression you're helping my mood?"

"That's what I'm trying to do."

"You're failing. I don't need your advice or opinion about whether my upset is valid or not. That's completely screwed up. Stop judging me when I'm upset."

"Stop being upset and I'll stop judging you for it." She finally stopped what she was doing and looked at me, smirking as if having scored a point. My heart pounded more at her dismissive amusement.

"What the hell did you just say? Look, if you don't have anything helpful to say, just shut up."

"You're being rude." She looked back at her laptop.

"So are you," I snapped.

"No, I'm not. You need to stop reacting to every little thing," she added, diminishing me.

I shouted in disbelief, *"It's not a little thing!"*

"Yes, it is."

"Not to me, it isn't."

"Well, I can't help that your judgment is screwed up."

For a moment, I was taken aback. "Fuck off."

She looked startled, glanced at me and stopped what she was doing, and then made a dismissive gesture with one hand before she resumed typing. "Don't talk to me."

I snorted. "Gladly. Just because you happen to be here when something happens doesn't mean I'm looking for your input, especially when all you have to say is insulting bullshit."

"Whatever."

What I could never get her to understand was that her remarks made me feel worse, rather than calming me. She once admitted to doing it on purpose to teach me a lesson about getting upset. She didn't specify what the lesson was. It didn't matter partly because I wasn't interested in this instruction, finding the whole idea condescending. Growing up, my family had been similar in that they did not take any upset of mine seriously, writing me off as just an immature baby even into my teens. As a result, I had gone through most of life's troubles alone because no one wants to have themselves and their experiences, thoughts, and feelings invalidated by uncaring, dismissive people. Somehow, I'd ended up married to someone similar, though she hadn't been like that until years into our marriage. I had a suspicion about what had caused the change in Sophia from empathetic and caring about me to dismissive – I was sometimes upset with *her*, and she didn't like it, so she'd opted for invalidating my feedback about her behavior. This had then slowly spread to any other upset I expressed. The irony of her upsetting me more while judging me for my increasing upset had me trapped in a feedback loop with her. And now the infamous subject had returned.

Marie interrupted my thoughts, asking, "What can each of you tell me about your family backgrounds, such as relationships with parents and any siblings? This often shapes attitudes and will help me understand your points of view so we can reach an agreement."

"I have an older brother and sister," I began, "but don't talk to them much, if at all. They aren't very nice and don't have much interest in anyone else in the family. She's in

Virginia and he's in Texas, so I haven't seen him in over a decade. No one talks to my sister anymore, as of 2010, because she's obnoxious. I think the one thing Sophia and I can agree on is my sister is not to have any contact with the kids."

"Yes," said Sophia. "I still agree with that."

Marie asked, "Are your parents still alive?"

"Mine are," I began. "They moved from here to Florida and we've visited almost every year, including with Dave, so he knows them. My father was an engineer and is a nice guy but, he never showed much interest in any of us, which is one of the reasons I'm so invested in Dave, so he never learns what that's like." As I said it, I realized his mother had already taught him parental indifference. "My mother was a stay-at-home mom until I was in grade school. She went back to college, got her degree, and started teaching grade school. The stress of that, some health issues, and my brother and sister always fighting made my mother unbearable. She was intolerable until she retired. We get along fine now.

"By the way," I added, "I'm Learning Disabled, which is hereditary, and I got it from my mother, so this is something I'm on the lookout for with Dave. It's important to me that if he is, too, it's identified earlier than it was for me and he gets the help he needs." He hadn't shown any signs of it so far, but then again, he was three. I hadn't either at that age.

"That's very important," Marie agreed. "He'll have a great advocate in you. What about you, Sophia?"

"I grew up in Russia and moved here by myself in my late teens. I was an only child," Sophia admitted. "I was raised by my grandparents, mostly, because my father left when I was three. I only saw him once in my teens, so I don't know him. He remarried and had other kids, but I don't know them at all. I get along fine with my mother."

"You have half-brothers and sisters? You don't know them?"

"No. I don't care. I don't even know their names."

Marie looked startled and I pursed my lips. I'd heard Sophia deny caring about her father's side of the family before, but I thought it bothered her. It had to have. Had the experience left a mark on her, one she also denied? Had denial led her to think that she'd turned out fine and that our son would too if he never saw me again? What damage would she do to him in the name of saving him from me?

Marie asked, "Why didn't your mother raise you?"

"She had to get a job in the city, so I went to live with my grandparents."

"What effect do you think all of this had on you?"

"None," she said, and I stifled an eyeroll. "I thought it was great, an adventure. I got to live in two different places, in the city with my mom on the weekend and in the country with my grandparents during the week. I loved it."

I shook my head. No three-year-old thinks losing their father forever is great, or not seeing your mom most of the week, or living in two places. I hadn't known this had all happened at that age. Was this another clue about Sophia's struggles with emotionally?

Marie said she wanted to meet with each of us alone for another thirty minutes, starting now. I volunteered to go first because I wanted to establish something before Sophia could bring it up behind my back. It was my turn to do that to her. I brought up Sophia's past and her denial that it had any impact on her. Marie said she'd noticed that at once and thought it was strange. I felt a rush of relief, that someone else saw what I saw. Sophia was certainly getting to me with her re-spinning of reality. The big thing I wanted to bring up, though, was Sophia's emotional dispute with me.

"There's been something going on for a long time," I began. "We met in 2000, and around 2004 or 2005, she began an argument with me that lasted for years. It stopped around the time Dave was born. It was about whether so-called negative emotions are real or not."

"What do you mean?"

"She claims that things like anger and frustration aren't real."

Looking perplexed, she only said, "Okay," as if waiting for an explanation on that idea.

"This wasn't happening in the beginning but, then she started implying certain things and eventually openly stated them. Basically, any time I got upset about something, she would start telling me that my reaction was not valid, it was wrong, inappropriate?"

"You mean your behavior when you're upset?"

"No, I mean that I was upset at all. Sometimes she did criticize my behavior, such as cursing, but it became clear that it was the existence of the negative emotions themselves that she was criticizing me for. I slowly noticed there was a pattern to her comments and eventually pointed out that she was acting like so-called negative emotions aren't real. She said 'they're not' as if it was obvious and she'd been trying to get this through to me for years and couldn't believe it had taken so long. After that, the existence of negative emotions became an open subject of debate between us. She'd always change the subject from whatever had upset me to this one. I'll admit to thinking the argument was inherently stupid. Of course those emotions are real. How could anyone think they're not?"

"Did she ever explain why she thinks that?"

"No. I mean, I tried to get a coherent explanation out of her, but she acted like it was so obvious that it didn't need one. She started telling me that there was something wrong with me, that I needed a therapist. Of course, that was offensive and just made the argument worse. I felt like I was being attacked because I was."

"She doesn't seem to be in touch with her emotions."

I snorted. "She's not. There's a long history of her ignoring mine, and even our son's. She has no empathy at all. I mean, telling you that your upset is wrong, and that it means that you need psychologist, isn't exactly comforting. I would just get more upset. That would prompt her to repeat it instead of stop."

"A cycle."

"Right. She won't stop with something like that, either. I mean, I've asked her, I've even told her to stop saying that to me, hundreds of times. I'd resort to leaving the room to get away from her."

"No one should be judged for their emotional state. You can't control it, only what you do in response to them."

"Exactly. But she thinks you can and that I choose to be upset. This is part of the theory that there must be something wrong with me. Sophia thinks emotions are a choice and she has chosen not to experience certain ones. Or so she claims."

I then related the infamous Coleslaw Incident. We'd been arguing while finishing dinner preparations. Sophia hurled a carton of coleslaw at the floor in anger, flinging food everywhere. The carpeted dining area of my apartment had made it harder to clean. For years after, when she was getting upset, I would jokingly ask if we were going to have another Coleslaw Incident, because the joke would calm her. This new lie that she never got upset was bullshit.

"So she used to admit to these emotions," began Marie, "but doesn't now."

"Right. I didn't know until just now that her father abandoning her happened when she was three, then got married, had kids, and stayed with them while ignoring her. Do you think this could be the driving force behind her suppressing her emotions?"

"Absolutely."

I sighed. "I guess that explains something anyway. To be honest, I don't really know what's going on right now or what her reasons are for wanting a separation."

"You may never know," she admitted.

I stifled irritation. I deserved to know and was determined to figure it out. It was why I'd joined Sophia at her therapist's office that horrible day. She'd since asked me to go back but I told her there was no way in hell, and she dropped it.

I told Marie about Sophia's panic attack and that Pam had formally diagnosed her with depression (a first), which I learned from a diagnosis code on a bill left on her car seat (I looked it up). I took fifty minutes of the next hour, not thirty, and Sophia finally knocked to get her turn, so I left. I assumed she rolled out lies about me being an emotional loose cannon, which my laidback demeanor belied. Was this what she meant about a peaceful environment? And yet all the nastiness was from her even though I'd given her the space she requested. I even buried my hurt about her rejecting my Christmas presents, refusing to eat with Dave and I over the holidays and her offensive comments.

In front of Sophia, I'd mentioned the spreadsheet of our respective time spent with Dave and Marie requested a copy. Sophia wanted to see it first, but I wasn't letting her alter it with lies and present *that* to Marie, so I agreed and then sent it to Marie, CCing Sophia, who then objected that it was "not cool." She had lost the right to complain about something being "not cool." It made me laugh. She altered her copy and sent it to Marie and me. To my surprise, she only altered her hours to be more present, like those 4:05

pm arrivals that never happened, and didn't try to reduce mine. I now had proof of her deceit in writing, which I would use in court, if necessary. Phone and text records would show her absences at those times.

Sophia cancelled the next meeting and when we reconvened two weeks later, she was armed with new lies. We did an exercise where Marie asked us what we wanted, what we could accept, and what was out of the question, regarding where we lived during the separation. Sophia pushed for Northern Virginia (NoVA) – and I said I would not consider moving there. This triggered a talk about the commute, her reason for NoVA, and that's when the lie came.

"I really resent you for making me have a long commute all these years," she said, "and that's part of why I want a short one."

"What?" I asked in disbelief. I also resented being blamed – and resented – for something that wasn't my doing. "How am I responsible for that?"

"When I worked in Virginia and shared an apartment across the street from my job, you made me move to Maryland to your apartment so that I had an hour metro ride."

"First of all, you're making it sound like this was done just to give you that commute, not like we were in love with each other or something unimportant like that. But did I put a gun to your head or something? You voluntarily moved in."

Switching subjects, she said, "Well I didn't want to buy a house in Maryland because my job was in Virginia, but you insisted."

"Bullshit. You were working in Maryland by then and so was I."

"That's not true."

I was really sick of the revisionist history. These serene lies in front of someone who didn't know better was already old. "They moved your work location to Maryland."

"I never worked in Maryland."

I laughed dryly. "Yes, you did. You worked in the building next to my grade school. I was going there when they built the place thirty or forty years ago. I watched it go up. You were so close to my parent's house that you sometimes dropped by for lunch with my mom or we met there for dinner with them after work. Both of my parents would testify to this. You worked there for *three years*. I can probably subpoena your work records if needed. Stop lying. All it's doing is pissing me off."

"Yes, okay, I did work there for three years, but you usually work in Virginia now and so do I, so we should move."

Part of me was surprised she'd just admitted to a lie. She'd only done it to pivot, in the same breath, to another attempt at forcing a move to NoVA. "Well, that's the kind of decision to make together, not you doing it unilaterally."

"It would be better for everyone."

"No, it wouldn't. I can reach jobs in Maryland, D.C., and Virginia from the house, but if I move to Virginia, I'm eliminating both Maryland and D.C. because of the traffic patterns. That cuts the work options by two thirds, and since I work as a consultant, changing jobs several times a year, that's a significant threat to my livelihood, which doesn't seem to concern you at all."

I owned my own company and had since 2008, when I began consulting instead of being an employee somewhere. I'd done it to avoid certain career problems and even though I found myself replacing one type with another, I still preferred it. I was on Sophia's health insurance but had arranged my own life and disability ones, among other things like retirement accounts. With the impending divorce, it seemed like less of a good idea to be a consult-ant. When in between contracts, I wouldn't have a wife's wages to fall back on, couldn't collect unemployment, and would only have my business savings. It had worked out well so far, but my company was another element of my life that Sophia was about to destroy even though I was working as an employee somewhere at the time.

She said, "You've always refused to move to Virginia even though the job market is better there."

I scowled. "Oh really? What about in 2007 when we had gone so far as to have the house listed for sale for six months, staging it, keeping it clean all the time, and we exclusively looked at housing in Virginia before deciding not to move after all? How does that count for not being willing to move there? Did you forget or are you just ignor-ing things that aren't convenient to your narrative?"

Dodging but implicitly admitting that truth for another opportunity to lie, she said, "Well, if you were willing to move then, why not now when it would help Dave?"

"It wouldn't help Dave. It would supposedly help *you*. There's a difference. What is good for you is not necessari-ly good for him."

"Yes, it is, because if I'm more comfortable and have more energy, that directly benefits him."

She had a point, but I conceded nothing and replied, "You are two separate people with different needs." She was conflating them, and I hoped Marie had noticed, not that it really mattered. The agreement we'd signed with her stipulated that she could not testify for either of us because such an idea threatened the open communication needed to get a resolution instead of going to court, and that's what we were there to try and achieve. But we didn't seem to be getting anywhere.

Sophia insisted, "I am not doing this two-hour com-mute to work, with a baby."

I stifled a sigh. "What happened to 90-minutes? Raising the stakes? Next time you'll say it's three hours. It's 45 minutes. And no one is making you take the baby."

"I had that long commute to Leesburg Virginia for a decade and I'm not doing that again." This was the job she'd quit last October to get her current one.

"Yeah, well, I kept telling you to quit that job every time you complained about it, so don't even think about blaming me for it. It was your employer's fault, too, because they're the ones who changed your job location to there and you accepted it instead of leaving."

"Well, I loved my job."

"And now you can find one you love in Maryland instead of trying to uproot Dave and me for your convenience."

"I'm not giving up this job."

"Why the hell not? You took it with the intention of giving it up and now you've changed your mind. You know, you're making it very clear that your priority is your career, not what is in Dave's best interest, and that's what we're here to discuss."

"Well, I want to move to Virginia."

"I don't."

"Well I don't want to be married to you anymore!" she suddenly yelled, turning to me for the first time.

For a moment I was shocked by the blunt hostility, thoughts jumbled.

An admission of her intention to divorce me, despite acting like the separation was temporary. Just a week earlier, she'd said with a straight face that she didn't want to throw away a fourteen-year marriage. I never believed anything she said anymore unless it was said in sudden fury, because in these rare moments of honesty, I got a reprieve from the lying jerk my wife had become...

From the explosiveness from someone who said our home was not a peaceful environment because of *me*. So much for Miss Serenity. She kept acting like she was some High Priestess of Angelic Behavior while alternately yelling screwed up stuff at me in front of others.

From the rudeness. Her refusal to acknowledge that the negative emotions she caused me were real made her capable of being shockingly cold because, in her mind, she couldn't cause me to experience emotions that don't exist, so why not do and say what she wants?

From the callousness to once again say something deeply offensive, and in front of someone. For someone who claimed I cared nothing for the feelings of others, she showed stunning hypocrisy. Where was her awareness of the shame this statement could cause me? Do we not need to honor someone else's personhood in body, mind, spirit, and *emotion*? Not when any of those are inconvenient, apparently.

From the arrogance. Her anger that I wasn't prepared to willingly uproot my entire life and that of our son's for her convenience came across as arrogance. It was all made worse by the fact that she was walking out of the marriage without even bothering to tell me why. Who gives up everything to follow the person leaving the relationship, especially when you now loathe them?

For the scorn for compromise. Scorn for trying to be reasonable. Scorn for me doing almost everything for her. Why the scorn? Because I sometimes exposed her to emotions she couldn't handle and which she had often caused but tried to deny. It wasn't working. Would she ever get it through her head and stop? I doubted it.

But I didn't feel humiliated this time. Not really. I was too closed off to her, but even the most indifferent person would feel a touch of shame on hearing such an awful rejection yelled so ferociously, and without warning, in front of a witness. She was the one who should've been embarrassed by the uncalled-for outburst. It was disgusting and in all likelihood, probably earned me sympathy from Marie.

I knew what Sophia wanted: the good old days when she lived across the street from her job. The onslaught of lies to achieve it wasn't okay, or the destruction it would cause to everyone, including possibly her. Her selfishness roared like a long pent-up volcano finally spewing its molten magma. That everything around her would be obliterated in the white hot, pyroclastic flow of deceit seemed inconsequential to her.

I was not moving because of lies. Or unreasonableness. Or to follow a woman leaving our relationship. I refused to use the phrasing, "leaving me," because it implied I warranted leaving. It was the other way around. I wanted to file for divorce first, because it implies rejection of someone deserving of it, and her doing that to me would have rankled. I was the one who had earned the right to end this marriage for spousal behavior, which had just gotten exponentially worse. I'd earned it by dealing with her crap for far too long. How did this privileged, lazy, unappreciative woman earn the right?

I was the reason we'd lasted as long as we had, overlooking one thing or another, swallowing my pride, stifling my upset. And she had the audacity to tell other people I was emotionally overbearing. She had no idea how many comments I'd kept to myself, how many names I hadn't called her (I'm not a name-caller, nor was she), how many insulting remarks she was spared. I uttered a fraction of my discontent and still, it was too much for her. I was a monster, she told them.

And I was increasingly certain that this was the game. This woman who provoked me all the time had now gone nuclear with provocation. If I showed the considerable upset she was causing me, I imagined her turning triumphantly to others and pointing the accusing finger at me.

"Aha! See? There it is! Negative emotions! I told you! Take him away!"

So, I had to feign calmness despite the horrible emotions she provoked so often now, threatening my right to see my children, making me think she was having an affair, attacking me as a father in every way she could think of and more. The strain of trying to not let her get to me in front of someone else was immense. She used my humanity against me.

Because humanity is what it is. It is human to get mad and more, but she tried holding me to an impossible standard that she claimed to have achieved herself, as if this moment, or that Coleslaw Incident, or others like it had never happened. She was not only demonizing me, but angelifying herself. A perfect being with an unwrinkled brow, no frown lines to be seen, no scowl line between the eyes. Peace and happiness followed her all the days of her life, her cup runneth over.

How did I outwardly react to Sophia's outburst? I didn't. My self-control was on full display. Sophia's was not because her panic attack had compromised it. Who was the loose cannon? Did Marie notice how calm I was in the face of Sophia's awful, unprovoked words? What did it all say about who was emotionally problematic?

CHAPTER EIGHT

Another Trap

We returned home in separate cars, excusing Emy, who'd stayed late. Sophia went onto the deck with her iPad and earbuds, sitting with her back to a kitchen window. I heard her talking and glanced over her shoulder, seeing a young man with short black hair on a video call, his smile ingratiating, his hands smoothing his hair, then touching his collar and adjusting the view of himself to be better, as he tried to make a good impression on a woman he was interested in. What sort of asshole flirts with a pregnant, married mother, who was in therapy for emotional problems in the wake of a panic attack, was diagnosed with depression and was planning to leave her husband? But then who knew what lies she'd told him?

I saw this as my only chance to get an image of her lover, if that's what this was, to show it to a private investigator that I was now determined to hire. I couldn't stand the suspicion any longer and needed to know. Was this her boyfriend? Was this guy the reason for everything that had happened this year? Was this the baby's father? I took a picture with my phone, but the camera focused on the window screen and not his face, so I retrieved the 35 mm camera from the TV cabinet and took multiple photos, able to focus. Then I grabbed the video camera for more, getting excellent close ups. Sophia appeared to have no idea. I felt no pain, only amusement.

Dave walked up to me. "Daddy, what are you doing?"

I'm taking pictures of mommy and her boyfriend, I thought.

He and I moved between rooms and a glance at the deck showed that Sophia had switched seats to face the house, still talking. I saw the same look of adoration she wore when looking at photos of her beloved horse, when she'd say, "Awww. I *love* my horse." I felt only cold resolve.

I showed Dave the young stud's photo, but he didn't know who it was. If I could prove this was her boyfriend and she'd introduced Dave to him, this was considered child endangerment that would get me custody. On the weekends, starting early that year, she often took Dave with her, supposedly to a friend's home for play dates, so it was possible that she could have introduced them.

The next day, I called my lawyer for a private investigator I retained for $3500, sending him the photos. He billed at $105 an hour, in four-hour blocks. I only cared about an affair because I could immediately file for divorce and custody instead of waiting a year after separation, as my lawyer told me. If I could prove neglect, or abuse of Dave, through an affair, it showed she was not a fit caregiver. I cared nothing for whether she was screwing this asshole or not. Part of me doubted she was having sex, but I had recently done all of our laundry and saw lace underwear that she hadn't worn in years. And she got a makeover – dyeing her hair black with a hint of purple. Everything pointed to an affair.

The investigator told me things he was allowed to do, asking questions like whether I was a co-owner on the car Sophia used. Since I was, he said I had the legal right to put a GPS tracker on it. It would ease the months of worrying about her vanishing with Dave and I would be visiting my parents soon, a great chance for Sophia to kidnap Dave with a week head start before I knew, so I bought one, hiding it in the seldom used, messy trunk of her grey-blue Infiniti G35 coupe. I didn't trust a magnet to hold it to the car's bottom. I could track its location online or via my phone and set perimeters to get a notification when she left home or work.

He suggested I try to identify phone numbers she regularly called to see if one of them wasn't a friend, but a potential boyfriend, so I looked up phone records and put together a list of her regularly called and texted phone numbers, trying to determine identities. Most records were for Alexa, or her best friend Cindy, who didn't know the Alexa/Amanda/Kate crew. But my research was pointless – Sophia's employer had given her a second smartphone.

I learned Sophia was looking for an apartment in the most expensive part of Fairfax Virginia near her job. She would eventually choose a luxury apartment in prime real estate, so pricey that it cost a thousand more per month than our mortgage payment. Or it would have, but instead of a thirty-year loan, we had a twenty-year, which had raised the payments by about $600. Her financial irresponsibility had forced me to do our finances, and now it threatened to drag us both under.

Adding to financial concerns was Dave. The plan had been pre-school starting that summer at age four, to get him ready for kindergarten at five, and no more Emy. We couldn't afford her for the baby, Dave in daycare, and an apartment for Sophia (*and* me?). And if we lived in different states, this meant no shared daycare or nanny, which raises costs, possibly by a lot.

To prep him for pre-school, I started taking him to a nearby child's gymnastics place where he'd get time with other kids and following group directions. The weekday slot meant I did it – because Sophia wasn't home at 4:05 pm! That didn't stop her from later claiming she did it, but I now expected such lies and took photos of Dave in class with me, and of the sign-in sheet with my signature. I could ask the staff to testify about who attended and my frequent emotional support of Dave, who had separation anxiety, even though he could see me through the big glass window separating lobby and playroom. He often cried, or refused to go inside unless I went with him. Sometimes he only sat on me, not playing with the others at all. Some days, we had to leave early, or on arrival, due to his emotions, so they knew I supported him emotionally. I slowly challenged him to grow his independence by staying outside for longer and longer. The staff knew to call me so I could return if he got upset.

With my marriage ending, I began resuming activities Sophia and I had done together until she killed them, like attending the Baltimore Symphony Orchestra (BSO) after a nice restaurant in Baltimore's Little Italy; my degree was in classical music and this had been my idea, which she'd supported until refusing to go anymore. I now went alone to an all-Beethoven concert. I loved it and bought myself a season subscription. But there would be no meeting eligible women there, as most were on a date, making intermissions a tad lonely.

Our annual family photo became awkward. Dave was the real goal, but we agreed that each of us would get shots with him without the other in the picture. We'd split the cost and go in separate cars like always, the idea of being in a close, confined space with her nauseated me. She was infamous for tardiness and got in the shower twenty minutes before the appointment when it took fifteen minutes to get there. Dave and I left without her. She showed up as we finished the photoshoot, forcing the photographer to do her photos with Dave anyway and pushing back the appointment behind ours. I smiled, for it so often seemed I was the only victim of her selfishness, as if it was directed at me specifically. Perhaps not. And of course, I was the jerk for all the years of objecting to this sort of behavior.

Toward the end of April, Sophia's mother was due to arrive from Moscow. Nina was the answer to how Sophia was going to handle a baby alone, an admission that she couldn't do it despite copious friends helping – or an estranged, nearby husband if she stayed in Maryland. Needing a team to replace me was nearly a backhanded compliment, but they were enabling her to destroy our marriage. They'd all supposedly save my children from negative emotions, which they would still experience because all people do, unless they could somehow end up in the Land of Supposedly Emotionless People, with Sophia as their Mad Queen. Not "mad" as in angry, of course, because anger isn't real. Duh!

I wasn't looking forward to Nina living in my house until Sophia moved out. Clearly, Nina had been told about my monstrous traits. How else could Sophia have convinced her to leave her own husband and life behind for however many months, even years, to a country she had only visited once and where she hardly spoke the language? Was Nina a de facto spy to testify against me? How much more uncomfortable could Sophia make me in my own home? I didn't agree to let her move in. My attorney said there was nothing I could do to stop it because Sophia was on the house deed.

One night my phone alerted me to the GPS tracker in Sophia's car moving. I watched on a map as she drove to a strip mall, for which I pulled up the address and Google

Street View. A bowling alley, restaurant, or billiard hall were the likely destinations. I texted her and asked if she was working late. She said yes, proof of one lie. I called my investigator but got an assistant, who explained that they needed a week's notice on busy Friday nights. If Sophia met her boyfriend, I only found out minutes before. This was not going to work. When Sophia got home, I asked why she'd had to work late and she said her boss had been hanging around her, lying to my face. No surprise there.

She invited me to her new, more experienced therapist. I suspected another trap, and for reasons I couldn't explain, my gut told me this one was working with her attorney. I'd learned she'd hired one by noticing a stack of papers jutting up from her purse, and on looking at the header, seeing it was from a law firm. She had apparently paid a $5000 legal retainer with a credit card I didn't know about, because it hadn't shown up on any of our cards; how much was she hiding from me? Curiosity was one reason I was interested in going; never mind how many cats it had killed. Technically, I had not retained my attorney yet, just paying as I went.

Even as this arose, we ran into a problem with Marie, the collaborative divorce coach – and that problem was Sophia. Like a mouse in a maze, she always went the same way looking for the cheese. Though she got zapped instead, she just kept trying that route. She once admitted to this pattern about something else, that if she had a theory she believed was sound, she'd keep trying it no matter how many failures occurred. If the definition of insanity is doing the same thing over and over and expecting a different result, she was bat-shit crazy. And she was about to exhibit it to the coach. We'd established that I would not move to Virginia, but Sophia had insisted on talking about it anyway, as Marie and I humored her. I calmly shot down every argument for it and by the meeting's end, we once again accepted that I would not do it. At the next meeting, Sophia wanted to rehash it again.

"Sophia," began Marie from her usual upholstered chair across from us, "we've already been over this twice and Randy has said it's off the table. We're supposed to work on areas of compromise."

"Well, I just wanted you to hear me out," Sophia responded. I threw up my hands in futility. "What do you like to do with Dave," she asked me.

I shrugged. "Play with him, teach him things."

"Right. And I like to do potty training, feeding him, and taking care of him."

I tried not to laugh. "Is that why you don't change or feed him on weekdays before Emy arrives, because you enjoy it so much?"

"I do," she said, objecting.

"Whatever." I enjoyed throwing her favorite way to dismiss me back at her. I really did.

Marie asked, "Where are you going with this, Sophia?"

I took that as a sign of her recognizing bullshit was afoot. I knew the answer to her question and said it first. "Let me guess. You're going to suggest you have him all the time and I can visit to play with him, is that it?"

"Yes!" Sophia said, as if I'd just agreed. We then spent an hour on this, neither of us budging, and when I observed how stubborn she was, Marie irritated me.

"Neither of you are being flexible," she said.

"There's a big difference," I began, frowning at her. "I'm not considering uprooting my entire life to move to a Virginia apartment, selling the house, closing my business in Maryland, and other giant changes, all to make *her* life easier. She is refusing to consider trivial things like using a breast pump, formula, or not taking the baby to work when no one *ever* does that. You can't seriously be comparing these."

Marie smiled almost sheepishly. "Fair enough."

I continued. "Her only justifications are bullshit and lies. If that's how it's going to be, we should just quit now because it is not happening. She won't move until we have an agreement, and she is the one determined to go, so how can she adopt absolute positions like she's got some incredible leverage on me? She has *none*." I wanted her gone forever, too, but I was the one who could run out a clock on her, not agreeing to anything.

"Why don't we take a break," Marie said.

We did, and when we came back, Sophia suggested we make a list of areas we would compromise on and wanted the other to consider compromising on. I went first, making various offers, like me moving out nearby for a while, or to switch the schedule so that she went in early to work instead of me. I also wanted her to consider breastfeeding for six instead of twelve months, not taking the baby to work, and Dave to have one daycare instead of two daycares in different states, which was the only thing she agreed about.

"Sophia," began Marie, "what are you willing to compromise on?"

We waited. "I don't know."

"There must be something," observed Marie.

Sophia thought again. "I don't think there is."

I shook my head. "I wish I had that on tape."

"We can come back to that one," Marie said. I got the impression she was suppressing a smile at my sarcasm. "What about things you want him to consider?"

"I don't know. I don't think I have anything."

"Then why did you suggest this?" I asked in disbelief. It was purely an attempt at getting me to budge, and an inadvertent admission that she would not. I didn't need to be asked to make compromises, as I'd offered them, but Sophia couldn't even offer ones when asked. I asked, "Has it become obvious which one of us is reasonable and which one isn't?"

Marie said to her, "You almost don't have to make suggestions because he's already being reasonable."

I said, "This is the way it always is."

We spent the remaining time rehashing things and getting nowhere.

That same week, we drove separately to her new therapist's home office, not far from my parent's house, in a low home back from the road. The driveway had been expanded for parking, a path of flat stones amid the grass leading to a few wooden steps and a side door. Inside waited a mud room and chairs, and a long hallway that led further inside past the bathroom on one side, and to the other, a few steps down into a wide room full of bookcases along the walls, knickknacks, a desk, two upholstered chairs, and a leather couch beneath the window showing the driveway. Everything about the room shouted "old" and lived in, a plethora of items available for the eyes of trapped patients to gaze at during recurring appointments, a kind of eyeball mercy offered up so you didn't have to stare at the psychologist the entire time while baring your soul. Were they a kindness or a coincidence?

Dr. Thompson had obviously been seeing patients here for eons and was somewhat frail, her brown hair mostly grey now, skin marks over her wrinkled hands, humbly dressed in slacks and a sweater. Her body shook slightly. She sat across from us in one of the chairs, a notepad handy, though I never saw her write in it. Despite the watery gaze in what might have once been sharp eyes, her mind was still quick, agile, and alert. I came to like her, partly because she came across as fair, rather than a co-conspirator squarely on Sophia's side whose role was to help her bully and manipulate me. She was definitely better than that stupid quack in Virginia.

But I still thought it was a trap. Did doctor-patient confidentiality extend to me? I wasn't the patient and I was never diagnosed. I never paid her, submitted nothing to insurance. She was Sophia's therapist, not mine or ours. It was not marriage counseling, though perhaps end-of-marriage counseling. I was still certain she was working with Sophia's attorney, the goal being to get me to admit to abusive behavior. Then she'd tell the attorney, who'd file an emergency motion to take Dave away, the therapist testifying against me. It seemed illegal, but I doubted nothing now. Is it paranoia when ploys already abound?

I stepped into this perceived trap from an abundance of certainty that the truth would emerge with a fair arbiter. Pam had not been one, but Marie was, so where would Dr. Thompson fall? I was giving her a chance, but if bullshit reigned supreme, I would walk out again. I would not be railroaded or goaded with lies. I was no abuser. The disputes were mutual, not one-sided. Sophia was the only one to whom one-sidedness could be attributed in all things, from not participating in housework before to getting her way now. Knowing confidence can be a downfall, I nonetheless arrived calm and certain that with logic and objectivity, I could make a reasonable person see the truth. I did not need yelling, name calling, or an aggressive tone to get my way. Bullshit did not lead to my heart's desire. That fell to someone else.

After the initial getting acquainted, Dr. Thompson began by telling me what was going on with Sophia, who sat quietly on the opposite side of the couch, never looking at me as usual, as someone spoke for her. She sometimes wiped a silent tear from her face with a tissue. She still couldn't tell me herself.

"Randy," Dr. Thompson began, "Sophia has been wanting to tell you something for a long time now but finds it very difficult."

I shrugged. "Okay."

"You may know by now that she's having some difficulty handling emotions. What she wants to tell you is that she is very sensitive to some of them and finds it difficult to deal with them."

I sensed I was about to be attacked again, but I only said, "I have not heard this before."

The therapist nodded. "She hasn't told you, not directly. Instead of dealing with these emotions, she has taken to suppressing them so that she doesn't have to. But her ability to ignore them has recently become a problem, due to the pregnancy. She is unable to do this anymore."

"Would these emotions be ones like anger and frustration?" I asked, knowing the answer.

"Yes, among others."

"Why is she, or rather you, telling me this now?" I hadn't expected Sophia to answer, but she did.

"Because I heard you say something to Dave that you've said to me many times. You told him he doesn't need to get upset when you're upset with him for a few seconds, and this is what you've done to me for years."

I stifled irritation. Me being briefly upset and asking her not to overreact was not me "doing something" to her. I remembered the incident with Dave where he'd hit me in the face. Toward the end of it, I had told him that I was only upset a few seconds and to try not to get too upset himself. This statement is what led Sophia to this moment with Dr. Thompson. Somehow, she overlooked all that was good in my interaction with Dave and focused solely on two seconds of my upset, the clear implication being that a normal person wouldn't have been. I'd asked her countless times, "What's the big deal with me being upset for two seconds?" And I never got an answer.

Or had I just gotten it? Sophia was very sensitive to such emotions. Was that the mystery of fifteen years, the cause of it all?

"Dave gets upset very easily because he's very sensitive," I said, "too much so, really."

"That's because he gets it from *her*," Dr. Thompson said, smiling.

"That's funny," I said, "because I thought the same thing last week."

"So he gets it," Thompson said to her. "He gets it, Sophia."

"Yeah," I started, "but it doesn't mean anything wrong is being done to him. There are scenarios where it's perfectly normal to raise your voice at your kid, like if he's about to do something dangerous and you're trying to stop him."

"That's true," admitted Dr. Thompson.

Finally, some sanity. "And if you've tried to get them to obey you repeatedly and they aren't doing it, you use the Dad Voice in my case, being stern to get compliance."

Dr. Thompson nodded. "Yes, this is part of effective parenting."

"Thank you," I said, relieved. So she could be reasonable. I wanted to make an important distinction I'd just noticed. "Her being sensitive to these emotions is fine, but that's not the conversation we've been having all these years. It has not been her saying that she's sensitive and would appreciate it if I toned it down or something. The conversation has been her telling me these emotions don't exist and that there's something seriously wrong with me for experiencing or expressing them." I paused for emphasis, adding, "And that is a very different conversation."

"Got it. Yes, that is a very different conversation."

Someone was listening for once. "I'm upset by the implication that she's been asking me to be considerate of this sensitivity and I've been refusing. That's not what's been happening. What *has* happened is her attacking my emotions, and when I ask her to stop it, she refuses. You understand? It's backwards. I'm the one asking for respect of my wishes and she's the one refusing. She even follows me from the room when I'm trying to get away from her for saying it. But this sensitivity to my emotions thing? This is literally the first time I've heard about it. I've certainly never refused to consider a subject that has never been broached before."

"Yes, that is a very important distinction," said the doc. "You are both not really hearing the other."

I wanted to say that wasn't true, because I couldn't hear something Sophia had never said, but I let it go. "One of her known quirks we used to talk about is that she thinks she's saying one thing to me when she's not. She tends to withhold information, too."

"It's true," Sophia admitted. "I am not as good at communicating as you are."

Dr. Thompson observed, "It seems to me that both of you feel like you're being disrespected."

I said, "What else can you call being told your emotions are all wrong?"

Sophia said, "I feel like I'm being disrespected because you won't suppress them."

"Why should I have to? Who are you to tell me I have to suppress emotions? It's not healthy."

"*Expressing* them is not healthy. And you shouldn't be experiencing them."

"Give me a break. Who are you to tell me what I should feel and express? I have a right to my emotions."

Sophia snorted in derision. "I'm the person you're abusing with them."

"It's not *abuse* when someone expresses something you don't like, especially if they're upset for reasons that have nothing to do with you and you're in another room."

"Yes, it is."

"Okay," Dr. Thompson interrupted, "let's take a breath. We can't expect other people to deal with their emotions the way we do."

"*Thank* you," I said, glancing around the room and its knickknacks. "To me it is very unhealthy to suppress emotions and I'd be very surprised if you encouraged it."

"Suppressing them is generally not good," she agreed, "but we can choose how we handle them."

"Yes," Sophia eagerly agreed.

"True," I said, "but she has made it clear it doesn't matter how I handle them, but that the emotions exist at all. You just heard her say that very thing."

The initial meeting didn't cover much more and I agreed to go back for another meeting. Dr. Thompson had been fair, logical, and respectful. I mulled over the revelations, focusing on this issue of me being upset for two seconds and how Sophia considered even that little to be a huge deal. It implied I had to be perfect, no negative emotions at all, no matter what happened. I'd been aware of it for a decade, as we'd argued about it many times. One particular version stood out.

"What's the big deal with me being upset for two seconds?" I once asked for the millionth time, after she came into a room and started in on me, having heard me curse.

"I have to make you calm down."

"No, you don't. I will do it myself. I'm already calming when you start telling me I shouldn't be experiencing what I'm experiencing, or thinking what I'm thinking. Those comments are upsetting and you need to knock it off and butt out. You don't have to do anything at all."

"I can't do nothing."

"Why not?"

"I have to defend myself."

I spread my hands. "Defend yourself against what? It has nothing to do with you."

"Yes, it does. I'm being attacked."

"What are you talking about? If I'm mad at my computer, what does that have to do with you, especially when you're not even in the room?"

"You shouldn't be feeling whatever you're feeling. There is something wrong with you. You need professional help."

"Stop saying that shit to me!"

But she wouldn't, and I often left the room to get away from her and this message, chased away. Oddly, we both wanted me to calm down. I was doing it without intervention, just needing a few moments to myself, but she thought that by delegitimizing my emotions, they would vanish. If she could just convince me they weren't real, I'd never express one again. Problem solved! She could never see that by attacking me, she upset me more. I saw it but there was nothing I could say to get through to her. She was maddening.

CHAPTER NINE

The Phone Call

Days after the meeting, Sophia took a phone call upstairs, leaving me to watch Dave, though I'd only been passing through the room on my way downstairs. She just assumed I'd stop what I was doing and take over responsibility, just as I assumed she'd shirk hers like she just did for the millionth time. Our son sat rocking himself to sleep on the couch, and once asleep, I crept up the stairs to eavesdrop on Sophia, who'd gone into Dave's room and closed the door. I lay down atop the upper stairs, chin just inches from the carpeted landing. I didn't know who she was talking to and assumed it to be her best friend, Cindy. I only heard Sophia's side of the conversation about the situation, the long periods of silence as Cindy blathered on out of earshot suggesting she was greatly influential in the demise of my family.

"He's a jerk for trying to make me do a ninety-minute commute with the baby," said Sophia.

I shook my head at the persistent lie. My current commute took me past her job, another ten minutes farther. I made it in 45 minutes each way. And I wasn't making her take the baby to work.

"I know," she said after a pause. "He's going to pay for the house while I pay for the apartment."

We hadn't discussed that. At our last refinancing, I had just started my consulting company. My first client hadn't paid yet, so it looked like I had no income for the mortgage application. We'd tried and succeeded at qualifying with only her wages. Technically, the mortgage was in her name, the house in both of ours, both of us paying for it but her officially responsible for the mortgage. Should I stop paying and destroy her credit? She was already secretly funneling paychecks elsewhere, trying to stick me with obligations. Hearing her unilateral plans for rent and mortgage came as no surprise.

Laughing, she said, "He said he'll help me move out, but won't move himself. He's not making any sense." She listened and laughed. "I know. It's like he hit his head on something."

Helping my pregnant wife move to minimize stress on the baby was an act of consideration she scorned. She equated that with the considerable effort to sell the house, close and reform my business, and uproot both my life and Dave's. Over lies. I was the one who'd hit my head on something.

"I'll get a Virginia apartment for three to four months, and then a house. I'm not spending the next eighteen years in Maryland. I hate this state."

I had noticed her acting like Montgomery County, Maryland, where we lived, was a shithole despite it being one of the richest counties in the country, with a highly-rated education system. The crack about eighteen years meant until the baby graduated high school, another inadvertent admission that she intended to make this separation permanent. Confirmation of deceit is always "nice."

After more listening, she said, "Randy said I can't leave without an agreement and I thought, 'watch me.' I'm going to talk to my lawyer. Until we separate, I also can't sue him for custody and him not agreeing to less than 50% custody is a problem."

My refusal just rose.

"I can tell that unless we go to court, I won't get more than 50-50. Time isn't on my side because the longer I wait, the harder it is to move Dave to Virginia. If I can get him there more than 50-50 and have the baby, I can take both of them away from him. I'm trying to establish myself as primary."

By chance, I had apparently chosen the ultimate conversation to eavesdrop on. My excitement faded on hearing her next words, which came after a long pause.

"Yeah, I talked to my lawyer about just leaving with Dave, but he can file an emergency injunction with the court that will force Dave back to him. I can legally just take Dave, but the injunction he'd file would be the problem."

My jaw hit the floor. She *did* want to kidnap my son. Only advice from her attorney had stopped her. And Cindy had just suggested she kidnap him. *Holy fuck. What the hell was Sophia telling everyone?*

"Once I have Dave living in Virginia a few months, I have more legal options." Pause. "Legally I can't do anything until I move out." Pause. "Not legally." Pause. "I wish, but not legally." Another pause. "No, that's illegal, too." Pause, then a laugh. "I know. The law is really in the way."

Sober coldness swept over me. *Oh my God.* What was Cindy suggesting? Were they just going to try them anyway? Damn the law? What the hell was wrong with Cindy? Had she also gone mad? Drinking the Kool-Aid too much?

A laughing Sophia said, "With the baby, he's going to text saying that he needs a break and I can save all the texts and use them against him in court, to prove to a judge that he can't handle it. He always did that with Dave, like three times a week, so I always had to leave work early to go rescue him."

More amazement. She'd said she wanted to avoid court while secretly planning it. The business about rescuing me was fantasy. It was true that when Dave was younger, she sometimes texted me from work to ask how it was going and I had occasionally expressed frustration, a normal reaction to any parent but her. This sometimes happens when you watch a child under the age of four alone from 4pm to 8, 9, or 10pm without a break, four to five days a week, for years. They have bad days and so do you. She had sometimes asked if she should come home early to help. I would say, "If you want." I'd hardly begged. Once a month was far more accurate than three days a week.

She also needed to make up her mind. Either she was at home at 4:05 pm every weekday and I wasn't watching Dave at all, or I *was* watching him and she had to come home early to rescue me. She didn't get to have both. And I could prove she was lying about each with text messages, some admitting her late arrivals, and none showing me begging for help.

"Yeah," said Sophia, "he's always screaming at me and Dave and sending him back to me to watch." Pause. "It *is* child abuse," she agreed.

So there it was. A child abuse claim. Not surprising. Didn't anyone she told this screaming lie to think it sounded incongruous? I was so laid back and logical, and I don't scream or yell, or whatever you want to call it. None of those who knew me had heard it even once. Why were they all believing this bullshit and helping her? So far, only Marie and Dr. Thompson seemed to see through it at all.

"It went okay," she said, "but he said he has a right to his emotions, and I thought, 'Yeah, and I have a right to leave your ass!'" She gave a huge belly laugh.

I shook my head in wonder. An ultimatum. Pretend I don't experience negative emotions or she's leaving. Her way or the highway. Her consistent questioning of my emotions was the abuse. The scorn, contempt, and amusement showed how little she thought of me. It was mutual. Towering arrogance not only roared unchecked, but was even supported by Cindy on the other end of the phone.

I doubt Sophia realized that she was the cause of many of the emotions she didn't like in me. Rather than questioning their validity, she should've acknowledged that they revealed she'd done something wrong and stopped doing whatever it was. That's part of how you keep a relationship alive. She tried to kill the messenger instead, perpetuating the recurring problem. And now our marriage was ending.

There were two kinds of negative emotions between us – ones she caused in me and ones she did not. Neither were okay with her, but the first was worse. People will choose their sense of self over anything. Hers told her she was a wonderful, innocent person. Why admit to being selfish, contemptuous, and lazy, a version of her that I reflected back with my upset? Maybe she'd been genuine when she said that she was defending herself, her sense of self. My emotions challenged her and therefore had to be destroyed, silenced, invalidated. Either her sense of self was invalid, or my emotions were. Something had to give.

And so she'd begun invalidating me. Eventually, even emotions that she didn't cause got sucked into the gravitational pull of her attempts to invalidate the ones she *did* cause. Had they all become the same to her? If she could convince me that negative emotions weren't real in general, would she be able to stop me from experiencing and expressing any of them, whether she was the cause or not? Caught in the orbit of her challenged self-esteem, my emotions threatened to pull, stretch, and even break her tenuous hold on her emotional control. I remain calm, she remains calm. I get upset, she gets upset. Here is a woman reacting to my emotions and telling me that I am not to react to any stimuli myself, even though she's reacting to the stimuli that is me, unaware of the hypocrisy therein. She didn't just expect me to deny negative emotions exist like she did. She expected me to not react at all to their existence even though she reacted to the existence of mine. I had to be better than her, not just *like* her.

The phone call with Cindy continued with Sophia saying, "He did bite on something."

Paranoia. To hear yourself spoken of in such a way causes it. What was she up to? Dr. Thompson was a trap after all. They set me up for something, and I fell for it, and I didn't know what it was. She didn't elaborate and I grew frustrated, mind racing.

"Well, she agrees with me. She said the baby should stay with me and the kids should stay together, so Dave should be with me during the week, and Randy should only get short, supervised visits. My lawyer agreed with me, too."

My mouth probably fell open. Of course her clueless lawyer agreed with the story she'd gotten. That didn't mean shit, but neither Marie nor Dr. Thompson had agreed. Had Dr. Thompson made that recommendation to the attorney, or Sophia, or both, behind my back? The idea that my time with my son needed supervision was beyond appalling. For a moment I almost wanted to cry atop the stairs, at the grotesque picture Sophia was painting of me to everyone. They were eating it up.

She continued after another silence spent listening to Cindy, "I'd probably have to settle for having them most of the time and letting him visit, but it's in the best interests of the kids if they never see him again."

This time my jaw hit the floor. The new #1 Most Hurtful Thing had now been said about me. I had suspected she believed this. There it was.

"Dave is afraid of him. Part of the plan is to do a custody evaluation and get Dave to say that. You know, Daddy got mad at me and I cried."

I wasn't sure I could handle hearing much more of this, though you couldn't have dragged me away. Now she wanted to use my *son's* negative emotions against me. How ironic. If I caused Dave negative emotions, I was the problem, not him. Likewise, if Sophia caused me negative emotions, she should be the problem. But no. It was still me.

Sophia said, "No, unfortunately I can't prove any of this."

That's because you're a fucking liar, I thought.

"Yeah, they've been great. They keep asking me what they can do for me. I've told them all about it. My boss and everyone there is just awesome, trying to help me any way they can."

Jesus. Her employer interfering had me incredulous. I already knew, but the reminder of a broad and deep conspiracy to take my kids away snapped me into focus. Who the hell did these people think they were? What right did they have? They were way out of line. I imagined them looking me up online to see what this monster Sophia was describing looked like.

I realized she was using sexist stereotypes against me, telling everyone I was the perpetually angry husband abusing his wife and kids. She was a damsel in distress and they were all determined to rescue her and the baby, the noble, heroics assholes that they were. A cold, seething anger slowly built, one which was entirely justified. It was not a sign that there was something wrong with me. God I was so sick of being judged for the pain she caused me.

"He's emotionally abusing me. He can't understand that his anger hurts me."

I almost wanted to laugh. And you can't understand how telling me my emotions, thoughts and experiences are not real, and that I'm fucked up and need a therapist, hurts *me*.

"It helps to have your perspective because you've already been through it."

I scowled in confusion. Cindy had been divorced and recently remarried, but she didn't have kids.

"Say hi to your mom for me."

Alexa. She was talking to Alexa, whose mother Sophia knew and liked. Alexa, the woman who'd introduced us, who tried to set us up, who helped us in the early stages of dating, especially when Sophia was pregnant and the abortion loomed. The woman who had said afterward that if we could survive that, we could survive anything. The woman who'd once been my friend first, before meeting Sophia at work and ditching me for her and their posse of girls, saying she couldn't be friends to both of us because she'd get in the middle of things.

And now here she was fifteen years later, in the middle of things, helping my wife figure out how to take my kids away from me forever, suggesting Sophia kidnap them, and clearly believing lies about me abusing my son. Making suggestion after illegal suggestion. She'd always been an ADD-driven motormouth. I should've known it was her from the way Sophia listened for long moments, time after time, as Alexa blabbed, leading Sophia into marital destruction like the Pied Piper of Custody Carnage. Alexa was leaving her husband, too, and taking the kids away. Oh how they must have bonded! What stunned me was that Alexa had called me to express concern over how I was doing. I'd been suspicious, apparently with good reason.

I wanted to kill her.

CHAPTER TEN

A Horse
Named Resentment

The next day, my mother called both of them "evil" when I phoned her from outside so Sophia wouldn't overhear me. Running into my neighbors one by one, I told them a little, including the lies that Dave was afraid of me and I was abusing him. Both were instantly shocked and didn't believe it, having seen us together outside many times. Both offered to be witnesses in my defense, and one gave good advice that wasn't easy to follow.

"Don't let the crazy make you crazy."

Easier said than done.

We again met Dr. Thompson, who hadn't known I was coming and seemed genuinely happy to see me, though Sophia had undoubtedly badmouthed me to her. I now had a better idea of the forces arrayed against me, Sophia none the wiser about my knowledge.

"I think we need to improve communications," began the therapist, seeming to include me as a responsible party for our poor communication. I was having none of that.

"I think you need to start with her on this one. She withholds information and even admitted it in January."

"That's true," Sophia confessed to my surprise.

I went on to add how horrible it was to be kept in the dark about what was happening and why. I told Dr. Thompson the things Sophia *had* said and how – the comments about never kissing me or sleeping with me again, yelling that she didn't want to be married to me anymore, and lying that I had caused her to have a panic attack.

Dr. Thompson nodded. "You did not cause her panic attack. That much I know."

I sighed. Sometimes it's nice to get such an acknowledgement. I noticed Sophia wasn't apologizing for the accusation. She seldom did for anything anyway. "I still don't know when it was, and I'm not sure I believe the reason. I don't see what Dave being in kindergarten has to do with us working on our relationship. What's wrong with talking about it right now?"

Dr. Thompson began nodding. "Right. Randy's right. What's wrong with right now? That's exactly right."

I noticed her agreeing with me more than Sophia, but I soon found myself threatening to walk out and never return. Far from backing down on false accusations or apologizing for one, Sophia raised the idea that I was emotionally abusing her, an offensive exaggeration at best. I immediately shot this down, not caring how unwilling to discuss it I appeared.

And so Sophia cited her proof. "You said you were going to get a gun and kill my horse. How is that not abuse?"

Eye roll. "Oh, come on. First of all, a single comment is not abuse. There has to be a pattern over months or years. And secondly, I don't have a gun. And I have no idea where your horse is even stabled, and you can't seriously think I was going to murder it."

"How am I supposed to know what you're capable of?"

I snorted. "Really? After fifteen years? Then again, this year you've proven you're capable of things I never would've imagined."

Dr. Thompson asked me, as if she knew the answer, "Then why did you say it?"

"It was just an expression of frustration."

"An abusive one," Sophia retorted.

"A single comment is not *abuse*," I repeated in exasperation. The whole horse thing was a huge issue between us, a button she could press, and she had just slammed it. I was quickly getting upset, which irritated me all the more because I knew I was going to be judged for it. "I'm not elevating all of your screwed up comments as abuse, even when there's a prolonged pattern of them, so stop doing that to me over a remark said in frustration. It's insulting."

Dr. Thompson interrupted. "Well, we don't want to get into a back and forth about who said what."

That irritated me because it sounded like dismissal of an important, valid point, one that was at the heart of this marriage implosion. "On this one, we do. There's been too much crap from her about this horse for me to tolerate being made out to seem like the problem here."

"It's never productive."

"It will be this time because it will tell you all *sorts* of things about this relationship. Her behavior over a decade or more led to the remark and she's acting like one comment from me is the real issue and she's refusing to acknowledge the events that led to that comment."

"Well, let's move on to other things. It doesn't matter."

"It does to me," I persisted. "I'm sick of being falsely accused or characterized like an abusive monster, most of it behind my back to people I hardly know, and I never get to defend myself, and they're trying to help her take my kids away from me."

"I really don't think we need to – "

I raised my voice. "Look, either I get to tell my side of this story or I am walking out of here right now and you are never seeing me again."

"Okay, okay," said Dr. Thompson, holding up supplicating hands. "I can see there's an issue here."

"You got *that* right." I knew my behavior played right into Sophia's assertions that I got upset over nothing, but that was what I had to clear up. This was what she did – countless fucked up things and then when I reacted with one minor thing, she said I was the problem. I was not letting it stand in front of a witness, especially one likely working with her lawyer, because to do so allowed her exoneration of herself and blaming of me to stand unchallenged.

And so I told her therapist the story as Sophia listened in silence, not contradicting my account.

When we'd met, I was taking horseback riding lessons. She had ridden for years, missed it, and dreamed of owning a horse, so our first date was riding near Dulles, Virginia, at a stable that let us take two quality horses out unsupervised. We went there for years until they closed, and our honeymoon and usually anniversaries included riding. She resumed riding and taking lessons, semi-private ones with the two of us, but she was more invested, getting really into it and even making custom breeches for us with a sewing machine.

One day, Sophia found a barn she liked. By "barn," I don't mean the building. There are people who own a house with land and a barn, but they hire a manager to handle the stables and horses, that manager being the "barn" – they are a business for liability reasons. Sophia liked a "barn" consisting of Rob and Amy, and their other students, who owned horses while Sophia and I rode one of Rob's "school horses" named Nellie. School horses were our only option during lessons before this, too. They are used for clueless kids and adults who give commands poorly with hands, feet, legs, and "seat" (your butt). They know what you want but often refuse to do it from laziness, making you doubt yourself. I increasingly loathed Nellie, and Sophia was no fan either, but we were stuck with her, even after Rob and Amy left to manage another property. They took their supplies and horses with them. Sophia followed them from location to location, which changed every year it seemed, and therefore so did I.

Figure 3 Me on a Horse

We took lessons from Amy (and rarely Rob), me on Nellie, Sophia on a better horse, but she often rode without me, on Nellie. While Sophia was a better rider from having more experience, I was more talented; I steadily gained on her. She often complained that I picked up where I'd left off after the last lesson while she had to repeat much of it. After hearing me complain about Nellie one too many times, she suggested around 2005 that we buy our own horse.

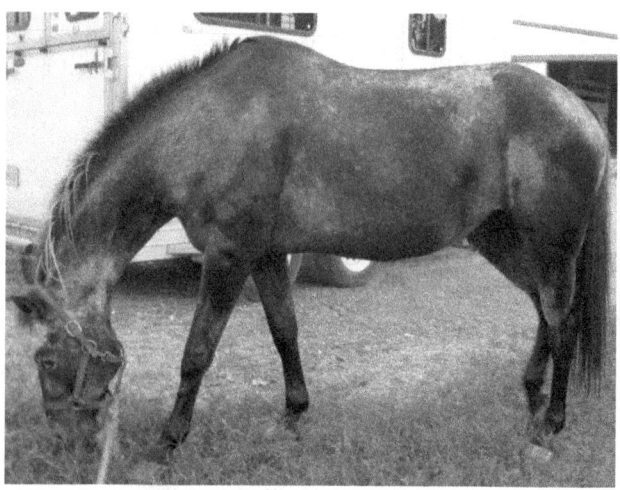

Figure 4 Nellie, the School Horse

"Are you kidding?" I asked, standing in the kitchen with her as I cooked fries, the burgers on the grill needing a few minutes before I flipped them. "Those are *way* too expensive."

"We can get a really good one for four or five thousand," Sophia said as if disagreeing, while confirming my point.

"That's even worse than what I thought! What's the stabling cost?" I set out plates, having already gotten the sandwich pickles, buns, cheese, tomato, and ketchup out.

"It depends on how you stable them, like a field board or in the barn, which is more expensive but better for them."

"Give me a number." I took a drink.

"I don't know. Three hundred to eight hundred a month."

I almost spat out my water. "Are you serious? That's insane! No way."

She began an impassioned plea. "Well, I'm just asking you to consider it. I've always wanted a horse, and we're both really into riding. It wouldn't be just for me, but both of us. You can stop riding Nellie."

"Thank God for small miracles," I interrupted. "I hate that horse. And I'm sure it's mutual."

"I know, that's why I thought you'd want this even more than me."

"Well, it sounds great when you ignore the cost, but we simply can't afford that."

She worked out the numbers anyway and over several months focused on the awful experience with Nellie, saying there was a way out for both of us. For our anniversary, we went to a B&B that included riding lessons on the owner's thoroughbreds. Mine was gorgeous, well-behaved, and superbly responsive. I had my best riding experience and made rapid progress, the horse confirming I made the right moves instead of screwing with me by refusing to cooperate. I consented to buying a horse as a trial after my great experience. If it wasn't working out, we'd sell it. Sophia agreed and wanted to handle the purchase. One day she excitedly told me about it and did the deal, spending $5000 of our joint funds on it. I groaned about it but I looked forward to riding whenever I wanted on a far better horse. We'd have to take turns instead of ride together, but it was fine. This was the plan we made together. Little did I know it was all a ruse and she'd made a secret plan of her own all along.

Sophia dropped a bomb the first time I said something about looking forward to riding the horse.

She casually said that, in her and Amy's opinion, I was not good enough to ride it and would never be allowed to so much as sit on it.

She spent $5000, half of it mine, to buy a horse she intentionally planned to keep to herself and prevent me from riding.

We would now pay $300-800 a month in stabling and medical care.

She spent months lying to me that the horse was for both of us, using my hatred of Nellie so that I'd agree to the purchase. Now she informed me I'd have to continue riding Nellie. She informed me that I'd still have to pay full price, $60 each time, to do so, not even getting a courtesy $1 off as someone boarding a horse at the "barn." Since every ride would cost me another $60, there was no riding whenever I wanted like Sophia now could unless I incurred even more fees. My cost had skyrocketed with zero benefit to me. Already a better rider than me but, with me fast gaining on her, much to her disliking, she'd found a way to stay ahead of me in skill.

I was insulted by the justification she offered – my supposed riding skills. Sophia was the one who'd been thrown from a horse three times, once breaking her arm. Me? Not once. I had just ridden a better steed than this at the B&B and excelled. I was born Learning Disabled and suffered terrible self-esteem problems in grade school, about my ability to succeed at anything, only to be diagnosed and helped. I went on to graduate college Magna cum Laude. Originally a music composition major, I'd switched to classical guitar with only two years of school left, and I passed every performance test on time, including two solo recitals – I excelled at quickly learning something physically challenging. Since childhood, no one had made me feel so incapable and worthless that I would not even be given a chance, but Sophia just had. She had preemptively and unilaterally cast me out.

This was contempt. Delivered casually. Without apology. And since Amy and Rob controlled the barn, and Sophia controlled the relationship with them, they could easily stop me from ever mounting that horse. Sophia rendered me powerless.

I was furious.

She didn't acknowledge having done anything wrong. She claimed that she didn't know I was "into" riding. I owned a helmet. A crop. Riding boots. Gloves. Breeches that she had made for me after measuring me and us picking out fabric together at the store. I had been riding when we met, not her. I went almost as often as her, for *years* of joint lessons. I had learned how to take care of horses, cleaning their hooves and more. It was unfathomable that she "didn't know." An insult to my intelligence.

I saw the future. We'd go to the barn. She'd get on that horse I privately nicknamed Resentment. I'd get on the hated, disagreeable, stubborn Nellie. She'd call Resentment "my horse" like she was already doing. I would glare daggers that it was supposed to be "ours." We'd go out into the field. She'd prance around in front of me on Resentment, the horse I wasn't allowed to touch, I was so unworthy, and it hurt me deeply. I'd urge the mule that was Nellie to obey my commands but she'd undermine my confidence through refusal. Sophia would be laughing. I would be cursing, every second a bitter reminder that the person I loved most in life, and trusted most, had betrayed me on purpose and with the malice of forethought, then lied about it, insulting my capabilities and memory, trying to gaslight me into believing it was all some innocent misunderstanding.

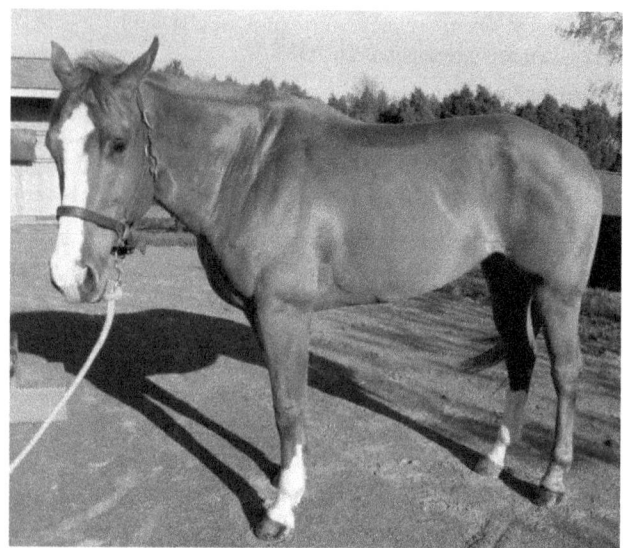

Figure 5 A Horse Name Resentment

However frustrated I sometimes felt riding Nellie would go nuclear. I could not endure this. Would not. There was no way I would submit to the insult of it, the frustration, the anger, the indignation, the contempt, the deceit. To ever ride horses again with Sophia, if one of them was Resentment, meant acceptance of it all. I could not do that, even had I wanted to. It was too much to ask. I know my limits. This far exceeded mine. We would have fought at every outing to the barn.

Sophia took away an activity that I loved. The day she informed me of her betrayal was the last time I ever went riding with her, and due to the cost, I just quit. She had tainted an activity – the first one – that brought us together and now it would start tearing us apart.

At first, she asked in bewilderment why I wasn't going with her to the barn, revealing a cluelessness about the impact of her actions. I chose not to explain to her because

I was still too hurt and upset, and as a result – I withdrew, as I usually do. I knew she would lie again about what she'd done, as we'd repeatedly argued about it already. I could not do it again. It was a knife to the heart when the one you love so casually lies to your face about what you know to be true. The pain of it was so deep I just shut down the subject, feigned indifference and talked about something else on purpose. I had decided that the subject of me riding horses ever again was forbidden. We never did it for an anniversary again either, a tradition going back years, now dead.

Week after week, year after year, she found the energy to go to the barn, ride that horse, clean and wash it, lovingly conditioning the leather of her saddles, tack, and more – and all the while, she refused to do much around the house because she was too tired. She put in a lot of effort for herself and the horse, but not for me. Not for us. Not anymore. Despite it all, I still went to the amateur riding events she later took part in, videotaping her and cheering her on.

I'm not sure how long we owned Resentment. A few years at least before she tried to sell him for some reason and buy another horse, but there would be no resumption of riding for me. I was out, by *my* own decision. Selling a horse can take months. One day, while in her white Mitsubishi Mirage, she was driving, I asked how it was going.

"So what's going on with the horse sale?"

"I gave it away."

My eyes popped out of my head. "You *what*!?"

"I gave it away."

I was briefly speechless. "What the hell were you thinking giving the horse away?"

"Well, I couldn't sell it and I just wanted to move on."

"That horse was worth five thousand dollars!"

"More like two thousand."

"What? Since when?"

"Whatever. It's done."

I noticed she wasn't exactly apologizing, and I struggled for words, finally asking, "When the hell was this?"

"Two weeks ago."

More shock. "You gave it *away* two weeks ago, behind my back, and you didn't say anything until now, and you're only telling me because I asked? What the hell do you think you're doing? You don't get to make unilateral decisions like that."

And then she uttered the immortal words. "My horse, my money."

I sucked in a breath through my nose and stopped speaking. In fact, I didn't speak to her again for two weeks. She justified stabbing me in the back when giving the horse away by pointing out she'd stabbed me in the back when buying it. Some would say I gave her the silent treatment and this was abuse, but the outright hostility that I kept to myself would have been infinitely worse. Four letter words, screaming, and name calling were all I had in me.

Over the years, we went through three different horses, and in 2011 she got pregnant with Dave and couldn't ride. That horse began to deteriorate, becoming unfit for riding even after expensive rehabilitation, which continued when she finally consented to sell it because we couldn't get rid of it due to its condition. I felt trapped, watching money vanish into the waste pit of Resentment III.

"What's going on with the horse sale?" I asked one day in the kitchen, where we often seemed to be during conversations that amounted to updates about life. This time we were making several meatloaves together, her mixing ingredients while I measured everything and prepared baking dishes.

"I'm not really getting anywhere," she admitted.

"Why?

"Well, he's not in very good shape."

"I thought we were spending all this extra money to get him in shape?" I poured breadcrumbs into the bowl as she churned it.

"Yeah, I just can't get a buyer."

"Why not give him away?" At this point, I'd settle for the loss rather than spend another $400 a month. He wasn't worth much anymore anyway and we'd actually save money by just getting rid of him. I wanted him off the books.

"I can't do that either."

"Why not?"

"The only place I can give him to is a rescue farm, but they'd just euthanize him."

"So we're stuck with this horse?"

"Basically."

"Until it dies of natural causes?" I poured in the tomato sauce.

"Yeah."

"How long is that going to take? Five years?"

She laughed. "If we're lucky. More like ten to fifteen, even twenty."

"Are you serious? We're going to pay $400 a month for two decades until the damn horse dies?" That was $24,000-$96,000. We were not rich. I noticed she seemed unfazed by this, as if she'd made up her mind to do it, without talking to me about it, of course.

"Basically. It will eventually die of old age."

In utter disbelief, I mused aloud, "Why don't I just get a gun and shoot the damn thing?"

She didn't respond, but now we were sitting in Dr. Thompson's office years later, the horse still on the books! She cited this rhetorical question as proof that I was emotionally abusive, suggesting this lone comment was the problem instead of her decade of bullshit about the horses. The idea infuriated me. And the more I talked, the more Dr. Thompson nodded.

"Okay," she said, laughing ruefully, "so I can see there's history with the horse. I think we can all agree you've both said things you probably shouldn't have."

I glowered. "The offhand comment about shooting the horse I don't know the location of with a gun I don't have and don't know how to use hardly competes with telling me she's never kissing me again, or sleeping with me, or accusing me of causing her panic attack, and that she doesn't want to be married anymore." I didn't mention her trying to find a way around legal loopholes so she could kidnap my son, since she'd technically said that to Alexa and not me, and she didn't need to know I knew about it.

Dr. Thompson smiled and I could tell she wanted me to drop the subject. "That is true. I agree. I just want us to not rehash things any more than necessary, as there are bigger issues than various comments."

"True, but I want to be clear that I will not sit in silence if I am treated unfairly. If that's what you want, do it behind my back like she's already doing. I will not let a lie or mischaracterization go unchallenged if I hear one, so if you want this to not be he-said, she-said all the time, then quit with the lying."

"Fair enough, and I agree with you."

I noticed Sophia didn't say anything, implying she did not agree. No surprise there.

As talk continued, Sophia admitted to not telling me much for fear of a bad reaction, implying my ignorance was my fault. It was a thinly veiled swiped at my emotions. Again. Maybe she should've stopped saying fucked up things and I wouldn't have had a bad reaction. Call me Captain Obvious. She confessed to being unable to find another way to tell me anything and had decided to suppress it all instead. She acknowledged holding grudges from things I'd said or done that had hurt her, not citing examples, which was just as well.

I sensed that Dr. Thompson increasingly saw that Sophia was not some innocent victim of an abusive husband, but a full participant in upsetting said husband and taking no responsibility for the reactions she caused and characterized as abuse. The picture I painted was infinitely more complicated and believable.

I had noticed something in her remarks and said, "I understand that you don't want to accept that you've upset me, maybe because it makes you feel guilty, but when you tell yourself that you did nothing wrong, you are also saying that my upset has no explanation, no rationale, and can't be predicted. That's not at all true. There is always a reason I am upset. That you don't know what it is doesn't mean it isn't there. What's really upsetting to me is that when I try to tell you what happened, you won't listen, insisting to me that nothing happened. It's almost like you're purposely telling yourself my emotions are random. The result is that you are on edge about them happening at any time, for no reason, according to you.

"But here's the worst part for you: you are telling yourself that you are helpless, a victim, and that you cannot control my emotions. Never mind that controlling another person's emotions is not your job, or responsibility, and could even be considered offensive and intrusive. But the real issue is that you think you don't impact me when you do. You've had the power to affect my emotions the entire time I've known you. You are just misusing it, making my emotions worse and stronger, when you don't want them worse and stronger, but you want them to be calmer, just like I do. We want the same thing, but I'm the authority on what makes me calm when upset, and you always reject my opinion of what will calm me in favor of *your* opinion, even though you are wrong and it has never once worked.

"What I need from you when I'm upset is for you to leave me alone for a few minutes so I can calm down, but you won't do it. If you did that, I would calm down. If you asked me what was wrong, I would calm down. If you listened to me say what happened and actually heard what I'm telling you, I would calm down. Maybe you can even make a joke like we used to do about the printers being out to get me, because I was unconsciously acting like they were with all the problems they caused me. And it would make me laugh and calm down.

"You are not some helpless victim. You want power over my emotions? You've had it the entire time. You have been badly misusing it for the worse. You just need to learn how to use the power you already *have* for the better."

Dr. Thompson sat nodding as I talked, and when I glanced at Sophia, I had the impression that it had honestly never occurred to her to try the things I had just suggested. It didn't surprise me.

Her therapist was so impressed that when I left at session's end, she not only shook my hand, but clasped mine in both of hers, one hand on top, repeatedly saying thank you and that I had been wonderful and very communicative, and that she really hoped I would return. She seemed to respect me. It was mutual, and I wondered if I was wrong to be suspicious of the motives for having me there.

But my guard remained up, with good reason.

CHAPTER ELEVEN

It Has to Get Worse...

At the next session with Marie, Sophia still wanted to talk about me moving to Virginia, even though I'd ruled it out a dozen times over multiple sessions. She'd thought of more angles. It resembled whack-a-mole, me defeating every irrational argument only to have another pop up. Even Marie showed exasperation and together we suggested stopping these sessions altogether as it was unproductive. Sophia agreed. We never saw Marie again. Collaborative divorce had failed, as I'd expected. We (I mean Sophia) had wasted nearly $2000 on the sessions because Sophia wouldn't even try meeting in the middle, insisting on her way. Did she think she'd wear me down? I'd lived a brutal life for twenty years before meeting her and withstood it all. She knew this, but I was increasingly wondering if she'd ever really met me. She didn't seem to know me at all.

I talked to my lawyer about Sophia's emotional abuse allegations. She said that was difficult to prove even when true and I faced no risk until then. Even if I was a terrible father, I would get more custody than having none at all as Sophia intended, so her extreme wasn't likely. The responses calmed me.

In late April, I drove thirteen hours to Florida to help my parents prepare to move to Texas near my brother, his wife, and their two kids. I'd seldom told them about my life because they had made it clear in my childhood that they weren't listening. I was used to dealing with terrible things alone until I'd met Sophia, who was now the terrible thing. But now I talked to them twice a week and they were definitely listening, and they were appalled. During my visit, my mother assured me all the relatives she'd talked to didn't believe a word she'd related about Sophia's accusations. Some wanted to testify. I felt grounded for the first time in months, Sophia's incessant gaslighting having affected me more than I'd realized until hearing another perspective. Dr. Thompson had given me this at times, too. Sophia's psychological warfare briefly felt like a distant memory.

With the free time of vacation, I put some pieces together. Sophia had once said she'd married me partly because she knew she could trust me due to my honest-to-a-fault personality, which included emotional honesty. Ironically, it seemed she was leaving me for the same reason. Her behavior all these years had slowly cost her my respect, earning her contempt that she felt and heard. Rather than try and change her behavior which had caused the metamorphosis, she invalidated my upset. This was a defense mechanism.

One sign we've done something wrong is the reaction – negative emotions. If, like Sophia, we've trained ourselves to ignore those, we see no sign that we did something wrong. Ergo, we did not. There's no reason to stop it at the time or going forward. No apology. We can develop an infallibility complex. Since she'd supposedly done nothing wrong, my upset made no sense. There must have been something wrong with me. Taking the kids away implied only I expressed these emotions. Otherwise, removing them made no sense because they would just be exposed to someone else's, too. This fit her narrative that there was something wrong with me, the one person like this.

Ignoring negative emotions might've worked before she met me. No siblings to provoke them. No father. Her working mother gone weekdays. Retired, doting, stress-free grandparents had raised her. Had she rarely been exposed to a negative emotion beyond her suppressed own? She had been a friendless loner, which made moving alone to the U.S. as a teenager easier, never seeing anyone she'd known again. She had few friends here until shortly before meeting me. I was her first boyfriend at twenty-four. "Emotions are a choice," she had repeatedly informed me. This flies in the face of reality and what any psychologist would say. That we live in a society that presents cool, emotionless indifference as desirable may have influenced her choice. America does this, but according to her, Russians are worse and view emotion as weakness. Like positive emotions, negative ones are an inherent part of life and intimate relationships.

After we were engaged, she said she loved rollercoasters like me, so we went to Kings Dominion in Virginia. But once on one, she felt nauseous and dizzy. Even tamer rides caused the same, ruining our day. She had joked that falling in love with me had made her weak. She had prided herself on being tough and years later admitted that she didn't feel the need to be anymore because she could rely on me. It had been the excuse for not doing her share of anything anymore, the original cause of my negative emotions toward her, and which I was honest about. She hadn't liked that part of my honesty. Love had softened her hard shell, leaving her vulnerable to the negative emotions she caused but couldn't face. Was that when suppression began, or had it been there all along? This wrong turn left her feeling lost, unable to see that if she stopped doing the things that upset me, she wouldn't face those emotions. Instead, the tactic was to invalidate this feedback. We were stuck in a negative feedback loop of her making, and her stubbornness meant there was no way out except ending the relationship.

It came down to world view. Hers was that these emotions don't exist. But if they don't exist, then how is it that I just expressed one? This is called cognitive dissonance. Let's say you don't believe little green men exist. What are you supposed to think when one is standing in front of you? You can accept the evidence and change your incorrect world view, or you can keep your world view and find another rationale for what you see ("It's just a guy in a costume!").

Sophia chose the latter, waging a long gaslighting campaign to convince me that these emotions aren't real, to silence me. She needed me to never reveal that these emotions exist through a display of them, even if only seconds long. This was the answer to my often-asked question, "What is the big deal with me being upset for two seconds?" She had never answered. Time after time, she made it clear that the problem was not how I expressed my emotions or their brevity, but that they existed at all. "You shouldn't be feeling, thinking, experiencing..."

She couldn't face a reality most of us had dealt with all our lives: we can upset others and should therefore watch our words and actions. She seemed to reject this, which explained her casual cruelty. "I'm never kissing you again," she had serenely informed me.

She'd admitted long ago to not carrying her weight because I was so strong. *The Art of War* talks about turning your enemy's strength into a weakness. Was this her version? Use my capability as an excuse to dump all responsibility on me and go from capable, strong, and an equal partner to lazy, incompetent, and indifferent. There's an esteem we feel when we have our act together. She had given it up. Was she as disappointed in herself as I was? Had this combination been the black cloud hanging over her life, the one prompting those conversations about why her life was great but she still felt depressed and couldn't figure out why? An invisible demon stalking her, wearing her down.

You could say I should've let stuff go, but I did all the time, just taking care of something for us and swallowing my grievance despite her claiming I gave free rein to it. She had no idea how much I withheld – the names I never uttered, the curses I stifled, the volume I kept low, the blows I wanted to use on an inanimate object and never did. Her head would've exploded had I done them.

And while I could walk away from situations, the angst festered. But what I could never ignore was that every request I made for change was met with "no." She never said it. She just refused to compromise. And in the end, that is all I saw. Every stack of papers, pile of clothes, or undone errand was a reminder of how little she cared about me, that she couldn't even give me one concession, no matter how small. The only changes where ones she instituted over my objections, because they were at my expense. It is a huge deal when your life partner rejects every last request you make. That is not a marriage. It is not a romantic relationship. There is nothing even remotely romantic about it. It says loud and clear that they do not care about you, that they do not love you.

And that message caused the negative emotions I expressed.

A year after Dave's birth, as we talked about her depression again, she blurted out, "I don't want to be anyone's wife! I don't want to be anyone's mother!" She also said she was fine with being roommates with me (I assumed that meant no life sharing, romance, or sex, but she didn't specify). I'd thought she was blowing off steam, but I now knew it had been a rare moment of honesty from someone far more deceptive and reticent than I'd realized.

When I was upset, Sophia and I wanted the same thing, for me to calm down. I had told her countless times what I needed – to not interact for a few minutes. Not only did she refuse, but she'd gaslight and attack me. I would leave to get away, and she'd follow, not taking a hint, even when I yelled at her as I fled. She interfered with my anger management process and then obnoxiously told me it didn't work.

I figured out much of the mystery to Sophia's attack on my emotions while on the week-long trip to my parents that April. While there, I jumped on a cruise ship for a few days. Sophia and I had done it several times and people had always been social, but not this time and I was bored. I did hang out several times with a beautiful black woman in her 20s, but she was leading me on, even giving me a lap dance in a club one night and then ignoring me after. I enjoyed it anyway, of course, and it inspired thoughts of dating, but romance was the last thing on my mind. Sex, however, was not.

I did several video calls with Dave, who kept saying he loved and missed me, in front of his mother, who no doubt couldn't process this truth. Her skewed perspective reared again the day I got home. Dave wanted to sleep with me and I loved the idea because I missed him. Sophia went to bed first, and as I neared the top of the stairs with him, he casually asked, "Where's mommy?"

As if Dave was terrified, Sophia cried out from behind his closed bedroom door, "I'm here, Dave! In your room. I'm here! It's okay!"

Gaping in disbelief, I watched helplessly as he ran into his room, changing his mind about sleeping with me. Via text, I revealed my anger at her stunt and she replied that she had to get his anxiety down. I felt incredulous that she'd heard fear instead of innocent curiosity. Was she more screwed up than I thought?

In my absence, my mother-in-law arrived from Russia to live in my house, sleeping on the couch. I'd known it was afoot. Nina was slightly taller than Sophia, stoop-shouldered, and had shoulder-length black-hair which was now mostly grey. She'd perfected "Resting Bitch Face," an expression that never disappeared except for sudden laughter that would end just as swiftly as it had begun. She seemed just as emotionally muted as her daughter. Coincidence? At first, we were cordial and talked despite her poor English, but in time, we never even said hello. I felt certain she was a spy in my midst.

Sophia's plan was to have Nina help with the baby and Dave, but it immediately became apparent she could not control our son, who ignored her, partly due to the language barrier. They literally didn't understand each other's words, but even Sophia and Emy didn't understand how to handle him after three years. And Sophia still couldn't control him precisely because she wouldn't raise her voice or speak sternly to him. She called that abuse. I called it being an authority figure. She was in for a shock when she moved out and had visitation, having squandered nearly four years of opportunities to establish herself as one because, as with everything, she shirked a responsibility in favor of me doing it alone.

My first week back, on Wednesday, my employer unceremoniously fired me over the phone. The first dishonest excuse was that I was working from home without permission; never mind that since autumn, my one-day-a-week work from home had been Wednesday. My work laptop had also been left on my desk overnight the day before in violation of company policy, but a co-worker had caused that. The third reason amounted to someone being offended that I'd once called into their meeting instead of being there in person and having left another one that ran over time (I needed to get home to take over for the nanny). The HR director, Susan, knew some of my personal situation from the day I barged into her office in turmoil. Rather than stopping this absurd firing, she was the one doing it. I told her what I now thought of her, reminding her of what I'd told her. F-bombs were dropped. I immediately stormed over to work to get my things, which she handed to me in a box outside beside a coworker.

Looking genuinely embarrassed and remorseful after my tirade, she began, "I'm sorry," before I cut her off.

"Don't. You don't get to say that shit to me." I yanked the box out of her hand and left. I suspected that the real reason for it all was that our team had completed the project for the client, the federal government, and my employer did not have another client project to put me on, so they used excuses to terminate me.

By day's end, I ditched my private investigator, needing the $3500 retainer back. He said something about keeping a percentage of it until I told him I'd been fired. He sounded genuinely remorseful about how much bullshit I had going on, meaning the pregnant wife, separation, paternity and affair concerns, and now being fired. That list and his pity made me feel pathetic, as I left behind turmoil for the cold calmness of depression. I was tired of feeling victimized but felt no self-pity, just deep weariness, despair, outrage, and indignation.

And then days later, it got worse.

CHAPTER TWELVE

Getting Caught

Before vacation, I had charged the GPS tracker, which normally lasted a week, but this time it had died within days. Now I went to get it and discovered that the perpetually messy trunk of her car was immaculate. She had likely cleaned it for the first time since I'd known her to make space for her mother's luggage on returning from the airport. My tracker was gone. I assumed it now sat in her lawyer's office as proof that I was overbearing or some bullshit. If it came up in court, I had the ultimate rebuttal – fear she'd make good on kidnapping Dave, for which I'd call Alexa as a witness. Besides, the receipt would prove I'd gotten it recently and it didn't amount to years of *anything*. It had also recorded proof of her lying to me, one of many examples to crush her credibility. My attorney said I had a right to track a vehicle I owned and not to worry about this.

But to this day, neither of us have ever mentioned it.

At the next session with Dr. Thompson, more lies and revelations emerged. Sophia accused me of hitting Dave. I shut that down at once. The subject died a swift death.

Dave had never been spanked. He didn't need it. He was a good kid, for one, but he was so sensitive to disap-

169

proval, especially mine, that he cried easily and didn't need spanking to get the point across. Growing up, my parents had spanked us, even buying a wooden paddle and forcing us to tearfully sign our names on it as if we condoned its use, a deep humiliation. I would never do this to my kids. When I used my Dad Voice on Dave – stern, harder tone, a bit louder – he got the message and sometimes cried, which Sophia now cited as proof of abuse. She called this "screaming," an offensive exaggeration. She'd said this enough that I once googled it and learned many people refer to it that way, but to me, screaming is over-the-top and can be heard from fifty yards or more. Sometimes a word is generic enough to encompass a wide range like this but suggests the extreme.

That brings me back to the idea of "hitting" Dave. "Hit" covers everything from a lethal punch to a light swat on the butt, one that doesn't cause physical pain. I'd done the latter a few times. But I knew Sophia's use of the word to her therapist was designed to suggest the other extreme and I was having none of that. She had become the Queen of Exaggeration. To her claim that if a child cries, that means you have abused them, I tested Dave one day, very politely giving him three warnings that I was going to take away a toy because of what he was doing with it. When the moment came, I wordlessly took it from his hands, purposely minding my body language. I didn't snatch it, for example, or stomp toward him. Despite how pleasantly I removed the item, he still burst into tears.

Aha! I thought. *I knew it!* Now I hoped to demonstrate this in front of a custody evaluator.

No one had ever raised a concern over Dave's safety – except me because she wanted to kidnap him. Funny how she considered that okay when it's not only criminal, but harmful to a child. She claimed to be an abuse victim and yet the police had never been called. The neighbors were willing to say they'd never heard screaming through the townhouse walls. And it wasn't because you couldn't hear it. One neighbor lived with her twenty-something son, who was a screamer. I heard him many times and listened at the wall for a scream of pain from his mother or a big crash, ready to call 911. The police did arrive once or twice a year, though I would never learn why.

That day at Dr. Thompson's office, we started talking about compromise, with me listing ones I'd offered, such as me doing the driving during custody exchanges, or me moving out nearby, and switching our schedules to make things easier for her. "I can't think of a time when she's compromised," I concluded.

"What about having kids?" she asked. "That was a compromise. A *huge* one."

I frowned. "How is that a compromise?"

"I never agreed to have kids. I only had them for you."

Gob smacked. "What? You can't be serious. Of course, you did." Was she about to claim I raped her? Made her stop taking birth control?

"No, I didn't."

More revisionist history. Would she ever stop? "In both cases, you voluntarily stopped taking birth control. You were even the one to suggest having *this* baby."

"That's true, but I only did it for you. I didn't want either of them."

Oh God, to get that admission with a witness who could testify. "That would explain a lot, but I refuse to accept that this is a compromise."

Dr. Thompson asked, "Why? Randy, this is a huge favor she did you."

Is it possible to scowl and glare simultaneously? "Don't call it a *favor*. That's screwed up."

"Now who is refusing to accept that I ever compromise?" Sophia asked triumphantly, like I'd been caught.

I let fly with exasperation. If Dr. Thompson couldn't testify about *that* crap, she couldn't about my reaction either. Wait – did I just have an epiphany?

"You can't tell me you want kids for a decade and agree when your biological clock is ticking, then tell me years later that you *didn't* want them, you *didn't* agree, and you did it for me. If it was true, you *lied*, and you can't call that a favor *now*. If I had known, I never would've married you, and if you'd admitted it before having Dave, I would've divorced you so I could find someone else. Don't tell me you did it for *me*."

I suddenly remembered all the times she'd watched Dave alone for a bit and me remarking that, as much as I needed an occasional break from parenting, I missed him just two hours later.

"*I* don't," Sophia would say in front of him.

Around the time she agreed (yes agreed!) to have another baby, she complained yet again about being a mother, always sounding like she regretted Dave. I forbade her from ever doing it again. If she wanted to bitch, she could do it to her friends.

With all the lies she told others about me, I became concerned about parental alienation, when a parent tries to convince their children that the other parent is bad and harmful. This makes the child fearful of the other parent and refuse to be with them. It is emotional abuse. For all her accusations that I was the abuser, gaslighting is a recognized form of it, and she'd been doing it to me over my emotions from around 2004 until Dave's birth in 2012. I didn't know why she'd stopped only to resume in January 2016. "Oh my God, it's back," I'd thought. But the attacks had magnified exponentially to accusations that I was abusing her and Dave. I kept picturing being on the witness stand explaining the history, and then turning to the judge.

"And look where we are now, Your Honor. She has finally put me on *trial* for having negative emotions. That's what we're doing here. If I'm found guilty, you take my kids away."

I considered Sophia capable of anything, including parental alienation. What if she could get him to say hateful things about me to a custody evaluator? I began reminding Dave of the fun we had together. I asked, "Does mommy play this with you?" And he'd always say, "No, just you." I would ask him who took him to gym class, the playground, or taped his favorite shows and movies, because he knew it was me. I saw these reminders as a bulwark of truth against the potential landslide of his mother's deceit.

Ironically, I unintentionally caused reverse parental alienation. Dave often said, "Mommy is mean to me," which meant she never played with him. I lied to him many times, saying, "Mommy wants to play with you but she's just tired," or something similar. He increasingly expressed similar resentment and disappointment about her, including the devastating remark, "I love Daddy. I love Mommy, but I don't like her." Ouch. He sometimes hit her, according to Sophia; I never witnessed it. I kept trying to explain away her behavior, so he didn't hate his mother. She'd earned his unhappiness with her just as I'd earned something else...

"Daddy's my best friend," Dave would say, unprompted, to me and Emy, who often told me this. I looked forward to him saying that to a custody evaluator. What Sophia couldn't understand was that Dave's deep connection to me explained his strong reactions to my unhappiness with him. But he'd run to me for comfort, not his mother. This was a sign of trust and love, not fear. You don't run toward someone you're afraid of, but someone who makes you feel safe again. This was a powerful statement about both of his parents. She was so incapable of comforting another person that our toddler already knew it. She was the opposite of empathetic.

Dave knew partly from a multitude of incidents when I had intervened, either Sophia or Emy unable to calm him, going back to when he was a baby. If I heard him crying longer than usual, I would check what was happening. This was partly my nature, but he was my son. Growing up, I had received contempt and disregard for my upset – like what Sophia was doing, only different in cause and method – and I wanted my son's concerns taken seriously. Great damage had been done to me and I wasn't letting my kids experience this. Not from me. It was critical that she not have 24/7 custody. Her attitude was a genuine danger to their emotional and psychological states if I wasn't there to counter it. Ironically, it was from their mother that the children's emotional well-being needed protection.

BabyGate exemplified it. We had three baby gates in the house, one upstairs and two on the second level, to control what floor Dave was on and prevent accidents. By age one, he *loved* going up and down with us, but sometimes we didn't want him to come, just stay with the other parent. I tend to move purposely, in this case striding to the gate, going through, clicking it behind me, and going. From my body language, words, and history, he knew he wasn't coming and remained calm, playing on the floor. But with Sophia, a full-on tantrum would erupt. Each time she'd head for the gate going down, Dave would beat her there because she moved so slow. He'd wrap both hands around the bars.

"Dave," Sophia would begin, trying to pull his fingers off, "I'm only going down for a minute, so you can't come."

He wouldn't respond verbally, vocabulary still limited, just increasingly distressed vocal sounds.

"Come on, Dave, let go," she'd say. But he wouldn't. She'd pry one hand off only to have him grab again. She'd give up and unhook the gate to open it, and now Dave was forcing his body around the gate's end. He'd let go to do this, a tactical mistake. Sophia would try to block his little body, but he was strong and determined. It would take several attempts to pull him back. He'd start crying. She would struggle to get around the end without him. Once achieved, they'd be standing on opposite sides of the gate, both pulling on the bars, her to close, him to open. And then finally the dreaded click of finality came when she got the gate closed. He'd been defeated. Up to here, I would not say she'd done anything genuinely wrong.

Figure 6 The Site of BabyGate

But Dave would cry harder, tears falling.

"I'm sorry, Dave," she said, sounding like she meant it, "but I have to go."

More screaming.

"I'll be right back, okay?"

"You should just go," I observed.

Dave started banging his head on the gate.

She told him, "I'll only be a minute, so it's not worth it for you to come."

He yanked at the bars more.

"I have to carry some things back up Dave, and I can't do that at the same time as I help you."

I said, "Just leave and he'll forget about it."

Ignoring me, she said to him, "I have to be able to hold your hand and I can't."

A sobbing Dave threw himself on the floor so he lay flat on his back, tears flowing.

"Maybe next time, okay?"

"Please turn around and go down the stairs," I said, raising my voice a little for emphasis, and to cut through Dave's screaming.

"Why don't you hang out with daddy?"

"Would you get out of there already?" I asked, getting frustrated. By refusing to leave, she was just rubbing it in his face that he couldn't go with her. That this wasn't her intention was irrelevant.

To him, she suggested, "Play with your toys or something."

He rolled onto his stomach, pounding his fists on the floor. Boogers were now coming out of his nose, his lungs heaving.

"Dave, it will take me too long if you come with me."

I irritably asked, "*Why* are you still standing there?"

"I'm trying to explain to him why he can't come with me."

Gesturing at our now hysterical son, I rhetorically asked, "Does it look like he cares?"

"Well, if he'll just accept it, he'll stop acting like that."

"He's *one*!" The idea of a toddler calmly accepting a rational explanation was absurd. I pictured him instantly calming down after one of her explanations and replying with a British accent.

"Oh, of course, dearest mommy. How silly of me. I shall presently cease and desist all emotive expressions, and calmly await thy return. I am so terribly sorry to have not understood your most wonderful explanations sooner, thereby causing you great strain and compelling you to explain what should have been manifestly obvious to me. I do so hope you are not unduly dissatisfied with me, for it shall break my heart in twain so that I might never recover. My present despair, now fading to joyous love, would be quite as nothing compared to the devastation your poor, devoted son would endure. I sincerely hope your travels to the first floor are most productive and satisfactory, a journey of a thousand ages, replete with bards singing of your travels and regaling the world of your bravery as you set forth on your epic adventure. Please do kindly tell me upon your return of the wonderous sites, revelations, and experiences you enjoyed. I shall presently attend to my toys in eager anticipation of our most joyous reunion. Farewell, dearest mommy! Ta-ta! Adieu! Many good tidings! Namaste!"

Dave lay on the floor, pounding his fists, kicking his feet, and screaming hysterically, tears and boogers pouring down his face in equal measure. I watched his mother turn him into this from the happy boy he'd been just a few minutes earlier.

To my observation that he was only one years old, implying logical arguments on a toddler weren't useful, Sophia said, "Whatever. Dave, you can't always come with me."

His screaming began to alternate with coughing because his cardiovascular system had become overloaded.

"You are *torturing* him!" I shouted.

"Dave, sometimes I just have to go without you and I need you to accept that."

"Oh, for God's sake!" I finally shoved aside my laptop and rescued my son, scooping him off the floor and continuing to the kitchen, out of sight of his mother, who only now turned and descended. I had broken the deadlock, but Dave was hysterical and it took ten minutes to calm him.

Some version of this scene happened over a hundred times, and that is being kind. How many times a day do you go up and down stairs in a three-level townhouse? It's generous to suggest this scene happened only twice a week. It lasted over a year. What is two times fifty? We repeatedly argued about this, as I pointed out that it never happened with me and the reasons for it – body language, demeanor, saying so, and establishing boundaries. The scene became shorter with repetition because I'd intervene sooner. It finally came to a head over a midweek lunch at a restaurant, both of us working from home.

When trying to convince another person of something, it's tempting to lay out the whole argument at once, but this never worked with her, so I got her agreement after every statement.

"You want to go down the stairs," I began, "without him reacting like that, right?"

"Yes."

"Does it happen when I do it?"

"No."

"Do you want the same result?" I picked at my lasagna, trying to be patient.

"Yes."

"I just go right down the stairs, right?"

"Yes."

"No explanations?" I cut a piece in half with my fork.

"Yes," admitted Sophia, her fork stabbing at a seasoned broccoli piece.

"You always try to explain why he can't come, right?"

"Yeah."

"And he always ends up on the flooring, crying and screaming, right?"

"Pretty much."

"So is it working?" I scooped lasagna onto my fork.

With a frown, she reluctantly admitted, "No."

"Is my approach working?"

Hesitation. "Yes."

"Then why won't you try it? We've been arguing about this for over a year and not *once* have you even tried it. *What* does that say about you?" I stopped there, frustration mounting —for all the times she'd driven our son to tears, all the times I'd tried to get through to her, all the times one line of logic or another had failed. As I shoved a mouthful in to keep me from saying more, trying to lose my upset, she let out a huge sigh.

"I *guess* I can try it," she reluctantly conceded.

Which was harder to believe, that she'd try it, or that she acted like this was some extraordinary sacrifice? I stifled an expression of disbelief and only said around my mouthful, "Just try it. It will work. Trust me."

She didn't respond, but within days it came up. The same fight to get through the gate without Dave happened, but once the dreaded Click of Finality happened, her on one side and him on the other, she started to explain why he couldn't come.

"Just go!" I interrupted pleasantly but urgently. "We talked about this! You can do it! Just turn around, not another word, and go down, around the corner."

With a visible effort, she stopped talking, turned around, descended, and disappeared around the corner. Dave turned to me as if to say, "Oh well," and went back to what he'd been doing, reasonably content.

And I threw my hands into the air in triumph. *Yes! I got one! I finally got one! I don't believe it! Yesssssssssssssss!*

And that's how it finally ended. She never did it to him again. This was the woman I was dealing with, the mouse that keeps getting zapped instead of finding the cheese because she has a theory that if she does this or that, she will achieve the result she wants. Never mind that it always blows up in her face. The definition of insanity...

At the previous session with Dr. Thompson and Sophia, I admitted to thinking Sophia was having an affair while watching Dr. Thompson's face, which registered clear surprise. *So Sophia hasn't told her, at least*, I had thought. Not that this meant anything. But the doc soon asked me to come back by myself so we could talk.

The day had come. But first we started talking about emotion and Sophia's response to mine. This led me to remark on a pattern that had played out.

"I once stubbed my toe and cursed," I began. "Sophia came in, telling me my reaction was inappropriate. My first response was, first of all, that's obnoxious. Secondly, you don't even know what happened. How can you tell me that my response is not valid?"

She nodded. "Yes, that doesn't really work."

"She's so determined to invalidate me and my responses that she won't even hear what's happened."

"Did the thing you stubbed your toe on belong to her?"

"No, it was the corner of the house. It's not like she built it."

"Right. If she had put it there, then maybe she'd feel some responsibility."

"Yeah, but that's why I've so often said it's none of her business, which she says is dismissive. That's true, but I'm right. Another thing that comes up all the time is me getting upset with my computer."

"Yes, she mentioned that."

"I'm sure. There's a point I want to make here. Let's say eight things have gone wrong in a row. I don't react until maybe the third thing, and then it's just a sigh or something. But then things keep going wrong, with me stifling my upset. But then finally it gets to something like eight issues in a row, so I finally curse."

"So you do try to control it."

"Of course, but she doesn't see it and won't let me explain that."

"You've tried?"

"Repeatedly. But there are two expressions that come up here. 'Seeing is believing,' and 'perception is reality.' Since she didn't see those things happen, she assumes they didn't. To her, my momentary anger is based on one thing and is outsized. Ignorance and arrogance go together, and so she tells me things I just experienced never happened. And she wonders why I get upset."

Dr. Thompson started to chuckle. "I can see how that is frustrating. Have you asked her not to do that?"

I laughed and could tell from her smile that she knew I had, many times. "Yeah, just once or twice. This conversation about emotion exclusively happens when I'm already upset about something else. Is telling me that my emotions mean I'm screwed up going to make me *more* calm or *less* calm? The subject will always upset me because I find it ridiculous and an attack, but she sees nothing wrong with it or her timing."

"And this has her thinking that you're unreasonable," she admitted.

I chuckled. "You know, she's criticizing me for reacting to something and getting upset, but she's reacting to my upset and can't stop herself. It's hypocritical. There's an unrealistic expectation she expects me to observe when she doesn't observe it herself. She just *thinks* she does."

"You got it. You got it. I think she doesn't say to you what she thinks she's saying, and sometimes she is withholding information. In our talks, I realized that she didn't tell you last fall that she had changed her mind about quitting her job."

"Last fall? I found out in January."

She nodded. "She said the reason she didn't tell you is that she assumed you would make her quit anyway."

I scowled. "Why would she assume that? Quitting her job was her idea, not mine. I have no problem with her keeping it."

"She does seem to jump to conclusions about what you will say."

I sighed. "I'm starting to feel like she's having imaginary conversations with me and assuming the worst reaction, then not even bothering to talk to me about it and punishing me for how I acted in a conversation that never happened."

She nodded, smiling. "You got it."

I noticed she said that a lot. "You know, she's implying that it's easier to move out and cause all this chaos then to ask me something. I find that outrageous. And insulting. I'm very reasonable."

Her smiled broadened. "Yes, certainly more so than her. Do you think there's anything that you're doing that contributes to this? I'm not saying that you are."

I appreciated the sentiment and thought about it for a second. "She tends to think she's saying one thing to me when she's really saying something very different. All those times she told me I'm screwed up, she apparently thought she was saying she's really sensitive to emotion and would I tone it down. She thinks she was asking for compassion when she was really attacking me, and I rejected the attack, so I'd assume she felt that I rejected her request for compassion, even though she hadn't actually made one. So maybe she just assumes I will reject every reasonable request, even though I never have."

She nodded more the longer I talked. "You got it."

I was starting to feel like I was more insightful than Dr. Thompson because she never said these things, just agreed with me. "In fact," I continued, "it is her who rejects reasonable requests to do one thing or another, like her share of the housework."

"Well, actions speak louder than words. You've both continued to do things you needed to, to hang on to your lives. No one left, stopping doing the laundry, or the housework." She stopped herself, maybe at my cocked eyebrow.

"She doesn't *want* to do her share."

"I don't think she has the energy."

I frowned. "See, I don't buy that. Just the other week she went out almost every day after work. She worked late for a team meeting, then a meeting with her boss, went to happy hour, and went out with Cindy one night. That was four of five weeknights, not getting home until 9pm. Then this weekend she went out half the day for a party, so I'm gonna call B.S. She has plenty of energy to do things for herself, but anything that would also benefit me, or Dave, is a no-go. She is ruthlessly selfish."

Smiling as if to commiserate, or soften the blow of her disapproval, she said, "We shouldn't judge each other by the worst of us."

I wanted to laugh, since that was exactly what Sophia was trying to do, except that she was inventing things, too. But I agreed with the idea. "Did you say that to her?"

"Not yet."

"Time's a wasting. She needs to stop judging me for my emotions. It's not appropriate."

"I agree with you. It's not fair to you. How we handle emotions is one thing, but being judged is another."

"Expressing yourself is not abuse, either, unless you're insulting the other person or something, but cursing at an inanimate object is hardly abuse just because the other person overhears it."

She smiled. "Of course. I see no reason that she can get the kids taken away from you any more than you can get the kids taken away from her."

The first part of that was a relief, since I still thought she was working with Sophia's attorney and these conversations were essentially a trap. But I disagreed with the last part. "She's unable to handle Dave's emotions, so I think this is a problem."

"Yes, it is, but not enough to warrant custody issues. She has admitted she can't handle Dave's upset. She gets anxious and that makes it harder to calm him. She just tunes it out."

"Not a recipe for success. She doesn't seem to understand the ramifications, like trying to separate while pregnant."

"*Yes,*" she said, sounding exasperated. "I've tried to tell her to just wait but she will not. I'll be honest, I don't understand why she's so determined to do it now. There is already so much going on."

"I think it's because she ignores all emotion, including the ones that she is setting in motion with this. To a normal person, emotion should be considered. To her, it is dismissed as irrelevant and inconvenient."

Dr. Thompson nodded. "She just doesn't want to deal with it and doesn't seem to realize that, by ignoring it, she causes more emotions that she doesn't want to deal with."

I started laughing. "God, someone else finally sees it besides just me. It's impossible to get her to change her mind about anything."

"I know. I know."

"And this whole thing of not telling me what's going on is a huge problem."

She nodded. "But there's absolutely nothing you can do about that. It is up to her."

I felt I had won over Dr. Thompson, since she was willing to be fair and listen. I had been so sure of this outcome if those conditions were met that I'd walked into what I considered to be a trap. And part of me still suspected she was telling the lawyer about these conversations. But if so, I also felt certain she'd told the attorney that they weren't going to get me on abuse claims. I had never felt nervous about these talks, but a part of me trusted the process and experience I was having even if I didn't entirely trust Dr. Thompson. Anyone paying attention could see that I was making a lot more sense than Sophia, whose stories didn't hold up on hearing my side of it. Dr. Thompson almost had to be telling the attorney this, if they were talking, and that through my attorney, I would destroy Sophia on a witness stand.

I asked, "Do you think her upbringing caused this difficulty in handling emotions, or in realizing what she's really saying to someone?"

"What do you mean?"

"The whole thing with her father abandoning her at three, getting married, having more kids, and staying with them while continuing to act like she didn't exist? I don't mean that specifically, but since her mother sent her to live with her grandparents and she was an only child, I just wonder if this affected her communication, not only bottling things up, but just not being good at it."

Clearly surprised, she replied, "I was not aware of this."

I shook my head. "I'm starting to think I should've expected her to withhold things from you, too, even as you're trying to help her. Her ability to shoot herself in the foot is becoming impressive." I then filled her in on the history that I knew.

"Well, that explains a few things," she ruefully admitted when I finished.

"Like what?"

"Well, that business with her father could certainly be something that triggered the suppression of emotions. Her mother, too. Even the apartment loss. A three-year-old can't really process any of that. What does she say about it?"

"She told the collaborative divorce coach it was great, an adventure, one that she's eager to give Dave. I find that absurd, and very threatening to my son's well-being."

Dr. Thompson nodded. "Yes. Yes, I will have to talk to her about it, but from what you say, this sounds like a strong denial that anything was upsetting to her. It certainly informs her thinking on the impact of a separation on your son."

"She has made it clear she thinks this will be good for him." I frowned. "It's partly because of this false accusation of abuse, but she's denying that the loss of so much will impact him. She seems to think she turned out fine. I couldn't disagree more. There's a part of me thinking that her father destroyed her family twice."

"What do you mean?"

"He did it back then, and he may have turned her into a ticking time bomb that went off last fall in her panic attack, and now it's destroying *this* family."

She nodded thoughtfully. "She's never had a man in her life. Not her father, no brothers, no boyfriends before you. She has said that she wasn't prepared for the way you act when you're upset, and she has tried to adjust. She has almost no coping techniques for this."

I sighed in exasperation. "Do you know how many times I've told her what I need and she has rejected it? I don't know if she doesn't trust what I'm telling her or *what* the problem is."

"You both need to establish trust again."

I smiled. "That's not likely."

She nodded. "It can be hard, but taking you as an example, her complaints about you are trivial. Sure, you get mad at your computer, but this isn't serious."

I felt relieved to hear a sensible perspective other than my own. "Thank you. She is blowing everything out of proportion."

"And for her part, aside from some rude comments, she hasn't done anything suspicious."

This time I laughed out loud. "I know you asked me here to talk about my suspicions that she's having an affair." I then gave her an earful – the calls taken in another room, changing the code on her phone, hiding her laptop screen, the man she'd been video calling with, getting a makeover, wearing lace underwear, staying out all the time, many of her comments, and something that had just happened. The week before, Sophia had texted me one weeknight claiming she was too tired to come home and would just get a hotel room near work, this despite the drive being *45 minutes*. I talked about all of her recent outings, which I suspected had been spent with her boyfriend.

As I listed the suspicious behavior, Dr. Thompson's verbal reaction escalated...

"She's not having an affair."

"I don't think she's having an affair."

"Well, it does *look* like an affair."

Ruefully, "Okay, *maybe* she's having an affair."

And finally, while leaning forward suddenly, "If she's having an affair, I swear to you that I don't know about it. *And her lawyer doesn't know either!*"

Inwardly I gasped. But I'd like to think I wore a perfect poker face as I sat there thinking, Well, how would you know what her lawyer thinks unless you're talking to her? *I knew it!*

I *got* her.

CHAPTER THIRTEEN

Damn Nina!

A week later, a crying Dave woke me by climbing into my bed at 6:45 am. He'd slept with Sophia the night before, so I was confused as to why he was now here. Then again, he needed comfort, and she wasn't much help.

"What's the matter, buddy?" I asked, patting him.

"Mommy's leaving," he tearfully replied.

"What?" I looked at the clock again.

"For work," he added.

She never left that early. Something was up. I picked up my phone and looked in the nanny cams, seeing no sign of Nina sleeping on the couch on the second floor. A light was on. The baby gates down there were both open. There was no movement. While there was a cam in Dave's room, Sophia had turned it to the ceiling months earlier so I could not see her crying, or so she had claimed when I asked.

I got out of bed and carried him as I left the master bedroom, finding the baby gate leading downstairs open. So was the door to Dave's room. I went in. No sign of Sophia, but I heard voices outside and went to the third floor window, gazing at the driveway, where Sophia sat in her Infiniti G35 coupe, the lights on, car running. Her mother stood at the passenger window, which was rolled down as she leaned into it. Sophia was yelling at her in Russian, her mother trying to placate her, from the sound of it. My impression was that Nina was trying to prevent her daughter from driving off in a rage.

Figure 7 The Infiniti G35 Coupe

Wondering what the hell was going on, I took Dave back to my room, stifling anger as I passed the open baby gate. They had left all the gates open and disappeared outside, leaving Dave to fend for himself. Fortunately, he'd come to me. I closed my master bedroom door and put him to bed with me. Moments later, I heard the front door slam and feet loudly stomping up to the third floor. The door to Dave's bedroom slammed. I looked in the nanny cams as Dave tried to go back to sleep. Nina was sitting on the couch.

Did Sophia have another panic attack? Was she going to blame me again? This time she had abandoned Dave, though it's possible she'd tried to leave him with Nina, who had instead gone outside to stop Sophia. Neither were fit to watch my son. I intended to make an issue of it and mention it to Dr. Thompson while watching Sophia's lying face.

And I did.

"What was that about?" I asked her.

Sophia said, "I'd rather not talk about it."

I snorted. "*There's* a surprise."

I never did get a straight answer. At least she hadn't tried to take Dave with her. I didn't have the GPS tracker anymore. But I doubt she would've gotten far and the stunt would've backfired. If she'd left for even a day, it was abandonment, and if she'd taken Dave, kidnapping. Neither would have played well. Damn Nina! This all could have been over right then.

It became increasingly apparent that Nina annoyed Dave. One day she offered him fruit that sat in the refrigerator as he played with cars on a floor mat with roads and buildings printed on it.

"Watermelon?" Nina asked him, using one word like usual.

"Yes," he said.

"Yogurt?" Nina asked. I assumed she was asking if he also wanted this, too, not instead, but her English was too limited to say, "Do you also want yogurt?"

"No," Dave replied.

"Yogurt?"

"No."

"Yogurt?"

"No!" he said.

I frowned, sharing his irritation, which increased when she walked back to the kitchen table and sat down without getting him either. I went and got it for him.

She also insisted on trying to get Dave to say the Russian word for something. When he wanted her to open the baby gate, she would ask, "Open?" and he would nod. But she refused. Instead, she would say the Russian word several times. I doubted Dave understood what she was trying to do. Her English was too limited to even say something like, "The Russian word for that is XYZ. Can you say XYZ? It means open in Russian." Instead, she'd just say the word, Dave wouldn't repeat it, and she'd say it again and again, refusing to open the gate. Dave would get frustrated and walk away. With each failure to cooperate or help, she lost his respect and any chance of affection. He didn't like her. Neither did I. Both of us grew to ignore her.

Sophia had to translate any advice I gave Nina on handling Dave. She claimed to agree with my observations and recommendations and then spoke to her mother in Russian, but I didn't know what she really said. Nina's behavior didn't change, and this threatened Sophia's plan to replace Emy and me with her mother. I hated them talking Russian in front of me, and I often looked at my mother-in-law and thought, *Get out of my house.*

The time had come to tell Dave he was getting a sister in summer, so I did.

"Really?" he asked as we lay on the floor amidst his toys. Our calico cat Minx watched us from a few feet away.

"Yeah. You know how you and me have fun all the time, making up games and being silly together?"

"Yeah, but not mommy. She's no fun."

"Yeah, I know. I'm sorry."

"It's okay. She never plays with me."

The sadness in his voice killed me. "That's part of the point I'm trying to make. This new sister is going to play with us all the time, so instead of it just being you and me, there will be another silly person in the house!"

A delighted grin lit his face. "Yay! Let's do something now!"

"Hold on. Listen, she will be a baby at first, and it won't be much fun, but after a while, it will be."

"Okay!"

"Also, babies need a lot of attention, so when it's born, me and mommy might have to sometimes pay more attention to the baby than you, but we did the same thing with you when you were that little, because we love you."

"Yeah, I'm not a baby anymore."

"Right. You can walk and feed yourself, but the baby can't, so we have to do it for her, so try not to get upset if we don't seem to be giving you as much attention. Just tell me."

"Yeah, but not mommy."

"You can tell her, too," I said, but he didn't seem to care. He knew better.

I had thought a lot about how to have this conversation, and I'd imagined such talks before having kids. Guiding his viewpoint was something I enjoyed. In this case, I didn't want him resenting his sister like my brother (the oldest) had *our* sister (I was the youngest). Their constant fighting contributed to the destruction of my family. Sophia had used their awfulness to suggest that Dave would be better off as an only child, like her. But I was determined to mold his attitudes and I did it again when telling him his mother was moving out. I had to lie to him a bit, just as I lied that his mother *wanted* to play with him but was too tired.

"Hey buddy," I began one day, feeling positive about how this would go because he trusted me, "I need to tell you about a few changes coming up."

"Okay."

"Mommy is going to move out soon, though we don't know when. It means she won't be living here with you and me."

"Is she getting another house?"

"No. An apartment." I then explained what that meant, finding myself explaining in kid terms the difference between renting and owning when he asked if she'd own it. "We don't know how long she'll move out for, but she should be coming back." Another lie. I knew once she was gone, that was it, in no small part because I'd never let her return, but Dave didn't need to know that. Not yet.

"Where is she moving?"

"It's to Virginia. That's another state, not too far away." I named some of Sophia's friend's kids, whose houses he'd been to.

"But why is she moving? She doesn't like it here?"

"You know how she's tired all the time?"

"Yeah, too tired to play with me."

"Yeah," I began, noting he'd believed that lie I'd told him repeatedly. "Well, she's pregnant now and that is going to make her even more tired, so she's decided to move near her new job. That will make things easier for her."

"Are we moving there, too, Daddy?"

"No, I will stay here. You will probably spend time in both places but me and mommy are trying to work out how much. You know how there are playgrounds here, and parks, and other fun places to go?" He nodded and I purposely adopted an excited expression. "Well, there will be all new ones there for you to check out! Twice as much fun!"

"Yay!" He put both arms in the air in celebration. Kids that young don't know what separation or divorce is, or how serious these are. There was no reason to make it seem morose and depressing. This was the kind of emotional nudge I gave my son, not the bullshit Sophia claimed.

That Dave loved his home became apparent one day when the garage door popped out of the track on one side and partially crashed down with a loud bang. While I surveyed the damage, he let out a wail of distress that he didn't want the whole house to fall down. Startled, I tried not to laugh as I consoled him, telling him that wouldn't happen. I loved the house, too, despite the perpetual mess Sophia made of it. A passage from my diary that May sums it up:

As I sit here, I can recall from memory the piles of her crap in every room. On the first floor, there's one next to the treadmill, by the back door, on top of the filing cabinet, another next to the TV, and her recliner is completely full of horse blankets and other shit. That's five major piles in one room. On the second floor, she has a mess under her table and on top of it, and two more on the kitchen corner stand (one on top, another on a second shelf). There'd be more here but this is where Dave usually is so there's some attempt to keep it cleaner. On the third floor, my studio and Dave's room are clear because she doesn't go in one room and the other is again his territory. In the master bedroom, it's a nightmare. There's a pile by the door, another atop the dresser, another by the TV, and then her desk is relatively clear right now because I cleaned it off when moving it months ago, but there's still a pile on top, one on the floor, two baskets worth of crap, and a gigantic pile hidden behind the desk. All of these piles have been there for months if not years. The only reason one goes away is me. I'm telling you, when she's out of here (and probably before), I'm just dumping all of her shit into a box or two and stuffing it in the garage. My house will be clean and free of random piles of shit. The only mess will be Dave's, and he's a toddler, so it's okay.

When she was pregnant with Dave, she had announced that she wasn't doing any cleaning anymore. I asked her why and for how long to which she replied that this was the price of her giving me a child. Was that an early sign that having kids was, after all, a huge *favor* I had to repay? I reluctantly hired a maid service that we'd had since. Her decision would have caused further resentment, a known love killer, as the responsibility of the entire house fell on me, in addition to everything else. Hiring the maid service, as with giving up horseback riding, was my attempt to avoid the upset she had caused.

She'd now referred to our home as a building more than once, as in "There are plenty of buildings in Virginia." To her, it was not a home, nor even a house, just a building.

She removed all sentiment – all *emotion* – devaluing its importance. In retrospect, it was telling – family and love is what makes a house a home and Sophia had stripped our home down to just a building. This implied that my attachment, and Dave's, was without merit and should be disregarded. She had seldom taken care of it and that made me feel for years that it was really *my* house, because I maintained it. I was looking forward to her leaving.

I soon told Dave the other news, that he was starting pre-school soon, while he lived with me, and that Emy would stop working for us but would visit sometimes, though not every day as he immediately suggested. He loved Emy and yet Sophia dismissed the loss of that relationship as inconsequential, just like the loss of his home or father. As someone traumatized by negative emotions, she didn't seem to understand positive ones either. The pre-school plan had been in place before Sophia's decision to separate, and we still agreed that a year of pre-school would get him ready for kindergarten. I'd begun taking him to a toddler gym class, where he showed improved independence from me and cooperation with teachers and group activities.

In May, shortly after my return from vacation, Sophia and I reached a compromise through Dr. Thompson. Sophia had pushed for a year of exclusive custody of the baby but I wanted six months and now she agreed. My guard went up and I felt suspicious when she began acting nicer. She stopped commenting on my emotions, the subject disappearing like it had around 2012. It was as if she had a switch for it. Was she up to something? Or had Dr. Thompson and I gotten through to her that she was at least as culpable as me for any disputes, which were not abuse? I didn't ask, but maybe I should have. I just didn't think she'd tell me the truth...but sometimes there is value in hearing a lie.

Dr. Thompson went on vacation for two weeks, during which time Sophia continued to act strangely, by which I mean nice. She began sending emails like, "Hi Randy, hope you are doing well." Even at the best of times, I never understood such messages. The sudden civility made me suspicious, but I played along, eager for an end to her warped hostility and aggression. She had always been the aggressor. Always.

The baby was due in early August. I felt no excitement at all, convinced she wasn't mine, and unable to learn the truth until after she was born. Why get attached? I would have no rights. I had closed my heart to her as a protective measure. Sophia robbed me of any excitement about this baby's birth. With Dave, I hadn't experienced much excitement either, but not because I doubted his paternity. It was just from the sorts of worries that any first-time dad has. People had asked if we were excited and all I could think about were the things I needed to get done. Car seats and inspections, diapers, cribs, and more. The babyproofing I had done included custom woodwork to fit the gates onto railings without damaging them. We'd taken classes at the hospital, including infant CPR; Sophia later claimed I did not attend them, but I went to one more class than her, for fathers only. Now years later, the birth of the new baby was so utterly different because of what Sophia was doing. The pregnancy had finished setting in motion the end of the family when it was supposed to augment it. Through no fault of hers, the baby was a destroyer of worlds.

I had now endured over four months of Sophia's constant assault on my parenting. The shock had worn off. In place of the giant, surging waves of emotion had come a high tide of depression. I was drowning either way. The threat of using false abuse claims to take my kids away gnawed away at any chance of peace, but it paled in comparison to the growing certainty that the baby wasn't mine.

In darker moments, I almost wished Dave wasn't, ensuring my custody loss, but only so I could disappear to the other side of the world and escape all this nastiness. In a rejection of the impact her father's abandonment had on her, Sophia was determined to force the devoted father of her children away. Was she emulating her mother? What had happened between her parents? Did Nina accuse him of abuse and drive him away? Was there a pattern here? Was it why she believed her daughter's accusations and left her home, country, and husband to come here?

I wondered what Nina, who was equally stone-faced and emotionless, saw when she watched Sophia, Emy, and I interact with Dave. Would she tell the truth to a judge or lie for her daughter, who might bully her into deceit? She had to see me playing with him and Sophia never doing so. Or making his dinner, sometimes feeding it to him. Or me giving him a bath. Or taking him upstairs to read a bedtime story. Or him insisting on sitting right next to me on the couch, and following me from room to room, or floor to floor even if I was only going to be gone for a minute.

Had Nina been as distant as Sophia was? They had not seen each other once in 22 years, Sophia refusing to return to Russia for fear they wouldn't let her leave again, Nina refusing to come, until suddenly she did. Sophia had seldom mentioned Nina or her grandparents. Neither she nor Nina knew how to raise a child because neither had. They were visibly awkward, cold, and distant, willing to attend to physical needs but nothing else. And I was meant to let them raise my kids? Over my dead body.

As if psychological and emotional misery wasn't enough, I was in significant physical pain for several weeks that May. A particular rollercoaster ride a decade earlier had been the apparent cause of my chronic bad back. Now it flared when I helped a tow truck driver get my motorcycle loaded after it broke down. I resorted to leftover painkillers, sleeping pills, and sleeping on an incline, to no avail. Two massages backfired and I nearly went to the hospital wondering if more was going on, like a damaged internal organ. I finally found a good place that did both physical therapy and chiropractic work. It sometimes took great effort not to feel sorry for myself.

CHAPTER FOURTEEN

Subterfuge

The next appointment with Dr. Thompson was just me because Sophia's car broke down on the way. The one after that, she was forty minutes late. We made significant progress that May anyway, the doctor negotiating with me, as she had apparently done with Sophia in my absence. I was given the impression that she'd finally gotten through to Sophia about everything from false claims of abuse to Sophia's complicity in tensions, and the value of my continued presence in the kids' lives. This led to a sudden change, including a drop in hostility.

Sophia agreed to 50-50 custody, though she wanted the baby full time for the first six months, down from twelve. Sophia eventually admitted that Nina couldn't watch Dave, who had apparently hit Nina a few times out of frustration. She agreed Dave would attend pre-school in Maryland while with me three days a week. She pushed for two days in another place in Virginia, but Dr. Thompson helped me reject this due to cost and it not being in his best interests. I offered to do most of the driving during custody switches and had learned that 50-50 is about overnight stays, not hours of time spent together.

I still felt suspicious of her, but part of me accepted the changes in her attitude because the bizarreness had been so alien and so awful. Was it wishful thinking, or had she seen the light? Time would tell and I mentally held my breath that this nonsense was over. We weren't getting back together, I knew, because I didn't want it, but at least we could be amicable about divorce and custody. That was my hope.

By June, she was apartment shopping, determined to move before giving birth. She ordered IKEA furniture, suggesting rare financial responsibility, but then she signed the insane one-year apartment lease of $1000 a month more than our mortgage. An argument and the infamous dismissive "whatever" ensued. Her refusal to sell the useless horse, that cost $300 a month to stable, continued. I was dying to divorce her by now and be rid of this.

I was also increasingly looking forward to her moving out. I finally felt I had won the months of battling, getting the custody I wanted, Dave in school in my state, and a cessation of false accusations, though part of me didn't trust the latter. She could flip it on and off, and now it was off. Was something still brewing? Suspicious as I was, I enjoyed the thought of impending freedom from her and made plans to rid my home of her mess.

I enrolled Dave in Kindercastle five minutes away, taking him for a two-hour visit, when his shyness didn't surprise me. I planned how to integrate him and help him overcome his separation anxiety, relying on Emy, who by now knew that her time as his nanny was ending. The basic plan was for her to stay in the room there with him, sitting to one side, but do so less and less. Next, she would stand in the hall, visible through the interior window, until not visible at all, and finally being gone longer and longer as Dave became familiar with the room, staff, and other students, needing Emy's familiarity less.

The first day, she began this too early and I was still in the lobby around the corner talking to staff, where she joined me. A blood curdling scream erupted from the direction she'd come.

"That's not Dave," Emy said.

"I'm pretty sure it was," I disagreed, going to look. I was right and had to sit with him for ten minutes to calm him. Despite Emy staying in the room when I left for good, he still cried at my departure. The next day, Sophia replaced me, later boasting that he didn't cry when she left. I stifled laughter. *That's because he doesn't give a shit about you*, I thought.

This was *my* plan, and Emy, the teachers, the staff, and the principal knew it. They also knew I called every day after drop off for weeks to learn how he was doing. Sophia never did. Just like with Emy, I took care of everything, including enrollment paperwork. They called me if something happened. I did virtually all drop offs and pickups even before Sophia moved to Virginia. He started at half days for three weeks and began asking them where his bed was because he saw them lay out cots every day, but he was leaving before nap time. This was a good sign of how he was adjusting. He finally went full-time and Emy stopped working for us, though she still visited. One teacher was instrumental in his transition, taking him to the window so that when I left and stood outside, we could wave goodbye. He cried anyway for a few weeks but eventually got used to the new routine, which we did for over a year. I purposely handled all of this partly because his mother was incapable of handling it.

Shortly after losing my last job, I'd found a nearby consulting job for a contract of about three months. The duration wasn't good, but the location was, until one day it went to shit. A coworker deleted most of my work, re-did part of it and handed me back my now broken software and told me to fix the rest of what he'd smashed. My client had ten employees and this was the #2 guy, outranking me. I was so incensed that I called Sophia of all people, looking for support from the least supportive person I knew. Had I gone insane? Maybe. But she'd been my best friend for so long that I really had no others anymore and she worked in the same field and would understand the outrageousness if not my emotions. And she'd been acting nicer lately, as if Dr. Thompson and I had finally gotten through to her. Maybe I was subconsciously testing her to see her reaction. But what I was consciously thinking was that I wanted to quit on the spot but couldn't afford it.

She passed the unintended test, even saying she understood why I was so upset and giving various helpful suggestions on dealing with it. I couldn't help thinking, *Who are you and what have you done with my wife?* Maybe both of us were having a revelation or maybe, this was an aberration...

At another appointment with Dr. Thompson and Sophia, her therapist asked me, "Sophia tells me you seem to be getting along better?"

"Seems like it. I haven't heard abuse allegations in two months, so that helps."

"Good."

"But it quietly went away and feels like an elephant in the room."

"How so?"

"She's never apologized or said she was wrong. For all I know, she still thinks it but has just learned to stop saying it."

"True," Sophia admitted, not clearing it up. "You've been better in the last two months."

I frowned. That sounded suspiciously like she was saying I had stopped being a problem, so I mirrored her remark. "If that's true, it's partly because you're better with how you react to things I say or do."

Dr. Thompson said, "Good. Very good, Randy."

I half expected a milk bone to come my way. "That said, there are things that linger for me."

"Like what?" Dr. Thompson asked. As usual, she talked more than Sophia.

"Sophia's been saying these terrible things about me to her friends and now I'm not comfortable around them, and yet they'll be at Dave's upcoming birthday party."

"I understand. You know, girls commiserate with each other much more than guys and they don't necessarily judge the way men do."

"I know at least one is giving Sophia as much help as possible and – "

"They're friends. Of course, she is."

I shook my head. "No, we're talking about suggesting Sophia kidnap my son. That is crossing a line. And it screams 'judgment,' not just talking trash."

"Okay, well I can't disagree with that," Dr. Thompson admitted. "Is there anything Sophia can do to fix that?"

"I doubt it. You two will have to come up with something on that one."

"We have talked and agreed that Sophia often says things she doesn't mean."

I noticed Sophia wasn't the one saying it, like always. How was I to trust she meant something when someone else had to say it for her? "Is that supposed to make me feel better? To me, she's been lying at every turn, and yet she claims she hasn't told any lies, and now you're telling me she doesn't mean much of what she says, which means she *was* lying."

Dr. Thompson laughed and Sophia smiled wanly in response. I had once asked the therapist if I seemed like a man who needed to scream, call someone names, and do other rude things to win an argument or make myself understood. "Not in the least," had been her reply.

I continued, "How am I supposed to know what she means and what she doesn't? If she doesn't apologize, I'll assume she means it, especially when it fits a pattern of similar remarks."

A smiling Dr. Thompson asked, "How can she fix this?"

I shrugged. "Giving me some hard-to-miss sign she didn't mean it. You know, like an apology." I paused, then joked, "I realize that's asking for the moon..."

This time Sophia briefly laughed. "As long as you recognize that."

Asshat, I thought.

"Well," Dr. Thompson began, "she has often told me that she could have done this or that instead of what she did."

"That's great. When do I get to hear one of these admissions? And on that note, why is it that I hear pretty much everything from you and not her?"

"I'm working on that," said the therapist.

"Good luck."

CHAPTER FIFTEEN

A New Life

Sophia moved out in early July while eight months pregnant, as if a woman in that condition didn't have more pressing concerns. My lawyer had suggested a written custody agreement to replace the verbal one, but her $5000 retainer to do it made me balk, partly because she said it couldn't be submitted to a court until I filed for divorce. We had to be separated for a year before I could do that. There's an old idea that trying to save some money by avoiding an attorney can cost you big later. Had I heard it and forgotten?

I let Sophia temporarily take a toaster, crock pot, one of two matching recliners from the first floor, the master bedroom TV, and Dave's dresser and nightstand, leaving his tall chest and 4-in-1 convertible crib, which was set up as a bed but destined to be a crib again for the baby. Dave abandoned his bedroom for mine, shoving his knees or feet hard into me at night until I lodged a long pillow in between us.

Sophia's absence thrilled me. I celebrated with wine and sushi. And an extended bout of cleaning, first randomly, then methodically, ridding a whole room of her mess. Each time I finished one, I stepped out and said, "This room….is clean." The line came from *Poltergeist*, when a little woman exorcises a house of evil spirits; I substituted "room" for "house." The double meaning of my version made me laugh.

I felt invigorated. At long last, I enjoyed cleaning up after Sophia because this time, I knew she wouldn't be there to immediately begin recreating the mess. I was not a neat freak. Sophia was a lazy slob. For a while, it felt odd to enter a clean room, so much so that I did a double take, half expecting the mess to be there once more, like the kitchen island where there was always another used teabag, the wrapping it came in and a sugar packet, some of its contents spilled. Now, nothing. I noticed it each time and I smiled. Marveled even. Checked my pulse to ensure I was not dead and in heaven.

Weeks later she was there again to get more clothes, made herself some tea, and I entered the kitchen to find that familiar pile on the island. The volume of anger that roared up stunned me. Only then did I realize how much I loathed living with her. Never again.

I told Kindercastle of the separation only to learn they'd figured it out from Dave talking about "mommy's apartment." That Sophia was visibly pregnant earned me some sympathy. I finally saw her new home on the fourth floor of an apartment complex that consisted of two five-story buildings connected by an enclosed walkway that spanned a road. Many shops were adjacent, making parking garages so full that I often drove around for 10-15 minutes for a spot. Sophia refused to get me a fob to enter the lobby so that I often stood in bad weather by myself or with Dave, sometimes holding numerous items for her or the kids. I'd wait for another five minutes until she exited the elevator and opened the door for us; sometimes other residents took pity on me and let me into the lobby, but not the two elevators, the only options to reach her apartment.

This waiting for her happened despite me perpetually updating her as to our arrival time, meaning she kept us waiting on purpose. This sort of indifference had caused many arguments over the years. And it continued now.

Her two-bedroom apartment was largely empty, with stark white walls and blinds, dark hardwood floors, and a small balcony overlooking the outdoor pool and hot tub. Nina's bedroom and bath, where the baby would sleep, were by the front door. The living area opened to one side, which she turned into a play area and living room, the kitchen open to it all. Aside from what she'd taken from the house, there was only a black kitchen set for four, a white couch, and a TV stand. Her bedroom and bath were farthest from the front door. Dave would not get his own room, sleeping with her. She would never hang so much as one photo on the wall or otherwise decorate. The place had a "temporary" (or maybe "I don't give a shit") feeling. I later and surreptitiously photographed it all to contrast her empty "building" to my fully furnished and lived in "home" in court.

I met Dr. Thompson without Sophia again, in mid-July, for the first time since Sophia moved out, which was the stated reason she wanted to see me, to see how I was doing. Ironically, she spent most of it upsetting me.

At some point, I said, "Sophia is walking back on agreeing to 50-50 custody on the baby."

"You've very black and white about things," she said. To my irritated expression, she clarified, "Just because she hasn't agreed doesn't mean she is opposed to it. I think she just wants to talk about it later."

"That's not what she's said and I *know* her. Not agreeing is her passive way of saying no. That is what it means. Half the time she agrees to do something and doesn't do it, so how am I supposed to interpret not agreeing at all? Yes means no. No means no. No answer also means no. And she's eight months pregnant. How much longer does she need? There's been plenty of time to reach an agreement on this."

"What's the rush?"

"Because I don't like being threatened with no custody of this baby, assuming it's even mine."

"You're still not sure?"

"She's given me no reason to be. She never denied having an affair."

She smiled. "She never admitted to it either. This is what I mean by black and white."

Scowling, I asked, "Are you saying she needs time to figure out how to answer *that* question? This is a yes or no situation. There's no gray area."

"Okay, fair enough. But why do you feel threatened about custody?"

"For starters, I see her using that to get the remaining 50% for Dave." I'd been acutely aware of this since January, if I'm not the father, I have no rights, and her refusing to agree to any shared custody at all, or walking back on an agreement, suggests that I'm not the father. Why agree to let another man, namely me, have custody if I'm not the father? If you think this baby not being mine isn't threatening, you're as nuts as she is. I've had this hanging over my head every day since January and no one seems to think it's a huge deal."

"Okay, you're right, that is very threatening, and I'm sorry you feel that way. Was there another reason?"

I got the impression she was fishing for information for Sophia and her attorney more than to help me, but I assumed they were aware of my next words because it was part of their plan. I wanted them to know I was aware of it in hope that they'd reach an agreement with me because they weren't fooling me.

"Yes," I said, "if you add up the kids to 200%, and Dave is at 50%, and the baby is at 100% for her, she has 150% of custody,.

Dr. Thompson admitted, "That is a possibility."

"You're not exactly making me feel better."

"You do tend to assume the worst about her intentions."

I snorted. "With good reason. She has destroyed my trust in her and given me every reason to doubt her. You're acting like my distrust is somehow unreasonable. I want an agreement on the baby so I can relax, which is something both of you claim to want."

"Well, if she doesn't agree, you are not likely to get anywhere."

Scowling, I asked, "Why is that? And all the more reason to press for an agreement."

"The father never gets more than 50-50 custody from a judge in Montgomery County. I've never seen it happen and you should probably just forget it."

I wasn't sure what to say to this. Was she in a bad mood or something? "With all due respect, you're not a lawyer."

She nodded. "Sophia knows this and has no reason to agree to less. In fact, even in the first two years, you're unlikely to get any custody."

My scowl darkened. Had she saved all the rude comments, observations, and predications for after Sophia moved out? "She never even wanted kids."

"That doesn't matter to the courts."

I'd heard this before but had a rejoinder at the ready. "Well it should matter when it strongly impacts your relationship with them, as it does with us. Sophia doesn't do shit for Dave and I do almost everything."

"That's not the story she tells."

She sounded dismissive and was pissing me off. "Yeah, well, she has no witnesses to back up her story and I do, including the nanny."

"I'm not saying you would never get custody," she clarified. "Even men in the military who haven't been around at all during the early years can get 50-50 custody down the road. In the long run, you would get it, just not in the beginning."

I relaxed a little. "Not good enough, especially when she can try to use it to take Dave right now."

"There is nothing you can do there."

"We'll just see about that."

"It's also bad for a baby to be with one parent and then the other during the first two years. There's no continuity and it's damaging for the child. The father is always the loser in this."

I hadn't read that anywhere and resented being referred to as a loser. "The obvious solution to that is Nina, who can move between our houses, providing continuity."

"That's not going to happen."

I glared. "Who are you to say that?"

"Sophia and I already talked about that and she said there's no way she'd do it."

"Didn't you just give me shit for supposedly assuming the worst about something or being black and white and now you're telling me flat out no, it's not even up for discussion?"

"We already discussed it."

"*I* didn't. You act like I'm not to be a part of anything unless you two, and her lawyer, decide I am. And don't you think these are things that I should hear from Sophia?"

"She's not here to tell you."

I observed, "Well even if she *was* here, you do all the talking."

She didn't argue that, only saying, "Nina doesn't want to live with you due to the language issue."

I didn't want my mother-in-law living with me either, but at least I wasn't bluntly saying it. And it seemed a trivial issue compared to the hugely important one of me having time with my daughter, but no, it was off the table and too bad for me. I was being threatened and I didn't appreciate it. "I hate to break it to you, but she just lived in my house for over three months."

"Sophia was there to translate and – "

"No, she *wasn't*. Nina was in the house with Emy all day and then with me from 4pm until 8, 9, or 10 pm, so what's the difference?"

"The language issue is a real problem."

"No, it's not. For starters, a baby can't talk at all and in theory Nina already knows how to take care of one. Besides, a baby isn't exactly complicated. You feed them, change them, put them to sleep, and all without using language to communicate with the baby. Besides, she'd be a back up to me. And Sophia is supposed to be teaching her more English anyway."

"She's too busy for that."

"Yeah, well, she wasn't when she made the suggestion of Nina coming here in the first place."

I knew what was happening. Nina and Sophia were now coming up with excuses for keeping the baby away from me for up to two years. My mother-in-law had lived off my hospitality for months and was now staking positions designed to help her daughter take my kids away. Was that the reason for bringing Nina to America all along?

This was the last time I saw Dr. Thompson. I don't think Sophia saw her again either. Within days, she went into one of several false labors several weeks early, each keeping her from going anywhere she didn't really want to, including to her therapist, and then labor began for real, and by the time she recovered from childbirth, Dr. Thompson had retired. As far as I know, she never got another therapist, but I suspect she did and just withheld the information.

Sophia had expelled me from anything having to do with pregnancy and childbirth, just as she planned to expel me from the kids' lives. Aside from what I learned from attending sonogram appointments (I was half surprised she let me), I knew nothing about what was happening, and with my certainty that the baby wasn't mine, part of me didn't want to know, as I walled myself off. Alexa had replaced me as her help, Sophia referring to her as a doula. But Alex had no training or qualifications, and no experience in the health care industry. She worked as a project manager for a telecommunications firm. If Alexa was a doula, then I had been one last time. As if. The Year of Exaggerations continued.

One night, Alexa drove Sophia to the hospital, which was five minutes from the apartment, then waited two hours to tell me at 1am that Sophia's water had broken and where they were. I loathed Alexa for suggesting Sophia kidnap Dave, but just as Sophia had communicated through Dr. Thompson, she now did so through Alexa, who told me Sophia was only four centimeters dilated and had to be at ten, as they were doing a vaginal birth instead of cesarean this time. Dave was at her apartment with Nina. I went back to sleep, up at 6am to head for the hospital. Sophia had reached eight centimeters.

I consciously tried to ignore the year's events, a herculean effort. Never mind fears this baby was not mine. I told myself she was, just in case, and tried to enjoy this literal once-in-a-lifetime event. Call it sticking my head in the sand, but it was the 11th hour of looking forward to the birth of this maybe-daughter, whose arrival had almost been completely ruined for me, and I just wanted to pretend for a little while. I deserved it.

As I drove away from home, Alexa began texting from the hospital. I try not to text and drive, but she was about to force me into it with a new outrage.

Alexa: Hey. Where are you?
Randy: Just left. 40 minutes.
A: K. Don't rush. She's not dilated enough.
R: K.
A: Listen, she doesn't intend to let you into the delivery room.

I couldn't even get an hour to ignore the constant aggression from her. She intended to bar me from the birth of my supposed daughter. On purpose. With the malice of forethought. I knew she had the authority to do it as a patient and powerlessness and vulnerability suddenly swept over me. And fury.

R: Fuck that. I am seeing the birth of my daughter.
A: Well, she doesn't have to let you into the delivery room.

Realizing this conversation would last, I put my ear buds in and began dictating my responses as I merged onto the highway.

R: She had better let me in.
A: She doesn't feel comfortable with you there.
R: She was comfortable enough to get pregnant by me. And I didn't do shit to change this, so too bad.
A: Giving birth is very stressful and you being there would make it worse.

R: That's insulting. I'm not going to do anything to make her uncomfortable.

A: I'm not saying you would. Just your presence.

R: Also insulting. Thanks for that.

A: She needs to be able to relax. This is vaginal birth.

R: Look, I am the best friend she has ever had and haven't done a damn thing to her, so this bullshit that I'm the one who causes her stress instead of the other way around is not going to fly.

A: There is too much tension between you two.

R: Because of her. And her comments and behavior. I am not missing the birth of my daughter because of bullshit going on in Sophia's head. This is literally a once in a lifetime opportunity.

Just for once in this awful year, could I just be left alone and not fucked with so I could try to enjoy this? But no. They had to ruin this, too. I was acutely aware of arguing with a woman who had suggested my wife kidnap my son. I despised her.

A: Randy, please be reasonable.

R: Don't say that to me. I'm not the one being unreasonable. There is no justification for this. This is very important to me. I cannot stress that enough.

A: Well that is surprising to me.

R: What is? Why would you think I don't care?

A: My husband didn't want to be in the room at all.

R: Then he's a fool.

A: You never hold back what you're thinking! LOL

R: Unlike some people I know.

A: Sophia is feeling really self-conscious. That's part of why she doesn't want you there.

Part of me wondered if I was to be kept out of the room so that the baby's real father could be present instead, but what I wrote was...

R: I've seen it all before, you know.

A: This is different. She puked twice last night and was embarrassed even in front of me.

R: I've seen her do worse than vomit and still had sex with her, didn't I?

A: LOL. TMI!

R: I'm halfway there.

A: I think you should go to the apartment instead.

R: What the hell for?

A: Dave is still asleep and if he wakes up and only Nina is there, he will get scared.

R: Bullshit. He'll be fine.

A: If you really care about your children, you should go there to be with him when he wakes up.

R: Don't ever question whether I care about my kids. You have no right.

A: You'll need to be there to comfort him, not be selfish.

I cursed, wanting to tell her to fuck off. She was trying to manipulate me into missing the birth of a daughter I couldn't even be sure was mine. How much of an asshole was she? What Sophia and her friends were putting me through was abominable.

R: Stop it. I am not going to the damn apartment. I am almost at the hospital.

A: I think this is a mistake.

R: I couldn't care less what you think. I have zero interest in seeing the business end of the delivery. I will stay up by her head, in the corner or some shit. But I will be in that room.

A: You need to calm down.

R: Don't tell me what to do. You have no stake in this whatsoever and this entire conversation is out of line and none of your business. Stop upsetting me. I'll be perfectly calm when you knock this shit off.

A: I'm asking on Sophia's behalf.

R: Listen, if Sophia prevents me from witnessing the birth, it will be the biggest mistake of her life. I will not be cooperating with her at all going forward. I will make things as difficult as possible. I have had enough of her bullshit.

A: That's very threatening. Don't you think this is the sort of behavior that got you into this mess in the first place? That made her leave you? It's like you haven't learned anything at all.

I lost it. She was just like Sophia, saying screwed up shit to me and then acting like there was something wrong with me for being upset about it. They demanded I be calm no matter what was said or done to me.

R: You have no idea what the fuck you are talking about. Don't ever speak to me about it like you do. Stop butting into my relationships. This is my family, not yours, and if you are going to say fucked up shit like that to me, you can just stop it right now.

I didn't care that this was all in writing and could be used against me in court. The context would tell the tale, and what it ultimately showed was how desperately I wanted to be there for the birth of my daughter, and that someone who wasn't part of my family was trying to stop me, even manipulate me, on Sophia's behalf. I was so angry and frustrated I couldn't stand it.

A: You need to calm down.

R: Stop saying that. You are the one upsetting me, so if you want me to calm down, knock that shit off.

A: How close are you?

R: Pulling up in a minute.

A: Okay, I will meet you in the lobby to get a coffee.

I parked minutes later, in so much turmoil I almost wanted to cry. It was too much. No one should have to put up with this. The last person I wanted was to see Alexa. I hated her. It took a huge effort to wipe the volcanic glare of fury from my eyes as I strode into the hospital.

On seeing me, she smirked. "Well you certainly don't hold back how you feel, that's for sure."

Bluntly, I said, "If you don't have anything nice to say – "

"Okay, okay." We headed for a breakfast shop, passing through turnstiles into a small area that looked like a bakery with fresh foods at the ready. "Try to relax. This is a big day."

"I'll relax when you stop trying to make me miss the birth of my daughter."

"It's not me, it's Sophia. I'm just trying to help."

"You're failing."

She laughed and started getting herself a coffee. "You don't mince words. I always liked that about you. So did Sophia."

"Not anymore." I decided to get some tea, reaching for a packet.

"Yeah, well, let's not get into that. Look, she's agreed to let you be in the delivery room."

"Good," I snapped, still glaring and feeling no relief. It was too soon. You can't continuously shove me into turmoil for forty minutes and then yank me out with a single comment.

Noticing my lack of appreciation, she said as if wounded, "Hey, I went to bat for you. That was hard. I have to tell you, I'm really surprised."

"By what? How much of a bitch my wife has become?"

She grabbed some creamer. "Okay stop that. No, I mean that it matters so much to you to be there. My husband didn't want to see either of the kids born. He was so squeamish."

"He's an idiot," I repeated. I had never met the guy, despite having been at their wedding, and I had passed the point of ever caring what Alexa thought about anything.

She laughed. "Honestly, I'm kind of impressed that you're so determined. I didn't realize you were so into being a dad."

"Maybe you should stop believing the bullshit Sophia tells you about me as a parent. She's got everything backwards and you don't know a thing." I took the creamer from her hand.

"Try to tone it down. I realize you're still mad, but you got what you wanted. You will be there. I swear. And I really do think you need to chill a little before we go up."

She was right, as much as I hated to admit it. I lightened my attitude with an effort. "This isn't some ploy to have me miss it, is it?"

"Oh my God, you're so suspicious."

"Can't imagine why."

"Look, it's not. I swear. We'll go up in a minute." She told me some believable details about how dilation was going and what they were doing to try and reduce Sophia's pain. And before long we were headed up. I didn't relax until the wide wooden door opened and I entered the large delivery room to see Sophia still pregnant in the bed to the right, the windows beyond, sinks and more to the left.

True to my word, I stood near the corner by the head-board and windows. Sophia and I didn't speak or acknowledge each other, in stark contrast to the last time we'd had a baby, me sitting beside her head and holding her hand as Dave was delivered, then kissing her on the forehead, an idea that repulsed me. So much had changed since the baby had been conceived, and it was now July 21st. Those changes were appalling. And a result, I felt numb, beaten into muted hollowness, a kind of suspended animation, waiting for it all to end, whether the birth, my fears about paternity, or this marriage. I only wanted a lack of complications for Anna's birth. We had at least agreed on her name without much arguing.

I'd arrived at 7 am but labor didn't start in earnest until 10. It started fine but slowly became problematic as she wasn't coming out and her vitals were showing signs of distress. The doctor finally used forceps to assist the baby's arrival as a half dozen professionals helped, and only now did I feel moved from my inner stillness, a touch of concern for the baby's welfare moving me.

Anna was born at 11:23 am, crying, bloody, but in the world. The nurses whisked her across the room to a counter where they appeared to be cleaning her, checking vitals, and wrapping her in a blanket. We had learned before now that Anna had a microscopic hole in her heart, a fitting metaphor for the effect her existence had caused in me. Between this and her heart rate and temperature being elevated, they decided she had an infection and put her into the NICU for infants, giving her antibiotics and oxygen. This meant no one got to hold her before they wheeled her away. One minute she was there, and then she was gone. Her birth had been as deflating as everything else in her short life. I felt empty.

CHAPTER SIXTEEN

The Speech

I quietly slipped out of the delivery room, desperate to get away from Sophia and Alexa. I gave way to the depression I've been trying to hide, finding somewhere out of the way to sit. An hour passed before nurses took me to see Anna. I feigned being in a good mood until I was left alone in the small room with her. Cleaned up, she lay sleeping and bundled in blankets inside a glass or plastic container atop a rolling cart, an IV in one arm, oxygen pumped into the sealed chamber. She had only just been born and already we were separated.

I stood in silence, alternating between watching her and slowly pacing, a moment of reckoning looming as I faced the unknown possibilities of multiple futures, each clashing with the hopes and dreams that had led to her existence. A destroyer of worlds, she lay blameless. I didn't love her. I didn't hate her. She was a blank slate, and would remain so until I could administer a paternity test. And even then, she might result in my son being taken from me, too. But it wasn't her fault. A slow resignation settled on me as I turned to stand beside her, watching her rest in a peace that her life had robbed me of.

"Hello, Anna," I quietly began. "Welcome to this world. I truly hope you enjoy your stay, and that you can bend this world to you instead of it bending you to it. It can be tough out there, and you're already getting your first dose of reality with your infection, and your first dose of help with your medicine. May you have more of the latter than the former. Try to have faith, little one. This world is what you make of it, for better or worse, and all you can really do is try.

"I do not know if you are mine. You may belong to someone else, and if that's the case, then I wish you well and bear you no ill will. I do not believe in the sins of the father. And your mother may have sins plenty enough for all. If you are not mine, you will need all the strength you have. I know who your mother is, and I may not be there to help you. You have a half-brother at least, and so we will know each other some, if not as much as we could, so you can always come to me, for I will always be here for you, if only for the principle of it, or because you are my son's sister.

"And in him you are luckier than you know. He is a wonderful boy, and he is very much looking forward to meeting you. If not me, then he will teach you to laugh, to be silly, to be happy, as I have taught him. You should spend your hours with him as much as you can, for he is like a light in the dark of this world, and he can help you find the light in you, as I helped him find the light in him. You will find out early what love is.

"And if you are mine, then I will show you myself. And you will be among the luckiest of children, for I have dreamed of you, fantasized of you, fought for you. I have endured much hell to bring you into this world, and were it not for me, you would not exist. I am the one who wanted you here. I am your reason for being. I am the one whose love you are here for.

"If you are mine.

"And so today, on your birth day, I must give you your first apology. I must ask you to wait a little bit longer for me, as I have waited for you. I must know if you are mine before we can make that dream a reality, because I could not bear to start it now only to learn a truth I have dreaded all year. I don't have it in me, because I am not sure how much more I can take. And so we must wait. If you are mine, I will make it up to you. In the meantime, I will pretend and give to you everything you need or want. Like a plane that has not been cleared to land, I will fly in circles around you until knowing if I must fly away from you forever, or if it is safe for me to land. Hopefully your waiting for me will end soon, just as my waiting for you does, and we will never wait for each other again.

"Sleep a newborn's sleep, little one."

Within a week, I resolved not to be a father to her even if she was mine. Sophia and her friends saw to it that I would not. She had shut me out of the pregnancy except for sonogram appointments. She tried to shut me out of the birth. And now they were shutting me out of everything else, and what hadn't happened yet, I realized would, and that my fatherhood had been eliminated.

Someone else set up a crib and other things in her apartment, denying me the chance. Alexa tried to stop me from driving the baby from the hospital to the apartment after the initial stay in the NICU ended, causing an argument, as she tried once more to replace me. Someone had brought clothes, blankets, and more, and I soon noticed that what I'd brought had been laid aside as if not wanted, and I did not see Anna wearing or using them going forward. No one would let me change her diaper. There were no bottles to give her or clean. I would not be doing her laundry. I would not give her a bath. I would not read to her. I would not be rocking her to sleep. I would not be

getting up in the night to help her. I would never be allowed to comfort her. I would not be told of things she
needed much less be allowed to get them. I was not given
updates by Sophia on how Anna was doing. I was told
nothing about Anna's day, her personality, her habits.
Nothing.

To protect myself, I walked away. I didn't want to see
Anna again, this child that likely belonged to someone else.
They certainly acted like she wasn't mine, gave every sign
I was to be removed. It was what Sophia wanted, what she
admitted to her friends, those same friends she'd lied to
about me, those same friends who'd believed every word.
They were so determined to shut me out and I couldn't
stop them.

But what finally set me off was a card from Sophia's
best friend, left on the apartment's kitchen island. The
exterior was a generic congratulations, but the handwritten
note from Cindy stabbed me in the heart.

*Congratulations for your new baby, your new job, new
place ... and NEW LIFE! All so well deserved. The best is yet
to come my brave, strong, and sweet friend!*

I knew Sophia was lying to my face about us getting
back together, and I didn't want it, but it still shocked me
to see "NEW LIFE!" in black ink, all caps for emphasis.
Confirmation of the lie. It bespoke of permanence, and
excitement, and how incredibly wonderful it was to leave
me, the horrible burden that I was. Cindy *congratulated* her
on what she had wrought.

Sometimes it's not what we say or do, but what we
don't that speaks volumes. Why didn't the card say, "I'm so
sorry you're going through this and I hope that you and
Randy can find a way to resolve your differences and reu-
nite your family?" Because she believed the lies. And Dr.
Thompson told me women gossip but don't judge, and I
shouldn't be uncomfortable around her friends. What a

load of crap. I now hated Cindy. I once helped her form her own business, giving hours of advice, freely and without compensation, an act incongruous with the monster Sophia told everyone I was. The recipient of my generosity had this to say.

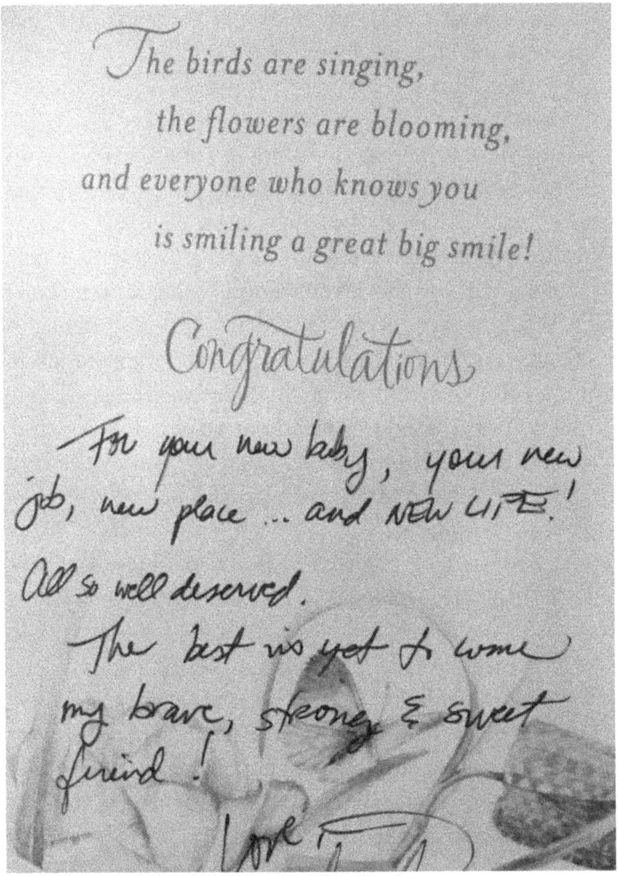

The birds are singing,
the flowers are blooming,
and everyone who knows you
is smiling a great big smile!

Congratulations

For your new baby, your new job, new place ... and NEW LIFE! All so well deserved. The best is yet to come my brave, strong & sweet friend! Love

Figure 8 The Card

The part about Sophia having well-deserved either the new life or baby were galling. Cindy called her brave and strong. Moving out while eight months pregnant could qualify, but it screamed out that Sophia was an abuse victim, me the abuser. This was her rallying cry to get so many women to swoop in and save her from me. And Sophia was "sweet?" Was she kidding? I alternated between being mad and laughing about the card.

But the ultimate effect was a turning away. I felt alone.

It was "all so well-deserved."

They were happy that I was not to see Anna, to care for her, to know her. If she wasn't mine, then so be it, and maybe that justified it? Did they know she wasn't mine? Did that explain the cruelty towards me disguised as help for Sophia? Or was help given without a care for how I, the ogre, would feel about my exclusion? Were they thoughtless monsters paving the road to my hell with good intentions, so obsessed with aiding the "abused" friend that any problems thus caused for the abuser were not considered, even justified? It had been nearly eight months, the card from Cindy a blow that finally struck home. I had been expelled and replaced.

All because I experienced negative emotions. And here she was, causing torment, and I was to act like everything was fine, because if I showed it, I proved she was right. The strain was horrific, pretending to be calm amidst such turmoil. Sometimes I laughed at the absurdity. And Sophia finally got what she wanted – me pretending that the negative emotions she caused me did not exist. Show them, lose my children. That was the deal. The manipulation and gaslighting had gone nuclear.

I was in a black mood when I returned to work from paternity leave, only taking two days for it. I was back a day or two when my client entered my office and fired me. He might as well have said, "How's your wife, the baby?

Yeah? Good. By the way, you're fired." He knew what was going on with the separation and birth and did this anyway. Remember that bit about his #2 guy, the programmer, redoing my code? Well, that asshole continued to refactor my code behind my back so that almost every day I arrived to learn my code had been rewritten. They finally decided I wasn't needed. Weeks were left on my contract, but it didn't matter. Part of me was furious, but I was glad to be gone from the hostile work environment. And I lucked out, quickly finding a new job near the house, but I took a five figure pay cut for it, the last thing I needed.

With the brief free time, I resumed cleaning out the house. I had often joked that she left a pile of crap everywhere like a cat peeing to mark its territory. Now I eliminated it to mark mine. I reduced maid service, but soon let them go to save money. The growing stacks of boxes in the garage began to grate on my nerves, as Sophia wouldn't take them long after childbirth recovery, when Dave also told me that Nina did all the cleaning and laundry at the apartment. Sophia was still as lazy as ever.

With Dave's 4th birthday on August 3rd, we threw no party. She wasn't in a condition to do it and most of the guests would've been her judgmental friends, so I wasn't throwing a party for their kids. Dave, who was surprisingly fine with this, had tons of play dates with them anyway as they showered the heroic and tragically suffering Sophia with attention, bringing their kids to her apartment. He and I also went out repeatedly, as he was in my sole care for the next month precisely because Nina and a recovering Sophia couldn't handle him. We went to the county fair several times, saw a monster truck show and demolition derby, and I introduced him to rides, one prompting him to loudly announce, "I *love* rollercoasters!"

I had noticed a difference between my outings with him and his mother's. I took him to fairs, the zoo, a trampoline park, the playground, and more, with us walking hand-in-hand and doing activities together, even at the playground, where I'd find a way to interact with him while staying off the equipment I was too big for, like tossing him a ball as he went down a slide. We played together in the pool. But when his mother took him to playgrounds, she sat on the benches while he played with other kids. She took him for swim lessons and sat while someone else taught him. Her mother got in the apartment's pool with Dave, while Sophia did not. She arranged play dates where he played with her friend's kids and she hung out with those friends. While these were good, they were marked by her not interacting with him more than necessary. And she honestly thought the kids would be better off with her.

When I visited the apartment with him, Sophia often asked if I wanted to hold Anna, and sometimes I said no, causing a genuinely perplexed look from her. "Why?" she asked.

I shrugged. "No reason."

"Don't you want to hold your daughter?"

My heart clenched at the characterization. "Later."

Seeming concerned, she only said, "Okay. Whenever you want." I didn't respond, keeping my face blank. "I'm sure she'd like her daddy to hold her."

Then maybe you should call him over. We can all have tea and cake.. For a moment, I thought I was going to cry.

Nina approached carrying Anna and I realized too late that she intended to give her to me as I sat, now feeling trapped, in the recliner I'd let Sophia take. A refusal now was too obvious, so I reluctantly took Anna in my left arm. I tried to still all emotion. I had always been so comfortable and natural with my son but felt horribly awkward, rising to pace away my nervous energy. I wandered into Sophia's bedroom, where I sometimes checked the conditions because Dave was supposed to sleep there. The paternity test was in my pants pocket as always, with me looking for an opportunity to discreetly swab Anna's cheeks, but I was never left alone with her.

Until now. Sophia announced from the other room that they were making lunch, so I pulled the envelope out and did the test, sighing in relief as I put it back in my pants. In a week I would know. Her birth certificate had me listed as the father, but I wouldn't have put it past Sophia to do that even if it wasn't true. She had shattered my trust.

Anna showed no signs of being affected by that small hole in her heart and it seldom got a mention at subsequent pediatric appointments. For the time, her life seemed normal, with me beginning to gain some idea of her personality, as much as babies show one. While a newborn takes over your life, that's only true when you're allowed to be a parent to the baby and live with them. Since this wasn't the case, her arrival had changed little; all of the impacts had occurred between her conception and birth.

Sophia began suggesting she enroll Dave in a second pre-school in NoVA over my objections and Dr. Thompson's advice. It wasn't good for him psychologically, emotionally, or even physically (twice as many kids to get him sick), but Sophia didn't care. She cited her inability to control him, which came to a head as summer ended and Dave returned to 50-50 custody instead of with me all the time.

One day Sophia called me in irritation. "You need to talk to your son."

"Why?"

"He called me stupid, said 'I hate you,' and he dumped my bag all over the floor. He even *hit* me."

Did you deserve it? I thought. She sounded like a child tattling on a sibling and I tried not to laugh, though I wasn't happy with his behavior. I knew the answer but wanted to make her admit it as I asked, "So why are you calling me?"

"I want you to control him."

"Why don't you do it?"

"He doesn't listen to me."

I couldn't help it. "Maybe that's because you refuse to raise your voice or admit you're mad at him."

"Will you just talk to him?" she asked, exasperated. "I don't feel like arguing about this."

I laughed quietly. "Fine. Put him on." She did and he was laughing. "Hey, listen Dave. Stop laughing. I'm not happy with what your mother is telling me about your behavior."

"Okay. Sorry Daddy."

"It's okay, but I need you to stop that, okay?"

"Okay."

"You need to listen to her, and the first time. I don't want to hear any more reports about you acting badly. Do you understand?"

"Yes. I'll be good."

"You had better. Just because I'm not there doesn't mean I'm not going to find out about any bad behavior and be upset with you. And no hitting. That is really unacceptable. No hitting mommy, or grandma. And if you ever hit your sister, you're going to be in so much trouble that you may never get out of it."

"I'm sorry, Daddy. I won't do it anymore."

"Good. Thank you. I will see you soon. Behave."

I hung up and shook my head in annoyance. She couldn't have it both ways. Either me speaking sternly to him was me abusing him, or it wasn't. She couldn't say my tone was abuse and then call me to use that tone to control him because she couldn't. *Make up your damn mind.* This happened more than once so that I routinely reminded him to behave when dropping him off. Sophia even used my disapproval as a threat, like the classic line, "Wait till your father gets home!" Letting her have 24/7 custody would have been the worst thing I could've done to her. Be careful what you wish for. She would've been begging me to take him.

That week, when I arrived with him one night, Nina immediately took Anna away to Sophia's bedroom and closed the door. This left me with Dave, who was still hugging my legs, and his mother.

"Where is she going?" I asked, irritated.

"We've decided to keep the kids separated."

"Why? They need to get to know each other. I am not okay with this." I gave my son a pat.

"Well, the other day Dave was being reckless and almost kicked her in the head, so I'm not okay with that and am keeping them apart."

I sighed. "Why don't you learn to parent him instead? Get her out here. This is my visitation and it's not okay for your mother to disappear with her."

"I want them separated."

"*Now*, Sophia." I used a tone she'd likely consider abusive, but I didn't care.

She frowned and headed for the bedroom. "Okay, but tell Dave to behave."

That night, Sophia suggested buying a minivan because Anna became upset in the back seat and her mother needed to calm her, but there was nowhere to sit between the two car seats in the coupe. I looked up the model she wanted and found a good condition used one for $8000, but she wanted the latest, top-of-the-line model for $35,000. I shook my head. We couldn't afford that, so we switched cars. My SUV was better, so I wasn't happy.

By summer's end, I received the paternity test results and stilled myself as I opened the envelope.

CHAPTER SEVENTEEN

Show Your Love

Anna was my daughter. I let out a breath, then flopped in a chair. The wall I'd been building for eight months could start coming down, but it was too soon to be thrilled. I heard myself sighing regularly over the next few days, letting the weight of worry fade away. I felt a little guilty for holding myself back, but that could stop and for the first time, I looked forward to seeing my daughter.

"My daughter." The words seemed weird at first. I would have to get over that. I had two kids, not one. My dream of more had been realized. And Dave had a full sister. It would all sink in over time. I could let myself feel more interest in her, hold her, play with her, see if I could make her laugh as I did with my son. Some anger returned at the deprivation wrought by Sophia and her friends. I was taking back as much as I could of the fatherhood which had been stolen from me. I would take no shit from anyone who tried to stand in my way. Anna was mine, not theirs. I was the second most important person in her life, and in time, would eclipse her indifferent mother, who simply couldn't compete with me for parental involvement. I was the one. And I was taking my rightful place. I was not that plane flying away from Anna for forever. I had been cleared to land.

I had legal rights to her. And I intended to exercise them. The custody situation had simplified in that where one was, the other should be. And that was an immediate cause for concern because Sophia had full custody of Anna. For now.

With one concern resolved, Sophia revisited another at her apartment one night, as I held my daughter a little more tightly, knowing for the first time that she was mine. She was too young to really play with yet, as I couldn't do much more than walk her around and get her to look at things I pointed to, telling her the names of them. I also did something I remembered doing with my son – touching a body part and saying its name at the same time, and if there were two of them, I'd do both back-to-back. She lay on her back on my thighs, head by my knees so she could look up at me. I did her nose, cheeks, ears, forehead, chin, arms, legs, elbows, knees, feet, and hands. Sometimes I'd do hers, then mine. Her deep brown eyes suggested she realized I was trying to tell her something and she paid attention, just like Dave had always done. They can tell when you're truly interacting with them. I suspected I was the only one.

"So you're headed back to work next week?" I asked Sophia, as my daughter lay in my lap and I made faces at her. "How do you plan to do this and watch Anna?"

"My mom is coming, too, so she'll take care of it."

I cocked an eyebrow. "Your boss is letting you bring a baby *and* your mother to work all week?" Now that I knew Anna wasn't her boss's grandchild, this was even more peculiar.

Sophia beamed. "She's awesome."

She's a home-wrecking enabler, is what she is, I thought. "How long is this supposed to last?"

"Until she's six months old."

Wow. "What then? That's when your mom is going back to Russia, too?"

"That was the plan, but it may change. I'm thinking of getting a live-in nanny."

I stifled irritation. Such a nanny would only live in one place, hers, so this suggested she was still intending to keep Anna at least during the week, because no one pays for a full-time nanny when the child isn't there. "She should be in daycare the same days as Dave, and at the same place. It is far cheaper and we can't afford a nanny and this luxury apartment."

"Whatever."

It had been a while since I'd heard the oft-repeated dismissive word and I reacted more strongly to it. "Don't ever say that to me again," I snapped. I half expected her to repeat it, but she said nothing.

A series of incidents began regarding my 90-minute visitations with Anna, and they appeared to be on purpose and designed to prevent me from seeing her. If I was holding Anna and she started to fuss, Nina would immediately try to take her from me, with me telling her no while gesturing at her with one hand to keep away. I'd turn my back, but she'd come around. I'd walk away. She'd follow, arms outstretched like a zombie from *Night of the Living Dead*. She'd back me into a literal corner and put both hands around Anna, trying to pry her from my arms. I was faced with a choice of holding onto Anna so hard that she was hurt, or giving her up, because Nina was not letting go. We were on the verge of an honest-to-God tug of war over my daughter.

This went on for weeks when it finally came to a head one night, when she repeated this for the umpteenth time, following me all the way from kitchen, through a play area, into the little foyer, and into her own bedroom to the farthest corner by the window, like a sheepherder from hell. All the while I was telling her no, to stop it, to get away from me, but she finally pried Anna from my arms, walked briskly away, out of the room as I angrily followed, over the foyer, through the play area, into the living room, into Sophia's bedroom, shutting the door and locking it with an audible click.

And I stood silently fuming at the front door. Nina's behavior implied that I was some sort of monster who had upset Anna and she had to be rescued and removed from my awful presence. I was out of sight so much and for so long that Sophia wondered aloud where I was and came looking for me, finding me seething just around the corner.

"You look upset," she observed after a moment, for once not sounding judgmental. When I didn't say anything, she asked in concern, "What happened?"

Quietly, to control my temper, I snarled, "Your mother. That's what happened." I then relayed what happened and pointed out it occurred all the time.

"I understand you're upset," she said, trying to placate me, and it really did seem like Dr. Thompson and I had gotten through to her about her responses to that. "She didn't mean anything by it."

I interrupted. "It certainly seems like you two are constantly trying to interfere in my visitation. It is not acceptable for her to take her from my arms. Or to walk away. Or to disappear in your Goddamn bedroom with Anna and lock the door. Bring her back here right now."

"Okay, I'll go get her. The reason she's doing it is that once Anna gets upset, she doesn't calm down for a long time unless we stop it immediately, so she's just trying to prevent that. You don't know because you haven't had her."

"And whose fault is that?"

"Sometimes it's really bad, Randy."

I was tempted to point out that it was because she sucked at calming someone, but she had managed to placate me for once. Throwing her usual behavior in her face wasn't likely to inspire this change lasting. And they did bring her back, but I wouldn't take her until I calmed down. It never happened again. It was a miracle – Sophia had accepted a request for change, finally able to restore my emotional equilibrium, like we both wanted.

When Anna cried, I didn't know what it meant because I was deprived of significant time with her. I couldn't read her and get what she needed. They should've helped me understand, not taken her away. I half-wondered if they were trying to make it harder so a custody evaluator would witness my struggle.

Similar events happened at my house and ended after a particularly egregious version. Once a week, she returned Dave to me and I visited with Anna, Nina in tow, but sometimes my mother-in-law refused to come inside with Anna and I had to go get her. Sophia still had a key and let herself in, Dave always running up the stairs to me. I would expect the others to come up.

One night, for a half hour, they did not despite repeated texts to Sophia, and calls down the stairs. I finally went down, upset that a third of my visitation had been stolen. It was bad enough that I only saw Anna about five hours a week. Dave stayed on the second-floor couch as I reached the door to the garage, my eyes flaring. Nina had put Anna in a stroller and was halfway down the driveway, seconds from disappearing down the street with her. The intended walk would likely have entirely deprived me of visitation.

"Where is she going?" I snapped at Sophia.

"She is taking her for a walk to – "

"No, she's *not*. Get her back here *right now*!"

"Anna needs to – "

"I don't give a shit what you think she needs. Now, Sophia!"

Exasperated, she turned to her mother as I calmed my disbelieving outrage. Sophia finally handed Anna to me inside the house, but at the same moment, Dave ran down the stairs, tripped, and landed hard on the tile floor on his stomach, arms out in front of him. He began to cry as he picked himself up, coming toward us, arms outstretched to be picked up. Sophia opened her arms for him but he sidestepped her and came to me, tears on his face, arms up in the universal "pick me up" sign of children.

"Dave," I began apologetically, "I'm holding your sister and can't."

He protested and Sophia said, "Come on Dave, let me help you."

"No," he tearfully said. "I want Daddy."

I sighed, reluctantly handing Anna back to Sophia and picking up Dave, who I carried upstairs, trying to calm him and unable to leave. Another half hour passed with Anna downstairs and away from me before I finally got her back. I quietly but sternly told Sophia they were to stop this bullshit. They needed my approval before taking Anna out of my presence or failing to bring her in. If she needed to be taken for a walk, I was doing it and Sophia could watch Dave, who I saw half the week. Another miracle – they stopped doing it.

Every time they visited, Sophia and her mother blatantly inspected my house for danger and cleanliness, going so far as to take a handheld vacuum cleaner to every surface. It's offensive having your guests do this and implied Anna needed protection from me. The irony of a slob like Sophia doing this grated.

In September, Sophia forced Dave into a second daycare in NoVA twice a week. The place was twenty minutes away without traffic. This meant driving 45 minutes to get there and to work – the same commute she would've had from the house. Do I laugh or kill her?

Dave didn't want to go and didn't like the school but adjusted more easily from experience. That was a major goal of preschool, to transition into kindergarten without a fuss. At Kindercastle, I continued my drop off routine of waving bye at the window and he was now all smiles. When I picked him up in the afternoon, he'd drop what he was doing and came running across the playground. "Daddy! Daddy! Daaaaaddddddddddyyyyyyy!!!!!!!!" When he got to me, he threw up both arms and said, "Pick me!" leaving off "up" as usual. The staff witnessed this and knew what it meant about my parenting, so they were always kind to me.

When I arrived alone to Sophia's apartment lobby to visit Anna and get Dave, he always came down with Sophia or Nina to bring me up, unwilling to wait for another few minutes to see me. He always ran to me, too, if my parking location in the garage meant meeting there for a kind of back way through doors and a service elevator. Sophia repeatedly witnessed it. Did she still think he was afraid of me? How many signs of love could she ignore?

Dave never wanted me to leave him there either, and sometimes Sophia had to help pry his arms off my legs the same way they'd had to at Kindercastle in the beginning. Before long he was calmer about it and we ended up with a departure routine, which consisted of me stepping into the hall from her apartment, and as I continued walked away, both of us alternated saying "bye" a half dozen times until he finally closed the door.

Dave continued to act badly toward his mother, once even biting her. I suspected he rightly blamed her for him living in two places, going to two schools, and only seeing each of us and his sister half the time. She didn't play with him even now, and I seldom saw her holding Anna, as Nina did it. Her lameness as a parent had likely been easier to overlook when I was there, too, but now there was no denying it, the sting more easily felt.

She was also trying to be a parent and authority figure, two roles she had ceded to me. She had an uphill battle because he already didn't respect her. I overheard her sometimes being very mean with her tone, raising her voice, and literally threatening him with timeouts, which I had never given him. I wanted to record it and play it back because she was worse than she'd accused me of being. Did she know the luxury she'd lived in for years, forcing me to control him while she sat back and decided I was abusing him? And now she was worse. The irony. I'd seen it coming and felt no sympathy, though I wasn't happy with Dave's behavior and often spoke to him about it. In doing so, I was kinder to Sophia than she deserved by a long shot. She had no idea how much I was responsible for Dave not resenting her more than he did, as I explained away her lack of interaction with him, which continued.

That October, I self-published a fantasy novella I didn't tell Sophia about. She had stopped caring long before now. When we met, I was authoring a novel with significant social, psychological, and philosophical elements. She had been impressed with my thinking as I discussed story and character elements, which led to talks about behavior, culture, and more. When she'd asked why I thought about such "deep" subjects, I told her about my very difficult childhood, teens, and 20s, full of speech problems, depression, isolation, bullying, and worse. She proved an interesting and thoughtful conversationalist about such things herself, and all of it had helped us fall in love with each other as we came to respect each other's mind. She used to read my books, genuinely interested in them and any talk of my aspirations for character and story arcs as I planned one, giving feedback.

She did the same with my music, which I pursued far more from 2001 until 2012, when Dave was born. I released six instrumental albums, all but one original music, with me earning three endorsements from music companies. All were recorded in my home studio with me engineering everything I performed – all guitars, and sometimes bass and percussion. Later I became a drummer, too, and recorded that at home. Several more albums were written and recorded but not released. From three years, my instrumental band performed locally before disbanding, and I briefly formed an Iron Maiden tribute band that struggled to get gigs. Sophia had supported all of this, coming to my concerts and both videotaping and photographing them, and not begrudging me the cost of album releases, even though I came nowhere near to recouping costs – one of the reasons I quit releasing them. She used to watch me record and wanted to know how my gear worked, and what it took to release an album. She'd hear about those plans and aspirations, too, and my struggles. I had rarely felt supported by anyone I knew and her attitude was one that brought us together.

Until the day it became another thing driving us apart. I learned the hard way, from Sophia, that it's possible to inadvertently kill someone with detail. I have a music degree and Sophia doesn't know music theory at all. One day around 2008, I was once again explaining what I was doing in a song I had just written and I was excited about it. In the middle of a sentence, she snapped.

"Enough already!" Sophia suddenly yelled, glaring. "I don't want to hear anymore!"

I recoiled, first in surprise, then in shock, scowling in disbelief. "What?"

"It's too complicated! I'm sick of hearing about this."

I flushed, feeling stabbed in the heart. I didn't trust myself to speak, didn't know what to say, so I quietly walked away. Resentment, now mutual, was what she felt on hearing me share with her the things I loved most in life besides her? How many times had I been excitedly telling her about my work, not knowing she just wanted to tell me to shut up? I began second guessing all those moments I thought we had shared.

Figure 9 Photo of Me in Concert

One could say I was overreacting, and while she never reacted that way again, any time I told her about my work after that, she'd dismissively wave her hand in a "get on with it" motion and say, "yeah, yeah, yeah." In other words, "shut the fuck up." And then I stopped giving her the chance. I got the message. By 2013, when I was releasing a new album, a conversation summed up the huge divide now between us. I had the album cover on my laptop screen when she saw it from across the room.

"What are you looking at?" she asked.

"Some artwork I commissioned."

"For what?"

I named the album.

"What's that?" she asked, repeating the title.

"The album I'm releasing next week."

She asked in surprise, "You're releasing an album next week?"

I cocked an eyebrow. "Did I fail to mention that?"

An album or book release is a big deal for an artist, and yet I hadn't said a word to her and didn't even realize it until that moment. To put that in perspective, I was the artist and record company, responsible for everything. I had written, performed, and engineered every note of guitars, drums, bass, percussion, and keyboards right there in the house in the spare bedroom that was my music studio. I spent hours over weeks at a professional recording studio "re-amping" and mixing it before having it mastered. I hired the album cover artist and had planned promotions. But what I hadn't done was play her a note or told her about any of it. With books still on hold at the time, this was what I spent virtually all my time doing aside from my day job or being a parent. And she knew nothing, her contempt, frustration, and impatience – all negative emotions! – driving a wedge between us.

I can't overstate how important this was for me falling out of love with her. This was one of my huge dreams, now banished as a forbidden subject. On that note, though, I released that album in 2013 and another in 2014, I finished recording them in 2012 and quit playing guitar when Dave was born, to be a father to the son I'd dreamed about having. I had mostly given up, without regret, my life's dream to be a dad; Sophia gave up nothing. Now in 2016 she was trying to take my kids away over perfectly normal emotions.

She continued finding ways to upset me even during the relatively peaceful period following Anna's birth. Sophia's 2005 car would need replacement soon, so I had it appraised. When I found her engagement ring in the house, I got that re-appraised for insurance reasons, as I had a policy I intended to cancel; I was now also paying to insure her property. When I told Sophia how much the ring was worth, she had a memorable response.

"Sounds like a car down payment."

I did a double take. The woman who'd so often lectured me on my behavior now bluntly referred to the symbol of my love as something to trade in for cash during a material transaction. It ranked high among the cold remarks of 2016. Had I still loved her, it would have hurt deeply, and since she still pretended to my face that we might get back together, it was cruel, and yet she seemed truly oblivious to that. She excelled at pushing me away and bore no resemblance to the woman I'd married, which prompted me to remark on how much she had changed.

"I haven't changed at all," she dismissively said, as if puzzled as to why I'd say such a thing.

I didn't reply. Either she was clueless about the changes or our relationship had been a ruse from the start. Had she gotten tired of pretending? She had received her U.S. citizenship through marriage to me, and her trust-destroying storm of lies this year had me questioning everything, including whether she'd married me just to get it. Her behavior had deteriorated steadily afterward as if her goal had been achieved. By 2008, I had begun to miss *my* Sophia, and by 2010, a stranger, a doppelganger I neither liked nor loved had steadily taken her place. This had become a marriage of inconvenience, at least for me.

I'd gotten over it, or thought I had, but the considerable disappointment had added to the poisonous resentment that had crept into me and our marriage. The comment about the car down payment came the week of our 15th wedding anniversary in October, sixteen years after our first date. The day passed without comment, as we weren't switching custody and had no incidental reason to interact, and I wasn't going to bring it up anyway. What a difference a year had made, as we'd agreed to have another kid twelve months earlier.

Instead, I was on dating sites, unsure how to handle dating while separated. Or dating in general, for that matter. So much had changed, the once frowned-upon world of online dating all the rage. I found it disappointing as women seldom responded, even when I moved on to an app where they had to make the first move after we matched. I joined Meetup and began attending events I'd enjoy and possibly meet someone. In time, I'd try speed dating with mixed results. I found myself having little interest in it all, just enjoying my freedom, solitude, and peace.

Sophia's apartment smelled good the next time I arrived, and when I asked what she was cooking, she beamed at me.

"Meatloaf! It's so much better than before!"

I frowned. I had done most of the cooking because she wouldn't. Was she passive aggressively telling me that her own cooking was so much better than mine, another way her life had vastly improved since leaving the relationship? "What's so much better about it?"

"It has onions!"

That brought me up short and I stifled a snarky reply. Meatloaf had been one of the few meals she'd helped me prepare. While she mixed everything in a bowl, I measured it all and dumped it in, chopped the onions, prepared the baking dishes, cleaned up, and orchestrated it. We made three loaves at a time, freezing two. But somewhere along the way, as with everything, she stopped helping, and so I made it easier on myself – I stopped adding onions. And now here she was, telling me my own recipe was so much better because she added the ingredient she had caused me to omit.

My mother immediately caught how obnoxious these moments were when I related them. I had regularly called my parents and my brother's family, sometimes on video with Dave, and had visits planned for the holidays. First, I went to Pennsylvania to visit my cousins and their kids, who were very welcoming of my son, in stark contrast to my brother's kids, who were the same age as my cousin's kids but ignored my son so much, despite us living in their house for a week, that his parents, mine, and my sister-in-law's parents all apologized for it. I was already updating documents like my will and decided that if both Sophia and I died, I wanted my cousin to raise my kids.

While there, every time I asked Dave to do a video call with his mother, he refused, but I did one anyway and he did talk to her. During a texting conversation I had with Sophia, she learned I was upset with Dave about breaking a present I'd just given him.

Sophia: You shouldn't be so upset with him.

Randy: You're 1500 miles away. How do you know how upset I am?

S: Okay, but just take it easy on him. You have a tendency to overreact.

R: This coming from the person who refuses to find out what just happened.

S: I'll admit I didn't really want to know.

R: There's a surprise.

S: I know Dave loves you. That's why it upsets him when you're upset with him.

R: Are you saying that's why you were upset when I was upset about something?

S: Yeah, pretty much.

R: You had a funny way of showing it.

S: I know. I think I purposely made myself fall out of love with you so it didn't bother me anymore.

What? Wait a minute. Was she serious?

R: When was this?

S: Sometimes after Dave was born. I just didn't have the energy anymore.

Wow. Finally, I knew why she stopped attacking my emotions around 2012. Had she felt she was fighting the good fight by doing so? But by giving up, she succumbed. This likely added to the feeling that she was a helpless victim. She had characterized my emotions as unpredictable, chaotic, and without reason, worsening that feeling.

The revelation explained the avoidance of activities together since then. And the refusal to listen to anything I told her about my life. And her staying up until 2 am to watch her iPad in bed, so she'd be too sleepy to spend time with me when Dave napped, because she napped, too. Making herself fall out of love with me was one of the countless reasons why I felt little responsibility for the marriage ending. I felt exonerated. All that blaming me for things, and yet so much lay on her doorstep, unknown to me. How much could she hide? She deserved this marriage to fail. She'd certainly done everything she could to ensure it did.

I bet it never occurred to her that the resulting behaviors would accelerate my continued falling out of love with her, too. It was yet another rejection of the reality that we can cause emotions in others, all because she couldn't handle that inconvenient truth. Had she thought that making herself fall out of love with me would save our marriage instead of end it?

While I was still in Texas, Sophia started an important text conversation.

Sophia: I'm going to need a better car than mine, due to snow.

Randy: After you give mine back and we swap again?

S: Yes. My car doesn't have good traction.

R: I know. I would also need my car when I have Anna 50-50.

S: Yes.

R: So we'll need it by Feb.

S: Yes.

I relaxed. She'd been suggesting a walk back on our 50-50 agreement with Anna for months, concerning me that she would not honor it. But January 21st was the six-month date for me to start getting her overnight and she now implied an intention of keeping to our agreement. When I got home, I began looking into daycare near the house. Kindercastle didn't accept children under two. I wasn't sure how I'd afford it all and thought about leaving my underpaying job. I was looking forward to much more time with my daughter.

But new trouble awaited in 2017.

CHAPTER EIGHTEEN

A New Threat

By early 2017, when I visited with Anna at the apartment, she was easier to play with, but not by much. She couldn't sit up or crawl yet, or even roll over, and I was concerned, looking up milestones. But I often sat with her, with a smartphone in hand, as we used age-appropriate games together, me tapping for her, sometimes using her finger to show her how to control the screen. Instead of using her own finger, she would take mine and tap where she wanted. I thought it was funny. Sophia didn't think so when I told her. I wondered why I bothered expressing my delight with the behavior of our kids to the one person who wouldn't have cared less. She couldn't even humor me that it was cute.

As I sat with Anna, I said to her, "Are you looking forward to coming to stay with me a few nights soon? Hmm?" I kissed her forehead.

From the kitchen, Sophia casually said, "I don't think you can start to have Anna overnight."

My heart clenched. "What? Why not?"

"I'm sorry, but she can't drink from a bottle."

"Of course, she can. Knock it off." I held Anna tighter to me, feeling a threat to my time with her coming from her mother.

"I'm serious. She starts to choke on the milk. It's like she can't control it, so she has to be breastfed."

I sneered. "Oh, how convenient. Prove it."

"Come on. That's not safe. You're putting her life at risk."

I scowled at the idea that I was endangering my daughter's life. "Stop saying stuff like that to me. I'm sick of it."

"Well, it's true. She could choke. You wouldn't want to be responsible for her dying, would you?"

I rolled my eyes. "Laying it on a little thick this year, huh? New Year's Resolution or something? Are you saying this is something new?"

"No, it's been true for a while. Since the beginning really. She's never been able to drink from the bottle. She chokes on the pacifier, too."

"You've known this for months and are just telling me now?"

"I thought I told you before." She stood making herself some tea, and I noticed that she immediately put the tea bag and sugar packets into the trash, unlike at my house, where she left them on the counter for hours.

"Pretty sure I'd remember something this significant. What did the doctor say about it?" I then added, "Or didn't you ask?"

"She said that it's probably the tongue tie."

My eyes widened. "What? You didn't tell me this either?"

Tongue tie ran on my family's side. If you look in the mirror, open your mouth wide, and lift your tongue, you can see a membrane holding (or tying) your tongue down. This membrane can be too short or restricted and impact tongue movement. Dave had it, too, and at his one-week-old appointment, when the pediatrician told me the problems it could cause with eating and speech and I related them to Sophia, she agreed to having it snipped.

"I thought I told you about it," she replied.

"I'm really sick of your communication issues, not that I think that's what this is. You purposely didn't tell me."

"That's not true. Why would I?"

I snorted. "Because now you have an excuse to keep me from having custody of Anna at all. As long as she has to be breastfed, I can't have her."

"I can't help that."

"Yes, you *can*.. If you'd had taken care of it, this wouldn't be a problem, or did you see an opportunity when it presented itself?"

"I didn't want an unnecessary procedure done. It would cause her pain."

"So what?" I asked, knowing how it sounded. "A few seconds of pain and that's it, it's over and it heals and she's fine, with no risk to her health or ability to talk later."

"Well, I didn't agree and made a decision."

"It's not your call to make alone!" I snapped. "I have legal custody, too. You don't have the right to withhold medical information or make decisions like this."

"Yes, I do."

Only the presence of Dave stopped me from calling her an asshole, though I normally didn't go for name calling. Or at least, not out loud. It just became crucial that Sophia never have more legal decision-making authority than me. She would repeat this. I was the one who could be trusted to consult her when making decisions.

I asked, "When is her six-month checkup? You had better tell me because I will be there in person to hear what the pediatrician says about this."

"Of course."

Despite the quick reassurance, even because of it, I half expected her not to give the info. She had a long history of agreeing to do something and not doing it. Two weeks later, we were at the appointment, Nina in the room, Dave downstairs in daycare, which happened to be in the same building in NoVA. I drove an hour to get there by midday, meaning I'd be gone for 2.5 hours of work time, but it was important.

The pediatrician referred Anna to a Speech Language Pathologist (SLP) for evaluation. Nearly every weekday for the next two weeks, I asked Sophia if she'd contacted the SLP yet, receiving different excuses for why she hadn't. She didn't get a name. She didn't get the number and would have to ask again. She'd asked but hadn't gotten an answer. She asked again. She got it but was busy. She had too many meetings. She'd left a message and got no call back. Twice. Three times. I asked for the number. She said she'd get back to me with it. She didn't.

I knew at once what she was doing – using Anna's tongue tie to prevent me from having custody. As long as Anna couldn't take a bottle, I could not have her. Since that's what Sophia wanted from the start, all she had to do was refuse cooperation with the SLP. I had suspected she would not honor the verbal agreement for me to get Anna 50-50 now. She had found her excuse, with plausible deniability. Of course, she pretended this wasn't what she was doing, but my foolishness had its limits.

I was done. Sophia was threatening my custody. I had to protect my rights and legal action was the only way to do that. I hadn't been happy with my attorney, who seemed wishy washy and had repeatedly told me she had to look into something and get back to me. I'd known about a better but more expensive attorney closer to me and spent much of February preparing for war.

I made copious, detailed lists of information: a timeline, biographical data (on all friends, family, nanny, doctors, psychologists), the current situation, and perhaps most important, a detailed breakdown of who really did what in the relationship regarding parenting. There were two of these, one for me and Dave, and one for her and Dave. If outline level 1A on my sheet was feeding, it was feeding on hers, too. You could lay my list and her list side-by-side on a table and lay a ruler across them, reading off 5E on my list and then 5E off her list. The category was the same but what they said was markedly different. It took me weeks to prepare it all.

Tensions mounted. I was angry. Angry that my suspicions had been realized. Angry at myself for not getting a written agreement. Angry that she would not get our daughter the help she needed. Angry at the powerlessness she had thrust me into a year earlier. It was time for action and for her to react.

I demanded my car back as agreed upon, but she refused, claiming Anna would cry without Nina in the back to soothe her and "think of your children" crap, implying I was being mean to them. The argument soon got lost in other bullshit. One day she claimed our four-and-a-half-year-old son was too emotional and got upset too easily (sound familiar?) and needed evaluation for emotional and psychological problems and possible medication. Outraged, I told her "over my dead body" with enough menace that she dropped it. I received a flyer for orientation at the elementary school he'd go to if associated with my house, and when I told Sophia, she outright said Dave would be going to school in NoVA five days a week, another threat. Was she trying to get me to file for custody and divorce? Because it worked.

On March 1st, I met my new attorney Michelle and her junior lawyer, who was half the price and who'd do most of the work. They both had black hair, hers long, his short, and both wore typical lawyer clothes, though his jacket sleeves seemed a bit short. She was a mother in her 30s while he was late 20s at best and getting married soon. The law firm had two old buildings of a few stories each and onsite parking in a lot behind, a few blocks from the Rockville courthouse where I'd married Sophia. For the insane hourly rates they charged, the offices didn't reflect it. I never saw anything but the mini-lobby and the same small, second floor conference room each time I was there.

They got me a water, we did introductions, and I gave them my stack of documentation, which impressed them as they reviewed it and asked questions. My preparations had them up to speed quickly. On seeing the name of Sophia's attorney and Dr. Thompson, Michelle revealed something.

"Oh, she often has her clients go to Dr. Thompson," she said.

My eyes lit up. *I knew it! Ha!* "I thought they were working together."

She nodded. "So what's going on with Anna right now?"

"We received a referral from her pediatrician to a feeding specialist over five weeks ago and Sophia has stalled on making the appointment. We're finally seeing her tomorrow. I am certain she's using this as a means to keep Anna from me."

At once, Michelle said, "Oh, I promise you that's what she's doing."

I felt relief at my confirmed judgment, noticing that it wasn't the first time a woman quickly and strongly agreed, almost like they thought I was a fool to not be more certain. How easily did women understand the manipulations of other women? Was it what they would have done?

"Any ideas on what the next steps should be?" I asked. "I intend to divorce her, but my priority is protecting my custody options."

"You're certain of divorce?"

"Absolutely." I relayed some of Sophia's behaviors, Michelle confirming that parental kidnapping would've landed her in jail, and Michelle knew the other attorney, who would've talked her out of it.

"I wish you'd come to us sooner. Sophia had the baby in Virginia?"

"Yes, on July 21st."

"And she's lived there exclusively? She hasn't spent a single night in Maryland?"

"Not one. Why?"

She sighed and I sensed bad news coming. "That means Virginia has exclusive jurisdiction over her because she was both born there and has lived only there for six months, which was the mark they needed to reach."

I went cold, recognizing I'd been manipulated, quiet anger growing. Now I knew why Sophia had been so determined to move before giving birth. "What does that mean?"

"That means we might have a jurisdiction fight on our hands. Dave has lived in both states half the time?"

"Yes, only since August. Before that he was only in Maryland."

"Okay, that's better, but it still works in their favor."

My heart sank as I wondered how bad my position was, feelings of vulnerability growing. "How?"

"Once he lived in Virginia half the time for six months, Virginia also acquired jurisdiction over him. Maryland has it, too, but none with your daughter." Seeing my grim expression, she said, "Don't worry, you still have some big advantages. For one, you have the house, which is a huge asset. The family home plays strongly. I'd like you to take photos of every room for us so we can show how good the home is. Do you have pictures of her apartment?"

"I'll have them within days," I said, feeling sinister. *That fucking bitch.*

"Great. Do you think the nanny would testify on your behalf?"

I nodded. Emy had been visiting regularly since we let her go the previous summer. And now it was time to call her for another visit to feel her out for this. "Yes, and she'll refute Sophia's characterization of me. She knows I'm the one."

"At some point, we'll talk to her and get a statement, but first things first. You need to file for custody here in Maryland. They'll likely dispute it, but this begins the process. If we have her served with papers here, she has 30 days to legally respond. If we have her served in Virginia, she has 90 days. I think we need to move now and aim for Maryland."

"Let's do it."

"Is there somewhere she can be served? I don't recommend it being at your house because it can be confrontational."

I nodded again. "Yes, at Kindercastle when she drops off Dave on Monday mornings."

"Okay. We'll coordinate this in a bit. We have a good guy we use for this."

"How do we file for custody?"

"I think we should file for divorce at the same time and have the custody issue be part of it. She can't do anything about the divorce happening in Maryland. Once you file it, that's it. She can't try to move that fight, if there is one, to Virginia. But with custody, she can try to move the fight there. But if custody is part of a divorce case rather than on its own, well, it doesn't make sense to try the divorce in one state and custody in another, so this gives us leverage to prevent her from moving the custody fight to Virginia if she tries. Does that make sense?"

"Yes, but I thought I had to wait until we'd been separated twelve months before I can divorce her. That's early July."

Michelle shook her head. "We can do it now. It's called a legal separation or limited divorce. You could've done this the day after she moved out, and then when the twelve-month threshold is reached, we just amend it to become an absolute divorce, which is what cannot be started until the twelve-month threshold is reached."

I held my breath, anger at my previous attorney soaring. She hadn't told me this crucial information, even saying I had to wait a year, which was the whole reason I hadn't insisted on the written agreement that had now come back to haunt me. I felt like I'd been set up by both Sophia and my previous lawyer. Now I was glad to be rid of her. What an incompetent ass. I also felt in good hands with Michelle, who clearly knew what she was doing by comparison. I had, at long last, made the right decision on an attorney and legal steps. I could divorce Sophia right now. Hell yes!

"Should I assume Sophia couldn't file and still can't, and that's why she hasn't done it?"

"Yes. There's a residency requirement. Twelve months. This is one reason you need to do this first and why we need to move on it now."

"Let's do it."

And so we set it in motion, me paying the $10,000 retainer I'd expected. She revealed other details, like being able to do "discovery," a list of questions we'd send Sophia via her attorney and which she had to answer, the questions effectively under oath. And one of those questions would be whether she'd had an affair. They'd respond with their own questions I had to answer. The paperwork I'd brought helped my team crafting our list.

Michelle wanted to avoid using Sophia's emotional issues because it doesn't play well with a judge, using someone's personal troubles. This irritated me and we politely argued, with me observing that Sophia's entire case against me was about my emotions, and those lies stemmed from *her* emotional issues, making them fair game. Michelle agreed but wanted to take the high road. I knew Sophia wouldn't. I didn't like playing by the rules or ethics when my soon-to-be-ex-wife did neither. Didn't that put me at a disadvantage? When honor costs you everything, what good is it? I could have my conscience but not my kids? Fuck that.

But I appreciated her point. Sophia could play dirty but we'd try it the nice way. It was my way, after all, but if it looked like I was losing, down into the mud I'd go without remorse or restraint. A judge should see that Sophia was a threat to the well-being of my kids. There had always been the inability to deal with his emotions, but now she'd suggested Dave be medicated so he'd be easier to deal with. And she was denying Anna medical care through stalling. I hated her more than ever. I could hardly wait for this to begin.

The next day, we finally met Kris, an SLP who came to Sophia's apartment midweek, with me driving 45 minutes one way from my job at lunchtime. Kris was an attractive, down-to-earth, logical, pleasant blonde woman in her 40s. She was good with both kids, Dave being present that day, and seemed like someone who quickly gets a sense of someone's vibe. Me and the kids liked her at once for these qualities. I sensed Sophia disliked her for the same. After all, this was the woman who, if she succeeded in improving Anna's ability to take a bottle, would cause me to start getting custody of my daughter.

Kris confirmed the tongue tie was severe and the culprit. Anna struggled to move her tongue up or side-to-side and couldn't control the flow of milk from a bottle, and she had to work hard on Sophia's nipple during a breastfeeding demonstration. We tried a bottle and she coughed a little. This was risky because it could lead to pneumonia and death, so until she could handle it, no custody for me.

Anna had missed developmental milestones. She should've been able to roll over by herself, or sit up, or crawl, or stand by herself without support by now, but she couldn't do any of them. Dave had been able to do all of them by that age because Emy and I challenged him. It was obvious Sophia and her mother did not. Neither knew what they were doing or gave a shit it seemed. And these two would raise my kids instead of me? There hasn't been a single visit to the apartment where I would find either of them sitting on the floor with Anna or playing with her. Not once. They didn't seem to have any idea they should do so, despite seeing me and Dave do it all the time, and my daughter laughing. What they failed to understand was that playtime formed part of important stimulation and development that babies needed. Besides, it is fun to play with your child.

Did the missed milestones play into my hands in court? They happened under Sophia's exclusive care. Kris advised that someone should try giving Anna a bottle once a day for practice. I suspected Sophia wouldn't. Going forward, I did it on each visit to ensure it happened some. Kris said it should still be breastmilk, which meant Sophia had to start breast pumping after all. I smirked.

"Can't we just have her tongue fixed like with Dave?" I asked, holding Anna, trying to make the most of every time I saw her.

"Yes," Kris began, "but it's harder now. She's much older."

"Why does that matter?"

"A newborn won't move much but it's much harder to get a six-month-old to lay still. No pediatrician would do it unless she's under sedation."

My eyes widened. I didn't like the idea of Anna under anesthesia at that age, but if it had to be done to help her, and protect my right to see her, so be it.

"I don't want her going under," Sophia emphatically said from where she sat on a folding chair.

Kris said, "It's very safe. We're right down the street from Inova Fairfax Hospital. They have one of the best pediatrics wards in the whole United States. My husband actually works there."

"I still don't want that to happen if we can avoid it," Sophia said.

I reluctantly admitted, "I'd rather avoid it for now, but if it becomes necessary, then..."

Kris got the point. "I'm not sure it's needed at this time. I'll have to examine her each week or two and see what progress she's making, and I'll give you exercises to do with her, to improve her ability to control her tongue."

"There's no rush," Sophia said, to my disbelief. I knew she thought that, but to admit it?

"Yes, there is," I disagreed. "I can't have any custody of her until this is resolved." From some of the SLP's assumptions about my presence to help with feeding, it became apparent that Sophia hadn't told her we were separated. Surprise, surprise. I told her and saw her recognize that far more was afoot, and that she was in the middle of a custody dispute. Kris appeared to gauge the situation carefully.

She said, "I understand. She's gaining weight normally now, so this is why I said it's not urgent, but of course I understand you'd like to have her. Even when she improves, it might take a month for her to be consistent enough with the bottle. She has some catching up to do.

Let's see what we can do about helping her improve. That should be first priority."

That might've been the only thing we all agreed on. Sophia admitted that continuing to bring both Anna and her mother to work every day wasn't a long-term solution, but her enabling boss was allowing it to continue beyond six months.

A couple weeks later, legal action began in earnest. Michelle wrote the Complaint for Divorce, with me editing the language describing Sophia's parenting to minimize offending her so she would cooperate, not start a fight I knew was coming anyway. We mentioned the move to Virginia not being in the kids' best interests, Dave being forced into a second pre-school, Sophia's reluctance to deal with Anna's feeding issue and that Dave had no bed in her apartment. We covered her physical fatigue and difficulty coping that lead to therapy, a polite way of stating that she had a therapist to lay the groundwork for defending myself against emotional abuse allegations. I requested legal custody (the right to make decisions about their welfare), and primary physical custody, but, secretly, I would have settled for 50-50. I asked for use of the "marital home" for three years after the divorce is final, which would tie up her share of equity. I wanted most furnishings, leaving her with an already empty apartment and cardboard boxes as some of her tables. It was "all so well-deserved."

Around 9am on a Monday, I sat in Sophia's car, which I was still stuck with, watching her pull up to Kindercastle in my beige SUV. The white, two-story building stood before an elementary school, the playground where my son always ran to me surrounded by a white picket fence. I texted the process server, who sat in his own car nearby. We had been coordinating for a while, Sophia being late, as usual. Though he had pictures of the car and Sophia, and license plate information, I made sure he knew the car was there and got a look at Sophia as she helped Dave out and into the building. I didn't need to be there, but I wanted the pleasure of it. I had my phone ready to record her being served with divorce papers, which happened after she exited and descended the brick stairs. The server walked away and she slowly meandered to her car, slowly flipping through the documents. Was she surprised? I didn't much care. I drove to work, feeling more in control than I had in a long time.

Game on.

At Emy's suggestion, the former nanny came to visit that weekend, bringing her son, who was about ten. Her twin daughters were a couple years younger and didn't come this time, though all three had played with Dave and were kinder to him than even my cousin's kids. As the boys played with Dave's toys, she and I sat talking about a few surprises she had for me.

"I'm leaving my husband," Emy said, surprising me.

"Sorry to hear that."

"It's not good. It's why I want to see you. I need help."

One thing I always liked about her was the directness, which might've been partly the language issue; maybe she didn't have the words to be more eloquent or hedge. Her English was good, with a noticeable West African accent, French being her mother tongue. Her grammar was sometimes poor, such as not using the correct tense for a word or leaving them off, but I never corrected her. She had more street smarts and common sense than book smarts. Emy came across as down-to-earth, hopeful, sometimes a little naïve, but quick to understand something if you explained it to her one step at a time. She also disliked bullshit. I'd always liked her.

"What can I do?"

"I had to call the police the other day. I got restraining order. Look." She fished it out of her purse and I looked it over while she continued. "He's alcoholic. Started drinking lot when I lost my job."

For a moment I felt guilty, but Dave had been headed to pre-school and the separation hadn't changed the timeframe. Emy was still unemployed since we'd let her go – it had been nine months already. I asked, "How is job hunting going?"

"Not good. I need your help there, too." She told me about a forum where people looked for nannies and asked me to go in there and interact with people, seeing if someone would consider her, so I did this for her over the next several weeks.

"What caused you to need the restraining order?" I asked, handing it back.

"One night he got drunk. Came home at 3 am, being loud, so I confront him. He says he doesn't want to be married to me anymore. He starts smashing stuff. The TV. Printer. A vase. Big mess all over floor. I call police, but they can't do nothing. But I got protective order. It's good for a year."

"But he still lives there?"

"Yeah. The kids are afraid of him. Me, too. And my mom. I don't want him there. I need an apartment, but I have no money."

Sympathetic, I said, "I'll start looking in that forum today." She wasn't good with computers, so her daughter had to send me the URL for it later, and while I did find a number of people who contacted her and sometimes me, none hired Emy. When I told Sophia about what was happening, I refrained from pointing out that the behavior of Emy's husband was the kind of thing Sophia was implying I did when she lied to others about my two seconds of cursing at a computer, for example. Sophia had no idea what abuse was, despite what she thought. As my attorney had pointed out, the police had never been called on me, nor had protective services. Sophia's claims that I was abusive to either her or the kids wouldn't pass the smell test.

But that wouldn't stop her from making them...

CHAPTER NINETEEN

It Begins

As Sophia and I continued visitation and appointments for Anna with Kris, neither of us mentioned that I had filed for divorce and custody, a new elephant in the room. In the minutes after she'd been served, I expected a text about it, but hours later, I knew there would be no response and felt relieved. I didn't want to discuss it. I wasn't changing my mind.

The next few days, she seemed tired, sad, even defeated. Had she held out hope despite her behavior? It seemed ludicrous, but no more so than making herself fall out of love with me to keep the relationship alive. She honestly didn't seem to realize her behavior had consequences. Had being served made reality intrude on delusion? Had it finally sunk in that the marriage was over? Was she doubting her actions? Or was she just disappointed that I'd beaten her to it and taken some control? Did she wonder "why now?"

Because you violated our agreement and showed all the signs of trying to manipulate me into losing custody.

We hadn't exchanged a word about the fate of our relationship since before Anna's birth. I'd surprised her. The funny thing is that divorcing her was incidental to ensuring

I kept custody, my lone source of distress. My marriage was collateral damage, an afterthought. I was divorcing a doppelganger that had replaced the woman I loved, and I'd long since stopped mourning her death. She'd made it extraordinarily easy to not give a damn.

I thought of so many things she'd systematically eliminated from our relationship. Love. Kindness. Compassion. Thoughtfulness. Affection. Sex. Riding my motorcycle. Horseback riding. Skiing. Going to the symphony, rock concerts, movies, or nice dinners. Latin dancing. Listening to me. Listening to my music. Reading my stories. Cooking and cleaning with me. Carrying her weight. Even watching TV together, as she'd taken to watching her own shows on an iPad. And she claimed she hadn't changed. "I'm fine with being roommates." Speak for yourself. She'd refused marriage counseling because of how it would look. *How will it look when I divorce you?* Time to find out.

I updated Dave's immunizations for kindergarten, prompting Sophia to observe we hadn't agreed on which state (it can only be one). I would never accept Virginia. Once he entered a school system, he couldn't be removed without agreement from both parents (not happening) or a court order, and a judge would only force it if something serious warranted it. Dave turned five in August and was legally required to enter kindergarten in September. The question of which state had to be answered by then. Sophia had telegraphed her refusal to move back to Maryland. Whichever state had him in school, that parent won primary custody M-F. This was the war, the other reason Michelle recommended filing papers immediately.

I began acquiring new credit cards to transfer mounting legal fees from my usual cards. Each had an introductory balance transfer offer to pay 0% for 12-18 months instead of a 15% APR or more. The transfer fee of 3% meant paying $300 once on $10,000 rather $150 every month for 12-

18 months. I raided my 401k as soon as I could, taking as much as I could without paying a fee. I also took out loans against two life insurance policies totaling $25,000.

Anna's appointments with Kris continued. I sometimes listened via phone rather than attend. She showed improvement with solids, causing effusive praise from Kris, who said Sophia and Nina were doing a good job. I frowned, knowing Sophia would see it as a reason not to have the tongue-tie fixed, though by now Kris had formally recommended it because Anna was not improving with liquids. Kris had also recommended a barium swallow test that would prove whether liquid was going into Anna's lungs, as barium would show up on the x-rays as Anna drank. Sophia said she wanted a second opinion.

Starting in April, Dave began saying he was afraid of Kindercastle without explaining why. I had multiple conversations with his teachers and the principal as we tried to figure it out, but they were as perplexed as me until I realized what was happening. Dave was used to playing before school, but when Daylight Savings changed, he was oversleeping and wasn't getting it. Sometimes I even had to wake him up and give him breakfast in the car. After a few weeks, he finally claimed he was afraid of school so he could play at home with me, his first attempt at manipulating me.

"Okay buddy," I said the night I realized the truth, "time for bed."

He looked at the clock. "It's only 9."

"Yes, but here's the thing. You can either go to bed now and have an hour to play before school tomorrow, or you can go to bed at 10 and have no time to play before school."

He considered. "I'll go to bed now."

And this is how Dave acquired a set bedtime.

I had missed the days of reading him a bedtime story in a rocking chair, a pile of books on his dresser, though he could be cranky like any kid. One night he slapped a book out of my hand to the floor. I grabbed another. He slapped it down. I took another for him to do it with, not for me to read it to him, and we began creating a huge mess, Dave laughing at our newest game. As the stack dwindled, I told him only a few were left so he had to pick one to read, so he did and I read it, and he started to fall asleep.

I was better at calming him than anyone, including Emy. Long before Sophia moved out, I sometimes rescued Dave from both of them (when Sophia and I were both working from home). In one incident, Emy was trying to make him nap but he kept trying to leave his room, fussing so badly that I heard him on the first floor. I went up, kicked both women out, locked myself inside with Dave, and sat down on the rocking chair as he tearfully tugged at the door. I got him to come closer and pulled him into my lap. He immediately squirmed to get out, so I let him. He went straight to the door.

"I'm not letting you out," I calmly told him.

"Yes!" he complained.

"No. You are not leaving this room. You don't have to sit in my lap, but you aren't leaving."

He again came closer and I again pulled him into my lap. He again tried to get off, so I let him, and he returned to the door.

"Not happening, buddy."

He cried and banged on the door. I knew he was tired. As happens with little ones, he was overtired and resisted the nap he needed. That sort of psychology was beyond either Sophia or Emy. They wouldn't have understood what I was doing either – establishing autonomy and boundaries. He could go where he wanted in the room, but he couldn't leave it. I made a show of respect and authority at once. Don't want to sit in my lap? Fine. But you aren't leaving the room.

The third time he came closer and I pulled him into my lap once more, he didn't try to get off this time. He knew I'd let him, his goal was not that but leaving the room to play. With that ruled out, he gave up, sat on me – the one person who understood him – and let me read to him. He soon fell asleep and I put him to bed. This is what happens when you acknowledge another person's emotions and psychology and react appropriately. This was the kind of father I was, not the abuser Sophia was telling everyone I was (an act that was in itself abusive). This was the reason Dave literally walked around his mother to get to me when upset. I was the one. I always had been. I always would be. When I left the room, I found Emy sitting atop the stairs. Not for the first time, I had to explain to two women, one of whom had three kids, how to handle my son.

Sophia's inability was on full display at her apartment one night. Dave had contracted norovirus, a nasty stomach bug that causes sudden and frequent diarrhea. While he was potty trained, the desire to poop came on so fast that he couldn't get to the potty fast enough and Sophia was using pull-ups on him, as this had started in her custody. Just as I arrived to take him home with me, he had finished on the potty and now stood clinging to the bathroom counter as she began cleaning him up. Nina had handed Anna to me and disappeared into her bedroom. I could see into the bathroom where Dave and Sophia were because the door was open and his blood curdling screams brought me closer. While Sophia was cleaning Dave up, I saw his butt was bright red and sore with a nasty rash – a result from days of diarrhea. Tears poured down his anguished face. Using wet wipes, she wiped him slowly, gingerly but he still screamed in so much pain each time that, for once in her life, she repeatedly apologized for causing him distress.

Finally, he was clean, and it was time for a new pull-up and Butt Cream, a brand of diaper rash cream he was familiar with. He knew that it soothed his skin. It could also prevent the rash, but nothing could keep up with norovirus except maybe a titanium butt. Parents can develop a preference for putting on a diaper or cream first, but eventually, you end up doing it in both orders enough times to be a pro at either.

"Dave," Sophia began, "lift one foot so I can put the pull-up on. Then I'll put the Butt Cream on you."

"No!" he screamed. "Butt Cream first!"

"No, I'm doing the pull-up first."

"No, Butt Cream!"

"Come on, Dave."

Scowling as I held Anna, I said, "Would you just put the cream on him?"

"He can wait a minute," she said, still kneeling behind him.

He screamed, "No! Butt Cream!" Boogers had now joined the tears pouring down his face.

Reacting to my son's distress, I urged her, "Come on. It will make him feel better."

"I want to put this on him first. Dave, lift your foot."

"No! Butt Cream!" He was distraught.

"What difference does it make to you?" I asked, frustrated. I looked for somewhere to put Anna down so I could help my son, but there was nowhere, and Nina was gone to her bedroom. "He's the one in pain."

"I want to do this first," she said, holding the pull-up.

"Why?" I demanded, trying not to accidentally yell in Anna's ear.

"Dave, lift your foot or I'm going to get mad."

"No! Butt Cream!" Dave's face was now as red as his butt.

I snapped, "Will you just put the damn Butt Cream on him already?"

Sophia irritably asked, "Will you let me handle this?"

"Give him what he wants!" I demanded.

"Dave, lift your foot."

"No! Butt Cream!" he screamed, hysterical, lungs heaving as his mother rejected his needs and desires in favor of her own. Again, and again, and again. He was powerless in the face of her cold obstinance, just like me.

"Is there some reason you can't see how upset you're making him by refusing?" I asked.

"Oh, he's just being a drama queen," she dismissively replied.

I silently yelled in my head, *There it is! That's the whole problem with you!*

Despite her words, she finally put the pull-up down and began covering his raw butt in white Butt Cream. But the damage was done. Dave was distraught. Once Sophia had finished and washed her hands, I forced her to take Anna so I could pick up a still sobbing Dave and put him in my lap, tummy on mine so as to not irritate his burning butt, as I rocked in the recliner. There are times when a child is so upset that, even when they stop crying and go quiet, their lungs will heave once or twice a couple times a minute, and he lay there on me experiencing this for a while, now exhausted. When I got him in the car not long after, he quickly fell asleep, emotionally worn out.

Dave's distress had been a 10 out of 10, a visible and audible display of upset so extreme that it was beyond bizarre that she couldn't, or wouldn't, see it. At least I finally understood how she could see something like this and think, "This is not real. It is not happening. And I do not have to react to it."

A few days later, she bought a bed for Dave, presumably because I'd pointed it out in my legal papers and her lawyer told her it looked bad. I'd be able to prove with dated photographs that she only did it for that reason, not because she gave a damn. It had been nine months since she'd moved there.

One day, Kris texted us jointly because Sophia had cancelled the last appointment with no rescheduling. I admitted that Sophia thought we needed a second opinion. Within seconds, the phone rang. It was Kris. I laughed. She was sharp, having recognized that I was choosing my words carefully because Sophia was on the texts.

"Hi Kris," I said, still laughing.

"Hi Randy. I wanted to talk freely."

"You picked up on that quickly."

"I've been in these situations before. Do you think Sophia is uncomfortable with me? Does she want another pathologist?"

That surprised me. "I'll be honest. I don't think it has anything to do with you. I've seen many medical people and I know someone who knows what they're doing. It's a ploy to keep me from having custody, that's why she's stalling. As long as Anna can't take a bottle, I can't have custody. On that note, between you and me, I filed for divorce and custody a few weeks ago."

"Oh, I'm sorry. I know this is hard, especially with two little ones."

"Thanks. My only concern is protecting my right to see my kids and Anna improving."

"I'm glad to see your heart is in the right place."

"Which brings me back to my point. You recommended Anna's tongue be fixed, and once that happens, it's just a matter of time before I start having custody, so she therefore has to prevent it, using whatever seemingly plausible excuses she can find. Questioning your recommendations is just part of it. Don't take it personally."

"The pediatrician is deferring to me to make the decision."

In other words, if Kris recommended it, the pediatrician did. "That's why she wants to find someone who will recommend against it."

She sighed. "I'm sorry."

"It's okay. Just keep doing what you're doing. I believe you are on the right track."

"She's also refusing the barium swallow test."

"I know. It's harmless, but since it would prove that having Anna's tongue fixed might be necessary, she won't allow that proof to exist."

While this phone call was happening, the text conversation between the two of us and Sophia was also occurring, making me chuckle.

The Wednesday deadline for Sophia to file a legal response to my filing came and went without a response from her. Part of me couldn't believe it, but then she never took care of anything. Had she really not told her lawyer? Was she this irresponsible? My attorneys waited until COB Friday and doublechecked, admitting it sometimes gets filed at the last minute and doesn't show up for days, but they confirmed it wasn't done. We even prepared an affidavit asserting Sophia wasn't in the military and had no reason to not respond. They prepared an affidavit for the judge to declare her in default. Michelle prepared a statement for herself to sign and submit to the court about it. I was getting what I wanted without a fight and felt relaxed but in disbelief. Would Sophia being the Ultimate Do-Nothing Spouse finally get me something?

On Monday, Sophia and I met with Anna at another specialist in tongue-tie issues, and this one handed her what she wanted, a recommendation not to have Anna's tongue fixed. He was super positive about Anna learning to compensate and suffer no consequences in time, which was key. Like Sophia, he was fine with months if not years passing by without having the procedure done. I was not. Anna was now nine months old and hadn't spent a night with me yet, when I was supposed to get her at six months. I was angry, my mood worsening as I drove straight into nasty rush hour traffic to get back to work. Along the way, the phone rang. It was Michelle.

"Well," she began, "it looks like she filed something after all, and you're not gonna like it."

"Let's hear it."

"She filed a motion to dismiss your custody case outright, based on Maryland having no jurisdiction over Anna. If it works, your entire case would be dismissed. I don't think this is going to work, but that's their angle. She also filed a counter suit in Virginia seeking full custody. I don't think this is going to work either because it doesn't make sense to have the divorce be heard in Maryland and custody done in Virginia when they are part of the same case. Judges are not keen to do that."

"What do we do next?" I asked, trying to remain calm.

"We're sending over the paperwork for you to review it. I do want to warn you. It's pretty nasty, so just be prepared. She is not taking the high road."

"Okay, thanks."

"We are already working on a legal response and we can talk more tomorrow. Look over what she filed and let me know your thoughts and we can talk then, okay?"

"Yes. Just let me know when and I'll take off from work if I have to."

When I went through Sophia's court papers a while later, I was furious.

CHAPTER TWENTY

Another Storm of Lies

As far as I can tell, there are three kinds of lies. Outright lies. Sins of omission. And gross mischaracterizations of the truth. Sophia's legal filing was all three. Ironically, all were listed under a heading, "Facts."

Sophia claimed that during her pregnancy, I was unable to care for Dave for more than two hours at a time before texting her that I was "done" and unable to handle it. This was pure invention and easy to prove as false. Text records survive and there would be no record of this. In that sense, the lie worked in my favor, destroying her credibility.

She claimed she often returned home to find Dave crying and me not soothing him because I "needed a break." The pot had called the kettle black. But this had actually happened. Once. Anyone giving advice to new parents, including nurses at hospitals when you take parenting classes, tells you that when you get too frustrated, to lay the baby down in the crib and walk away until you cool off – I couldn't calm Dave if I wasn't calm myself. The baby won't die from crying. This is what you are supposed to do, and it's exactly what I had been doing the one time she came home and "caught" me doing it. I'd done it other times. Walking away was my thing, long before parenting, because it's the calmest and least antagonistic. Dave, at least, could not follow me as a newborn like Sophia and continue to upset me, so it at least worked with him. The worst alternative to this is known as Shaken Baby Syndrome, when a frustrated parent shakes the baby so violently that the child does indeed stop crying – because their neck snapped and they're dead. So here is Sophia criticizing me for following the advice professionals give you. Take me away, Your Honor. Taking a break, while a child is safe in their crib, is neither abuse nor a crime.

To my astonishment, she claimed I'd explicitly commanded her not to comfort Dave if he was crying. This was a flat out lie so backwards it stunned me with its boldness. She characterized me as getting mad over "minor infractions" – raising my voice, and Dave crying. There was some truth to this – it is part of how babies learn to self soothe and also laid the foundation for them being able to learn certain things later on in life. It's unfortunate when they cry, but I always made him feel better moments later and, by her own admission, he was very sensitive and cried over very little. She had even suggested to me months earlier via text (proof!) that she wanted to have him evaluated for emotional problems and possibly have him put on medication. She had also called me to speak sternly to him to get him to behave because she couldn't control him. You can't have it both ways Sophia.

Emy could also confirm how often I came to help her calm Dave, saying I was the only one who could do it; there was a period of maybe six months when I worked from home every other day, so I was literally in the house with Dave and Emy for 40 hours of the 80 in a two-week stretch, making Emy a powerful witness for me. Sophia's account vs. mine would be her bug of deceit getting splattered by my windshield of truth. Unfortunately, I found myself driving through a biblical, locust storm of lies.

She said I cursed around Dave, who repeated my bad language. This was also provable as false. Dave thought "stupid" was a bad word for years. It's not, of course. The reason he thought this is that I replaced every bad word in my vocabulary with "stupid." A phrase like "this fucking/damn/asshole/piece of shit/crap computer" became "this stupid computer." I thought this was safe, until one day I heard Dave refer to one of his toys the same way and I realized that didn't work either. I didn't want him going around irritably saying, "This stupid toy." It made me laugh, but I had to stop saying that, too, but the damage was done. Both of us took to telling Dave that "stupid" is a bad word and not to say that. In the days after Sophia's torrent of lies were filed, I asked Dave if he knew any bad words.

"Yes," he said, grinning a little and knowing he shouldn't say it.

"Can you say one?"

He hesitated. "Stupid."

"Do you know any others?"

"No."

I eagerly awaited a custody evaluator to witness this. Emy would also confirm it. Even if Sophia had been right that I cursed in front of him, it wasn't abuse. It wouldn't have been ideal, but so what? Oh wait, she was Little Miss Perfect...

She accurately stated that I went to work early on weekdays, but characterized it as me abandoning her all alone to deal with Dave, the poor thing. She valiantly got him and herself ready for the day and then drove over two hours per day. Aww. Emy would soon state in writing that Dave was still in his dirty diaper and clothes when she arrived every morning to take over, and had to feed him breakfast. Sophia wasn't doing shit. My commute was just as long but I hadn't wanted sympathy for it.

Sophia alleged that on weekends, I slept in "while expecting her to care for Dave." This was true on Saturdays by mutual agreement. Why? Because during weekdays I had to get up at 5:30am to be at work by 7 so that I could be home by 4pm (because she *wasn't* there at 4:05 pm), and even when I worked from home, I still had to be done working by 4pm so I could watch Dave without trying to work at the same time. On weekdays, Sophia got to sleep in until Dave woke around 7am and she got Sunday to sleep in. The nerve of me wanting a single day to sleep in compared to her six! The other obnoxious part of this was that, once awake on Saturday, I exercised, did our laundry, and took care of the accumulated mail and bills of the week before heading to the grocery store, so I was doing errands for my family rather than doing something fun. What a bastard!

She claimed that she was unable to communicate with me about these issues because I would "blow up" and shut down and refuse to discuss them. First of all, what issues? None of this ever came up because none of it was happening. In fairness, if she'd tried to start a conversation based on an extreme lie, exaggeration, or claim of abuse, I would indeed have gotten upset and refused to have much of a conversation. Secondly, if I was so unwilling to discuss relationship issues, how did she account for me going to Dr. Thompson so many times? Why did the therapist have to be the one telling me what Sophia thought most of the time, even when my wife sat right there? Thirdly, you can't agree to a set schedule, live with it for four and half years – without comment or protest, and then claim it's unfair to you. It's also not abuse. She was just trying to make it sound like I didn't do shit, especially as a father, which was unbelievably ironic.

Sophia said she nursed Dave, put him to bed, and got up to deal with him in the night. For starters, it wasn't believable that she was nursing beyond his second year, and by her own admission she'd been breast pumping for two years, which meant plenty of bottles for guess who to give him? Yeah, me and Emy. He was four now and had been on cow's milk for years. Emy would back me up on that one, too, and if I had to, I'd subpoena former coworkers to make them testify about her need to breast pump during the day, and when it stopped. I also had years of text messages acknowledging Dave was asleep long before she got home. Honestly, at times the lies made me laugh because they were easy to prove and she was actually helping me. We'd also taken turns getting up to help Dave.

Her legal papers complained several times that I refused to move to Virginia. She first admitted that she'd "informed" me (it's not a discussion) we were separating and that she was moving out. I had messages from her proving this was true. But then she contradicted this with a long paragraph, in which she made it sound like she was a long-suffering pregnant woman valiantly struggling with a long commute and a careless, thoughtless, selfish husband who never did anything and wouldn't move for her while we stayed together.

She'd pleaded with me to move with her. I refused. She said it would be better for her while pregnant. I refused. She said it would be better for me. I refused. It would be better for Dave. I refused. She made it sound like we were discussing moving while married and my repeated, callous, uncaring refusals forced her to heroically undergo moving out alone while pregnant. To another state! And I couldn't or wouldn't see her wisdom and go with her. There was no acknowledgement that she could've moved near the house to solve the problem of us living in two states. There she was creating that problem and then blaming me for not resolving it.

She then said I lost my job in NoVA and still refused to move...to the state where I now had even fewer ties. Nothing of mine was in Virginia. If I live in Maryland and lose my job in Virginia, why would I move there? Wait! She had an answer for that. The job market was supposedly better there, and yet I purposely took a new job in Maryland to thwart her. Instead of, say, the reason I took that job was because it was near my home. Because only jerks want a shorter commute. Wait, hadn't she wanted an apartment near her job for a shorter commute? Her doing it was great, but me taking a job near my house meant I was an unreasonable asshole? Didn't that make *her* an asshole? I'm asking for a friend...

All of this was to characterize her as reasonable and me as unreasonable. Her as doing everything and me as doing nothing. Her as good. Me as evil.

She acknowledged that I was a consultant and the new job last year had been temporary, as if that was somehow odd, when it's the nature of consulting. She omitted that I owned an actual business in Maryland for this, with multiple insurance policies, bank accounts, a CPA, website, business cards, and more, or that my hourly rate took into account brief periods of not having a client. She then claimed I never had steady clients (provable as a lie via invoices), was often out of work for months at a time (provable as a lie), and she always made more money than me (provable as a lie); after fifteen years of me making as much as fifteen grand more than her, she had made more than me for only two months when she initiated separation. She made me sound like a deadbeat that she was carrying financially. Never mind that I made six figures, handled all the bills, and ran two companies – one being my consulting firm and the other - a small publishing house, where I was as an author (more bank accounts, websites, people I hired, etc.).

Oh, and we were technically employers since we employed Emy, and I handled all of the paperwork with my CPA – timesheets, vacation balance management, leave approval, pay checks (my signature was on every last one of them), tax paperwork, and modifying the yearly employment contract she and I signed. Sophia wouldn't even pay bills until the collection agencies had come after us and I decided to take over all of it. When she left and I cleaned up the house, I actually found a two-year-old letter from one agency that I hadn't even known about. These lies took balls to claim but were stupid.

She then said that, when she had wanted to quit her job while pregnant, I pressured her into maintaining it for her salary and health benefits. In reality, she had informed me she was moving out to an expensive NoVA apartment, and that she was keeping her job to pay for it and her mother's free room and board, all over my objections. But now this was all supposedly *my* idea! I had done this to her. It was rich.

She exaggerated my time unemployed after the obnoxious NoVA company fired me, provable with employment and consulting records – was she *trying* to destroy her credibility? This preceded another complaint that I still refused to list my home for sale and move for her. How was I going to qualify for a new home loan or an apartment while unemployed? Just as importantly, I'd seldom been out of work for a few weeks at a time, even when caught off guard by unscrupulous employers or clients, and it takes far more than that short time to list and sell a house, and by the time I would've sold it, I almost certainly would've had another job...possibly in Maryland. And in fact, that's exactly what happened *twice* that summer. Unreasonableness oozed from the pages.

She said I had no close family, but that she did in the form of her mother. That was rich. My parents, brother, and sister had moved away but grown up there with me, which meant I knew a lot of people, including family friends. I had an uncle two hours away, a slew of cousins two hours away, and my sister-in-law's parents 40 minutes away. She was a transplant from Russia, and now the mother she'd seen exactly once since 1994 was a close relative. I supposed that depended on your definition.

She again complained that I "insisted" on staying in Maryland and my "refusal" to sell the home even though the mortgage would be more difficult to afford on my salary, which wasn't true. The language implied I was being unreasonable and Her Highness simply expected I'd do as she commanded. She expressed bafflement.

She acknowledged in writing that we'd agreed I got Anna 50-50 at six months old but did not admit why it hadn't happened. She claimed that the pediatrician recommended against Anna's tongue tie being fixed when this was a lie that both pediatrician (who had no opinion) and Kris (who recommended it) could testify to prove. In discussing this, she made it sound like Dave had one pediatrician in Virginia for the last nine months (true), and made no acknowledgement that his pediatrician since birth was in Maryland. She falsely claimed that she took the kids to most medical appointments, which was only true of Anna, and that was because I had no custody of her, a kind of self-fulfilling prophecy. There was no mention of me driving two hours round trip to get to those appointments vs. her twenty minutes, or me calling in to listen and participate. In fact, she omitted everything I did while listing the few activities she did with Dave.

One tactic, which was evident throughout, was a careful excising of almost all factors from Maryland. She only acknowledged two: the house and Kindercastle. She neglected to mention Dave's dentist in Maryland. Or her horse. Or that we owned two businesses there. Our cars were registered there. She said her friends would testify, selectively choosing only those in Virginia as if the others didn't exist.

I wondered what her friends could testify to. She implied they'd back up her assertions. It had to be a bluff. They'd seldom seen me with my son and when they did – it was only at parties or Cindy's outdoor, summer wedding when Dave was two. He hadn't stayed still and I ended up following him around on the lawn the entire ceremony while wearing a suit, thirty yards away. I missed the entire reception too, having to walk around outside with him in the brutal heat again, Sophia refusing to relieve me until the end, when I went in to find my food cold and everyone finishing their dessert. Cindy apologized for Sophia, who wouldn't acknowledge anything was bad about this. If she called Cindy as a witness, I'd make her recount this.

Everything Sophia wrote was an attempt at defining me by my worst, taking something that happened once and elevating it to a nearly daily occurrence. And when that wasn't good enough, she made stuff up or omitted elements. There were sometimes three lies in the same sentence.

I learned from the papers that her job title was now Vice President of Development. I had suspected the job had gone to her head from a salary perspective and now maybe this. I wondered when she'd gotten promoted, as it hadn't been the original one. It certainly explained why she didn't want to quit anymore, having gotten absurdly lucky with that job, which she'd been reluctant to take until I talked her into it. She now weaponized it, using it as the excuse to move to NoVA and cause havoc, which had ironically been done in the name of making life simpler.

As I read, my anger grew at the lies as they turned increasingly ludicrous. My mood almost turned to amusement on realizing how easy she had made it to destroy her credibility, without realizing it. "Thank you," I even said out loud. But I was furious.

Her lawyer was cunning. They had planned this a full year earlier. Now I knew why Sophia had been so determined to move that she did it while eight months pregnant. Why she enrolled Dave in a Virginia pre-school, to make Virginia seem more like his home state. Why she immediately got a new Virginia driver's license ("Look, see! I'm truly settled here!"). Before moving, Sophia had told Alexa she was running out of time. To do what? To move out before birth, so she didn't have to leave the state, making it far more likely she'd go into labor in Virginia, that the baby would be born there. It also ensured Anna would have been solely in Virginia for six months by the time I was supposed to get 50-50; I walked into the trap by agreeing to that.

The first plan to take the kids away had been kidnapping, but her lawyer talked her out of it, probably around February 2016. The second attempt, in my opinion, was inviting me to Dr. Thompson in March 2016, to get me to admit to child abuse in front of a therapist, who would then be legally required to report me to authorities or at least Sophia's lawyer, who would call protective services or file an emergency motion with the court to immediately take Dave away from me. In lieu of that failure, the third attempt was the jurisdiction fight, planned in April 2016, me only finding out twelve months later. And now the fourth attempt had unfolded, starting in July 2017 when Anna was born, her tongue-tie was discovered, Sophia hid this and Anna's inability to drink from a bottle, preventing me from having custody of her in January 2017 at 6 months old, as agreed upon. It was continuing in the form of stalling and avoiding treatment from Kris.

The abusive, gaslighting attacks on my emotions had started around 2005, then ended abruptly in 2012 as Sophia decided she didn't have the energy for it. Then in January 2016 they suddenly returned a thousand-fold starting with the awful appointment with her first therapist. Four months later, they stopped just as suddenly as they began. She and Dr. Thompson, working with her lawyer, pretended we'd gotten through to Sophia that no abuse was occurring. I had asked the question of whether she'd accepted that or just learned to stop saying it. She had not responded. Now I had my answer. For the next twelve months, she pretended she no longer believed it, that Dr. Thompson and I had gotten through to her, that my reactions were normal, that the problem was her over-sensitivity to "negative emotions" and the way she communicated with me when I was upset.

But a year later, it was suddenly back, this time in black and white. I had now been publicly accused of abusing my wife and son, not that I thought anyone was paying attention to my court records. But I had a security clearance she could cost me, and therefore a job and even career options. Every seemingly pleasant and cooperative interaction over the past year had been a con to get me to verbally agree to let her keep the baby for six months and not agree to a written agreement.

"You have to con him," I imagined her attorney advising her. "You want a year of Anna 100%, and he wants six months. Give it to him. He'll think you're being reasonable. He'll have no idea that when the six months comes around, we'll have established Virginia as having exclusive custody over her, especially when she's born there and you do everything you can to make it look like Virginia is the real home state for both kids and yourself.

"If he files for custody in Maryland after that, we'll contest it. You can't file for custody until you've lived in Virginia for a year, but he can do it in Maryland the day after you move out. You have to stop him. If he gets a written agreement, you're bound to it, so it must stay verbal, and you gain that with trust. You have to pretend there's hope in the relationship. More importantly, you have to pretend you're going to honor the six-month agreement. If he thinks you won't, he'll insist on a written agreement and then you're screwed. Convince him you'll honor it, not by saying so, but by acting reasonable, and if you make it to the six-month mark, we got him. Stop saying all this stuff about him being abusive. Act like he and Dr. Thompson got through to you, that you've had a breakthrough, that he's a good dad. Be nice, be fair, be a partner. Pretend for a little while longer and you'll get what you want.

"You need to con him."

And that's why Sophia had suddenly turned nice last May and the attacks on my emotions stopped.

It's not every day that you learn you're the target of a long con and the goal of it is to take your kids away. Your humanity is used against you as proof that the people you love most in life and are so protective of, are in peril from *you*. I felt ashamed that I fell for Sophia's tricks. I should have been more suspicious. Ashamed of my reasonableness, my honor, my integrity, my decency. They had been used against me and I felt like a fool. I felt naïve for having hoped for the best, and sanity, and an end to the bullshit when already confronted with so much deceit and evil. Dr. Thompson had played her role well. Sophia had said the therapist was much better than the first one. I now saw what she meant.

A powerful, simmering anger slowly grew in me, compacted into cold, sinister malice by the knowledge that if I showed the negative emotions she was once again causing me, they'd be used as proof she was right about me. The strain I'd been under was immense. I felt perpetually setup.

The only constructive way to deal with my fury was determined, purposeful, calculated action. Two could play her game. And I had a smorgasbord of deceit to feast on that night, ripping her legal papers to shreds in writing to my lawyers. I spent all night on it in minute detail, writing a line-by-line analysis. While I was doing it, Dave kept asking me to play with him while sitting among his blocks, train tracks, and other toys.

"I'm sorry, buddy," I said, sitting on the couch and typing, "I have to do something really important."

"But can you play with me?"

"Not today. I'll make it up to you tomorrow, okay?"

"Okay."

Feeling bad for his disappointment, I added, "Today no playing. Tomorrow *all* playing."

"Yay!"

I laughed and went back to what I was doing. By midnight, I'd sent my written response to Michelle, who laughed when we were on the phone to discuss the next steps the following day.

"I can't believe you did this in a day," she said.

"Five hours," I corrected.

She chuckled again. "This is great. Very helpful."

"What do we do now?" I revealed my intention to talk to the Kindercastle staff and she agreed.

"We have about ten days to respond."

I hadn't known that. And there I was furiously acting fast anyway. "And we can?"

"Absolutely. I do have some bad news."

"Perfect."

"It's not that bad. We are not barred in Virginia. This means you'll need another law firm there, but we know people and will arrange this. You may even be able to have us deal with their retainer to make it easier. You have enough to worry about, but once we agree on one, and there's no huge rush, we'll bring the attorney up to speed."

Another law firm and retainer. Just what I needed. But I appreciated their help and felt I was in good hands. "So where are things filed exactly?"

"Her attempt to dismiss your custody claim, the one we filed, is in Maryland, because our claim is, so we'll soon get a hearing date for that. It will happen at the Rockville Courthouse."

"That's where we got married," I observed. "I'll enjoy the symmetry of divorcing her where I married her."

She laughed. "You probably aren't the first one. Her own custody claim is in Virginia, so that's what we'll need the other law firm for. We will be filing our own case to have her claim dismissed."

"What's our rationale?"

"We're going to work on the details of this with all the info you've provided, so I again want to point out you've really helped yourself with all of these notes. We can respond quickly. But our approach is partly to point out that it doesn't make sense to have the divorce in Maryland, which she cannot change, and move the custody case to Virginia when they're part of the same overall legal action. It also doesn't make sense to try Dave's custody here and Anna's there. They know this and are basically saying custody should be decided in Virginia for both kids, but we filed first, and that does matter to some extent, so the burden is on them to prove Virginia is the real home state."

"Is that a term?"

"Yes, and proving home state is our focus. He's lived in Maryland all of his life, 100% for the first three years?"

"Four years, then 50-50."

"Yeah, and Virginia has been less than a year at that. Anna has been 100% there since birth, so Virginia is her home state, but Dave's is Maryland and he's more important due to age. He knows people and is aware, unlike a baby. Also, all of the real witnesses are in Maryland, as are most of the assets. We're also going to point out that this whole Virginia thing is a fabrication done specifically to create this jurisdiction fight. They clearly think this is their best shot, and it's not a good one, but we do need to take it seriously to defeat it."

"I found out she got a new driver's license there immediately. I took a photo of it."

"Good. Send us that. This sort of thing points to intent to create an illusion."

"Yeah, she was eight months pregnant, so why was it so important to get a new license there?"

"She's trying to create the appearance of being firmly entrenched in Virginia."

"It's all bullshit. I suspect this is the real reason she insisted on enrolling Dave in daycare there."

"I can promise you it was. Now we know what she was up to. You are actually well-positioned to refute this, especially because she seems to have bent over backwards to avoid admitting all sorts of things are in Maryland."

"Even her horse," I interjected.

"You know, it strains credibility that she lived there for how long?"

"Fifteen years, give or take."

"Yeah, and she knows no one? A judge will see right through this."

"I assume we're going to point it all out in detail."

"Absolutely, and you just provided everything we need to do exactly that. By omitting as many references to Maryland as they can, they made a mistake, because we can show their dishonesty there. That will be a major focus and it's why your response last night is so helpful."

After we hung up, I felt invigorated, powerful, and full of clarity. No more wondering what Sophia was up to. She was going down in flames and I was warming up the flame thrower.

CHAPTER TWENTY-ONE

Machinations

The next day, I called Emy, who agreed to write an affidavit, which refuted many of Sophia's statements. She, Michelle, and I drafted it over a week before Emy came to the house to sign it. Emy was the star witness, and an objective one, unlike Sophia's friends, who couldn't testify to anything about me. As a *former* employee, she wasn't compelled by anything to keep her job. She strongly disapproved of Sophia as a mother and for what she was doing, a fact Sophia likely knew, for whereas I'd kept in touch and Emy regularly visited Dave and I (bringing her kids and even cooking for us), Sophia pretended Emy didn't exist. The former nanny was eager and happy to testify and knew Dave belonged with me. She had gotten a new job and was leaving her husband (he would eventually abandon them by returning to Africa) and taking her kids, so we were both on the path to a better life.

The same day, I met with the principal of Kindercastle and apologized for dragging her into this, then told her a light version of what was going on, including the emotional abuse claims and that I was supposedly indifferent to Dave's emotions. She knew how often I'd checked on him when he'd started there and all the attention I gave to his difficult transition. So had Emy, being a part of it. We'd also just gone through Dave saying he was afraid of school, and she and the teachers knew how seriously I'd taken that emotion. That he'd been lying didn't change that.

When I started to ask if her and three teachers would testify, the principal cut me off with an eager, "We'd love to. Absolutely. We can tell when a child is being abused, partly from observation but also training. I know this is bullshit." She was a bit younger than me, had two daughters, and was divorced, so she got it.

I now had four powerful witnesses, all independent and unbiased and eager to testify for me.

Then I got a call from Michelle days later. "I have some bad news."

"I hate it when you start that way."

"I know. I'm sorry. Listen, we talked to the principal and learned that her and the teachers were all ready to make a statement for us, but she told her boss about it to double check it was okay and was told no."

Shit. "What? Why the hell not?"

"They have a new policy not to get involved in litigation unless forced to by a court."

"And how do we do that?"

"A subpoena. She also said we could get the school records and she keeps detailed notes about all contacts. For example, all the times you contacted them to check on Dave, she logged. And that recent time where you said he was afraid of school."

"That's good."

"Yeah, but the stakes went up with this."

"Why?"

"A subpoena can't cross state lines." She stopped there, as if the implication was obvious.

"Why does that matter? They're in Maryland, and so are we..." I trailed off, realizing it.

"If Sophia is successful in changing the custody jurisdiction to Virginia, we'd have no way to subpoena the witnesses in Maryland. They would have to come voluntarily
but it's against the school's policy."

Fuck. With a single stroke, she would eliminate three of
my most powerful witnesses, leaving me with mostly Emy.
This was war. "What can we do?"

"It's not all bad. To be honest, it might even be a good
thing."

I laughed. "Okay."

"It improves our case for having custody decided in
Maryland. After all, three very important witnesses are
here and are needed to refute Sophia's abuse allegations,
which are almost her entire case for custody. You can't be
left unable to defend yourself due to jurisdiction, but that's
what would happen."

I appreciated a good line of logic. "Ah! Very nice."

Within days, they'd gotten the school records on my
behalf after I did some paperwork, and the motion to dismiss Sophia's case was filed along with Emy's statement.

By May, I began taping my arrivals at Kindercastle and
Dave's excited response to me, which all of the staff had
witnessed for nearly a year. We all tape our kids, but it's a
little sickening to do it to refute your ex's lies about your
relationship with them in court. The kindergarten orientation I'd told his mother about came and went without her
attending, so it was just him and I, yet another act of indifference from her.

Sophia began to regularly cancel the tongue-tie appointments with Kris so consistently that Kris began planning around this. She wanted to see Anna every other
week, but when Sophia cancelled, she would already have
the next week booked for someone else, causing four
weeks in between appointments for us. This was too long,
so since Sophia cancelled so often, Kris put us on the

schedule every Wednesday, and if we showed up, she just cancelled the following week's appointment.

Sophia's excuses always amounted to her job having scheduled a meeting or something, sending a clear message (in writing!) about what was most important. I was supposed to believe that her boss would let her bring a baby and her mother to work for forty hours a week for going on nine months, bring a bed to her office, and buy a temporary inflatable bed for her apartment, but she was supposedly and repeatedly scheduling meetings when Sophia needed to do the appointment with Kris for Anna's health, despite that appointment occurring at the same time every week and therefore being easy to plan around. Sophia obviously thought we were all morons.

Then I got a call from my attorneys.

"They're requesting we do moderation instead of resolve this in the courts," Michelle revealed.

I groaned. "I don't like that at all. Do you think this is good or bad?"

"I think it's good. It suggests they want to be reasonable."

I laughed. "Don't read too much into it. But did they sound like they're uncertain of victory after what we filed to dismiss their case?"

"Hard to say, but even if moderation fails, we will learn what cards they intend to play, so it's worth it."

"I have my doubts about that." I then relayed what happened when we were seeing Marie, the collaborative divorce coach, and how Sophia kept returning to the same argument over and over until even Marie became exasperated and we all agreed to quit. We never went back.

"Fair enough, but few people go into moderation and ensure that it fails. The whole point is that, while it's expensive, it's far less pricey that litigation, so we will probably come out with some sort of agreement."

"I'm not going to get my hopes up, but I take your point. I don't think you realize just how financially irresponsible Sophia is. She acts like money is no object. If this goes bad quickly, I will want to pull the plug."

"Either side can do that at any time."

"Good. Also, I do not want to be in the same room with her because I know she'll just stake positions that are going to piss me off and then judge me for reacting."

"Don't worry, you won't be. The way it works, you and I will be in one room, she and her attorney will be in another, and the moderator we agree to is another family law attorney who moves between rooms."

That was a relief, but then I got unrelated bad news.

My mother fell and broke her collarbone and a rib or two. With her stuck in the hospital, my 88-year-old father began a rapid mental decline that had everyone worried. He'd call her and tell her there was nothing outside the window, no grass, no trees, nothing but emptiness. She'd call and when he answered, he would say that he wasn't there and would be back if she wanted to leave a message. He was evaluated at a hospital and by many doctors since but no one ever figured out what was going on, though many agreed with my theory, that his life had revolved around my mother for so long that he was lost without her. This was not to say they were lovey-dovey, because they bickered terribly, but that was apparently better than nothing. She returned home and they soon had him on medication, so he more or less recovered as long as he took it.

My latest job, the one I'd had since last summer and which was five minutes from the house, also took a sudden turn for the worse due to an unreasonable, petty NIH client. They complained about the website I was creating for them, things like the exact shade of blue being off, or a different amount of white space between sections of it, or that I sent two emails (at different times) with one question each instead of one email with both questions in it. They even got mad at default web browser behavior that they blamed me for. It became so contentious that the project manager, my boss, and a higher-level executive were all on a call where they were literally yelling at me, and I had the great pleasure to catch them lying in front of my superiors. And then a week later, they accepted the first stage of work we'd done, only to cancel the remaining project the next day, throwing me under the bus to our CEO as the reason. I'd been scapegoated. And it was all happening right at annual performance review time. The result was a review so offensive that I began looking for another job. I was sick of people being obnoxious to me.

Speaking of which, Sophia was dragging her feet on agreeing to a mediator but finally did. She made a comment about not wasting money, so I suggested she be reasonable at mediation, prompting her to say I was the one who needed to be. Based on history, this meant give her everything she wanted the first time she insisted on it, not later or never. It certainly didn't mean she was budging and she had virtually admitted this.

The next time she arrived at the house, she suggested I replace all the carpeting to make selling the house easier, an assumption that I would move to Virginia. To my question about whether she could go month-to-month on her rent, she confirmed it but said it would be more expensive. She still hadn't gotten rid of the horse, nor seen it in nearly two years. I was eager to divorce her and get that horse off my books, as I was approaching $50,000 in credit card debt, with only $10,000 of that from before we separated. I didn't know how much debt she had incurred herself.

Then we had a court date in Maryland, just to schedule more important dates. We now had a three-day custody trial scheduled for January. To my surprise, we were both being forced to take a court-mandated parenting class that was standard. The next day, in June, we tried mediation. Or at least, I did. Sophia tried something else.

I arrived before my attorneys and met Diana, the mediator, a blonde, middle-age family law attorney we'd both agreed to use. The tall office building was far nicer than Michelle's. Diana offered me a choice between an exterior room with a view or an interior one without, so I let Sophia have the windowless room, as she deserved. Michelle arrived soon after.

"She brought the baby," she told me in disbelief, putting down bags and setting up a laptop, as I had done.

"Never seen that at a mediation before," agreed Diana.

"I guess you weren't kidding that she brings the baby to work?" Michelle asked.

I said, "No. You'd think she'd be more interested in Anna being able to take a bottle, so she wouldn't have to bring her everywhere. Lugging a baby and her mother around is apparently easier than breast pumping, not that she has a choice now thanks to the tongue-tie issue." Not until I said it did I realize Sophia had really stuck it to herself by refusing to have that fixed after birth. I wanted to laugh. She now had a pattern of making things infinitely worse in the name of making them better. I saw no sign of the intelligent woman I had married.

"How is that going?" Michelle asked.

"A little better. Anna can feed herself solids now, and I gave her milk from a spoon the other day and she didn't choke."

"It's just a matter of time."

I hoped to resolve it soon. "I took Dave to kindergarten orientation recently. Sophia was a no show."

"Do you think she's enrolled him in Virginia?" Michelle asked.

Surprised, I said, "I don't think so. She hasn't said anything. That would be messed up to do it behind my back, not that she hasn't done other things that way."

"That's why I'm asking. Maybe you call the school there and check."

I nodded slowly, adding a to-do item to my list. It would explain why she skipped orientation in Maryland. If she enrolled him, she might even try to claim this was another reason VA should have jurisdiction. Had she done it behind my back as if cancelling out his enrollment in MD? There was one critical difference – I'd told her about it, even given her the dates and more, and handled Dave's required vaccination records, including scheduling a few missing shots. Suspicion grew.

Moments later, Sophia and her attorney were ushered into my room by Diana, who went over some ground rules before asking who wanted to go first. I said nothing. Sophia was the one who needed to budge due to stinginess, so let her make the first offer. Her attorney volunteered, so everyone but me and my attorneys left the room again. We waited forty-five minutes, with me paying nearly $500 an hour for my attorneys to do computer work. I wondered how much of it was for me.

Finally, Diana returned and closed the door, seeming somewhere between amused and exasperated as she sat down with her yellow notepad and its scribbles. "Okay, there are two parts to their offer."

This ought to be good, I thought.

"One offer is about you moving to Virginia, the other is if you stay in Maryland. However, in both cases, Sophia wants 50-50 legal custody with tie-breaking authority." She paused, and then almost snidely added, "And I can tell you that's not where we *started* from."

I did a doubletake. "Wait. Are you saying she was offering me zero legal custody and you talked her into *this*?"

She tilted her head in a way that meant yes but she was trying not to admit it. "Well, let's not get into that. This is where we're at."

Un-fucking-believable.

It should go without explanation that at mediation, you try to meet in the middle. She had adopted a position stronger than any stated before, though I'd known all along she wanted me to have no say in anything. She certainly acted like it all the time. But I still couldn't believe she was now coming right out and saying it, and had to be talked down off the ledge by Diana. Her offer was worse than the worst case of me litigating and getting my ass kicked in front of a judge, which wasn't going to happen, but even if it did, I'd still get better than zero legal custody. The whole reason people try mediation, aside from being cheaper than court, is to not get a one-sided agreement. And yet that's what she offered. She had balls. And to think that Michelle had repeatedly told me we should not be unreasonable so as not to piss off the other party into refusing to negotiate. That's exactly how I was now feeling.

"It's never going to happen," I said. "I will never agree to her having tie-breaking authority or more than 50-50, because that will be like me having zero. She's proving it right now by denying Anna medical care." I explained a little more and Diana "got it."

"That's fine," Diana assured me. "We'll counter. Would you be fine with 50-50 and you having tie-breaking authority?" This meant that we had to discuss things but that if we didn't agree, one person got to make the decision.

"Yes. That's as far as she gets with me."

"Well, there is another option. Basically 50-50 and then when you can't agree, you see a third-party and try to work it out with them, up to a set number of times, and that person ultimately has tie-breaking authority."

I considered. "That might work. Are they allowed to speak to medical professionals and the like to get an unbiased opinion on what is needed?"

"Typically, yes."

"I would insist on it." I knew that any objective person would agree with me about what was happening, so I would essentially win disputes. But I told Diana not to offer it now, just me having tie-breaking authority.

She agreed. "The other part is about physical custody. She will let you have 50-50 if you move to Virginia, but if you don't, she wants them weekdays, and you get them on the weekends."

Part of me was surprised by the 50-50 part, but it wasn't good enough. "I'm not selling the house, and I'm not agreeing to less than 50-50, which does not work if we live in two states."

"She said you can't afford the house on your salary."

"That's a lie and I've already proven it with a loan officer. It's also none of her business, so it's irrelevant." I'd contacted the guy we'd last refinanced with and he ran some numbers for me.

I then made my counteroffer with some discussion with Michelle: 50-50 legal, tie-breaking goes to me, and 50-50 physical if Sophia moved to Maryland. If she remains in Virginia, I have the kids M-F. In effect, I made her the same offer she'd made me, even though I'd found her offer obnoxious.

You could say I'm a hypocrite, but is there a difference between an apartment and a house? Between somewhere you have lived 14 years vs. 10 months? Between a fully furnished place you spent 14 years decorating, and a mostly empty, non-customized apartment? Between knowing your neighbors for 14 years and knowing no one? Between having roots somewhere going back almost 40 years versus 10 months? Does it matter that you have two businesses incorporated in your state versus none in the other? Does it matter that preparing and staging a house for sale is so much more difficult than just telling your apartment complex you are not renewing your lease? Does it matter that packing up an entire house is significantly harder than a half-empty apartment? Does it matter to be forced to downsize from a house to an apartment due to not being able to afford one in the new location? The answers should be self-evident. I wasn't a hypocrite. I was reasonable. Besides, she'd created the problem by moving to Virginia over my considerable and repeated objections. It was her job to fix it, even if I had to force her.

Diana left and returned with Sophia's lawyer twenty minutes later, asking me to leave. Eyebrows raised, I did, and then five minutes later, Sophia's attorney left the room and I returned.

"We called off mediation," said Michelle, packing up her computer as Diana stayed behind with us.

"You're kidding."

"No," answered Diana. "They weren't willing to budge at all."

Shaking my head, I said, "So it was an ultimatum. Give us what we want or we leave."

"Yes," agreed Michelle. "We talked it over and decided we're too far apart and there's no reason to continue."

I sighed. "I can't say I'm surprised. Good call, I guess." I smirked at her. "I hate to say I told you so."

She smiled. "You did."

Diana chimed in. "One reason is that they know you have the court date in Maryland next week to find out if her attempt to dismiss your custody case will work. They feel confident it will, so they see no reason to give anything. They'll see what happens and may be open to resuming."

I scowled. "They knew that before agreeing to this! What the hell was the point of this?"

"Probably fishing for information," suggested Michelle, "to see where we stand."

"That was one hell of an expensive fishing trip," I said. I started doing math in my head, realizing how much this mediation-in-bad-faith stunt had just cost us between the attorneys. "I could've told them that without spending $4000! All they had to do was *ask*."

I couldn't help wondering about this idea that Sophia had been "very interested" in mediation, according to Michelle. Another lie? Or did she honestly believe I'd give in? I increasingly wondered if we'd ever known each other at all. And this idea that we might resume after next week was bullshit and I told Michelle so. I wasn't doing it again. I hadn't wanted to do it *this* time and she'd talked me into it. I was pissed. On the plus side, mediation failed after only 2.5 hours, so at least they were "quick" about it.

As we packed up, Michelle chatted with Diana, who basically said she thought I would win the court cases. She had reviewed all of the legal filings by both me and Sophia. Diana then commented that whoever won the jurisdiction fight essentially won the custody battle. It was mid-June. In a week, we would learn if Sophia succeeded in dismissing my Maryland custody case. A month later at the end of July, we'd learn if I would succeed in getting Virginia to decline to exercise their jurisdiction over Anna, meaning Maryland suddenly had that jurisdiction. And a week after that in early August, Dave would turn five. A month later, he would start kindergarten, which had to be M-F in a single state. And once he started in one school, that was it. No judge would pull him out without serious performance problems, which weren't going to happen in kindergarten.

If I won the jurisdiction fight by late July, we would file an emergency petition in Maryland to have the MD judge decide which state Dave went to school in. Which one he'd choose was almost a given. Sophia would likely do the same in Virginia if she won. The jurisdiction fight was the whole thing. While we had a three-day trial scheduled for next January, none of us thought we'd ever make it there. This thing would be decided in the next five weeks.

When I got home, I looked up the grade school nearest to her apartment and called them, leaving a message about learning if he'd been enrolled. While on Facebook that day, I saw an innocent status update from Sophia. I unfriended her, all of her friends (discovering one had already unfriended me), then blocked all of them. I didn't want to see anything about their lives. I changed my status to single and admitted online that I was divorcing Sophia, letting the secret out. I had kept the drama off there (and would continue), but the secrecy had begun to grate. Only relatives or those who saw me in person had known anything was happening, but now everyone knew. I felt relieved.

On Monday, the school returned my call and said Dave hadn't been enrolled. I hung up, not really reacting to the news. Two minutes later, she called back. She'd started looking through a stack of packets and found one for Dave, saying the paperwork had been dropped off on Friday. On the way home from mediation, Sophia had done it behind my back. I gave Michelle credit for "calling it" hours ahead of it happening, like she was Nostradamus.

It wasn't until that week that I belatedly realized something: If I lost the jurisdiction fight and a custody trial played out in Virginia, I didn't just lose access to the Kindercastle witnesses in Maryland. I lost my attorneys, who weren't barred in Virginia. A success by Sophia would be a masterstroke.

CHAPTER TWENTY-TWO

I'll See You in Court

For over a year, Sophia had been saying I couldn't handle being a father, but that week, Dave developed pneumonia, a life-threatening illness. And yet she agreed I would keep him all week so he didn't give it to Anna. I purposely had the discussion via text message for evidence. Judges love a good contradiction. My jerk boss wouldn't let me work from home to watch him, so I had to use vacation. I looked forward to quitting, my job search continuing.

The pneumonia caused another issue – I had to be in court in Rockville Maryland at 10am on Friday and not only was Dave not well enough to go, but Michelle was very clear that bringing a child to court looks bad to a judge. It is also disruptive, depending on how well-behaved they are. She wanted me at the courthouse by 9:30 or their offices by 9:10 to ride over in their minivan together.

I called my sister-in-law's parents, who lived forty minutes away, and they agreed to watch Dave for four hours. But then they repeatedly got lost on the way and were so late that I had to bring Dave with me, scrambling to dress him, pack supplies, and warn Michelle. She suggested they watch him in the courthouse waiting room, so they finally met me there, very apologetic. I was sweating in a suit, flustered, and hoping this was the worst of my day. I wasn't in the mood to hold a grudge and let it go. I suddenly felt very tired. Sophia might have been on the verge of dismissing my custody case, eliminating my witnesses and lawyers.

The Rockville Courthouse was quite large and had different areas for different case types. In the waiting area I'd found Sophia, Anna, and Nina, plus the attorneys. With Dave and I also there, all the players stood together for an awkward moment, lawyers seeing the kids whose lives they were helping to ruin or save, depending on your point of view. Sophia's attorney was a petite blonde woman who I learned was not the one pulling the strings, but a junior lawyer like one of mine. I never did see her real attorney.

While I was getting Dave situated (he was happy to see Anna and hang out with her), Michelle went into the courtroom and soon returned to pull me aside. We still had a few minutes before the 10am time slot.

"The judge wants to stay the case before even hearing it."

"What does that mean?"

"It means he won't make a decision today and will just postpone the case for four weeks."

I stifled annoyance. All the bullshit I went through to get there this morning only for nothing to happen? "Why? And why four weeks?"

"He can't do anything about custody for Anna because he has no jurisdiction over her, so he wants to delay until our Virginia court date in three weeks, when we try to get Virginia to decline jurisdiction. This is good news, really."

"How so?"

"It means he's refusing to dismiss our case today like Sophia wants. It also strongly suggests he believes it should be here and he therefore doesn't want to decline the case like she's asking, but he needs us to get Sophia's case dismissed in three weeks."

I almost smiled but was too fatigued. I had seemingly won this court date, or at least delayed it, before it even started. "Good point. So what now?"

"In theory, we can all leave, but I told them I want to make some oral arguments anyway."

"Why? To say what?" I watched Dave making faces to Anna and smiled about how great a brother he already was.

"To get some things on the record and to get a feel for what the judge is thinking."

"Why does it matter?"

"Because it becomes part of the record and he intends to speak with the Virginia judge, and our arguments today would be part of the official record. We'd basically be saying things to both this judge and the other one."

"He's going to talk to the Virginia judge before the Virginia court date?" I had sudden hopes of Sophia's motions being dismissed without ever setting foot in a courtroom.

"Yes. They do this sometimes and can reach an agreement without any of us going to court at all. He actually meant to do it before today but ran out of time."

On hearing this, I first felt encouraged and then annoyed with that last bit. The whole thing could've been over today, and with a strong possibility of it in my favor. "All right. Let's put on the record what you want to say."

We went into the courtroom, Sophia and her attorney already there, but we had to wait a long time because it's a cattle call. Dozens of people had the same time and the law clerk would ask for those with quick business, under a minute or two, to go first. Those who needed more time, like us, were forced to sit through other people's cases. That would not have been so bad if you weren't paying your attorney almost $500 an hour for the privilege. That's some prime impatience right there.

When it was our turn, only Michelle and the judge spoke, and he said several important things. He thought Maryland was the right jurisdiction and that all assets were in the state, and that the majority of time had been spent there. He said that it looked like Sophia had manipulated the system, that it was "planned and plotted," and that the tongue-tie issue was the only reason Anna hadn't spent any nights in Maryland, causing him to have no jurisdiction over her. He concluded by saying he'd take the case, not dismiss it, as soon as Virginia waived jurisdiction over Anna, and there was no discussion regarding what he'd do if they did not, suggesting he expected it. This was the second time in a week that an impartial expert in family law agreed with me. I walked out feeling pretty good about it.

I did some back and forth with Michelle and my financial advisor, Joe, because I needed money from my 401k. I learned from him what I could get, and from her, what I was allowed to do. Until the divorce was over, my 401k belonged partly to Sophia as much as hers did to me. Joe revealed I could take a chunk of money without paying a penalty, which was steep if I took the rest. But first we leveraged my life insurance policies for a loan of over $25k, which would cut my legal debt in half but reduce my death benefit by that much. I did some math on the house and became a little worried about affording it alone due to the legal bills and the job I was trying to leave; they were underpaying me by at least $10,000, another reason to go. They had served a purpose of quickly getting a job, and one near the house, after my last client unceremoniously pulled the plug.

By July, Sophia was still resisting treatment for Anna's tongue-tie, but now Kris, the feeding specialist, and I were in cahoots. I purposely arrived early to appointments, which had been occurring at Kris's large, elegant house in NoVA for months. This was a 15-minute drive for Sophia and 40-minutes for me, and yet Sophia still kept cancelling and I always took time out from work, having to burn more vacation hours. I had an attitude about work and it was only getting bigger. It was the third job in a row where they knew I was going through a nasty divorce and custody battle and they were being obnoxious anyway.

At the next appointment, Kris and I spoke alone before Sophia arrived with Anna and Nina. A room by the kitchen served as her home office, with a desk and tables along the walls, cabinets of toys, and an open area in the middle with a small, easily moveable table and chairs. The room was a bit messy as one might expect from little kids spending time in it. We typically sat facing each other in the center, Anna on one parent's lap, the other assisting with spare spoons, cups, drinks, and snacks for Anna to try while Kris observed, but now she and I sat alone so we could talk freely about Sophia's antics. Kris was sharp and I suspected she knew I purposely arrived early to do this very thing.

"I'm concerned about Anna's progression," Kris admitted, not surprising me.

"So am I and I'm pretty sure it's on purpose."

Kris barely stifled exasperation. I had sensed for some time that she fully agreed with me. "I'm sorry."

I nodded to recognize that but said, "It's not *your* fault."

"I understand the situation you're in. It's so frustrating. I have three or four babies who've all had their tongue-ties fixed and they're doing so well that they aren't even seeing me anymore."

"Things may improve soon because custody will be decided in a few weeks, including legal custody. The best thing that could happen is me getting to make decisions because I'll have her tongue fixed within a week."

"That's great. I hope it works out."

I got the impression she didn't want me to get too far into details so she wasn't in the middle of it. I didn't blame her, so I changed the subject. "Have you talked with the pediatrician about any of this?"

"All the time. Off the record, we're both really frustrated with Sophia."

I knew she wasn't supposed to say that and appreciated her candor, which was the reason I came early now. "I know you're keeping good notes. Please continue to do so. I will likely need them in court later."

She nodded. "I've been involved in a number of custody cases, unfortunately, so I'm familiar."

"Did you ever talk to the ENT? The one that Sophia used for a second opinion?" I had given her the guy's information when she'd expressed surprise at Sophia's account of what he'd said.

She perked up. "Yes, and she has mischaracterized what he said about the recommendation not to have Anna's tongue fixed."

I smirked. "There's a surprise."

The doorbell rang, it was Sophia, and we immediately got down to business as Nina moved to the living room across the house from us, sitting on the leather couches, the rest of us in the office, sitting on our respective folding chairs, Anna in my lap.

"So how is the cup feeding going?" Kris asked Sophia, meaning giving Anna a little bit of milk from a cup. Most often, we used a half empty teaspoon. Her difficulty controlling the liquid risked it going down "the wrong pipe."

"I haven't been doing it," Sophia admitted as if reluctantly.

Visibly startled, Kris politely said, "It's very important to help her learn to swallow milk from something other than a breast."

"I know," Sophia said with her "whatever" vibe.

"When was the last time?" I asked, tone hard.

"It's probably been a month."

The sheer negligence startled the glare off my face.

Trying to be polite, Kris said, "It really needs to be every day."

I said, "I will be sure to do it when I'm there from now on, but that's only three times a week. Better than nothing."

"Can I see the food diary?" Kris asked. Sophia was supposed to be writing down every solid food Anna tried, how often, and how successful she was with it.

Sophia at least looked sheepish. "I haven't been doing it."

Exasperated, I pointed out, "She asked you to start that a *month* ago."

"I know."

"You seriously haven't written down a single thing?"

"Do I really need to repeat myself?" she asked. I felt like smacking her.

Anna could now eat some solids if small enough, but we were trying to expand her abilities. Kris had supplied a list of food items to try, but when asked, Sophia admitted she wasn't attempting any of them. Not once.

Irritated, I asked, "Why not?"

"I'm too busy."

"With what?"

"Work."

"You only work forty hours a week like the rest of us. There's no excuse for after work, before it, or the weekends. And what's Nina's excuse? The whole reason she's here is taking care of Anna. Is she too busy, too, or are you instructing her not to do these things?"

As usual, she dodged a pointed question and Kris settled for going over the previously given instructions, emphasizing the need to follow through. She knew it was pointless, as I did, and when I left, I exchanged a knowing look with her. Her testimony about Sophia's refusal would be invaluable toward establishing that I needed legal custody. Sophia had denied me any decision-making ability through exclusive physical custody. But maybe this was about to change.

On July 19th, 2017, two days before Anna's first birthday, I met my Virginia attorney, Caroline, at her firm's offices. She was tall, middle-aged, and wore a black business suit with light makeup, her straight blonde hair to her shoulders. In one hand, she carried a satchel that seemed loaded down, perhaps with law books in addition to notepads that every attorney I saw seemed to have. She seemed business-like yet approachable, confident, and in-command of herself. Nothing about her gave me pause that the fate of my kids rested in her hands, aside from having no idea how well Michelle had prepared her, but I trusted Michelle's competency.

We piled into a law firm car and were driven to the nearby courthouse. I had spoken to Caroline once on the phone, trusting Michelle to bring her up to speed. The time had come to see if my petition to dismiss Sophia's custody case would work. The main argument was that Virginia was an "inconvenient forum," which meant that virtually every asset and witness was in another jurisdiction, but Virginia had exclusive jurisdiction over some elements (in this case, Anna) and needed to relinquish it. That would allow the case to proceed in the other locality, which had jurisdiction over other elements, some also exclusively. One state had to give it up. Maryland had already refused to do so, and that judge still hadn't made the phone call to the Virginia judge for a backdoor agreement that would've saved me a small fortune in money and stress.

So there I was, once again sitting in a packed, much larger room of attorneys and their clients, listening as easier and shorter cases went first and we waited. And waited. And waited. Caroline had told me our assigned judge was a good one, but he hadn't shown up. His replacement didn't know how to manage the courtroom so that multiple attorneys lied that they only need five minutes and then took twenty or more. Lawyer after lawyer around us quietly complained to each other. After an hour of this nonsense, Caroline and Sophia's attorney agreed to slip a note to the bailiff. We had another hearing scheduled for that afternoon. I honestly don't remember what this was for, partly because it never happened. But our lawyers asked if the other judge could hear our case if he ran out of other ones on his docket. The bailiff said maybe, but by lunchtime, this became yes.

We left the courtroom to return to the T-shaped lobby, at the intersection. Straight ahead was a waiting area where Nina watched Anna; Dave was at pre-school. To the right, all the way at the end, waited the other courtroom. As we waited outside it, our new judge reviewing our filed paperwork inside, I overheard our attorneys talking about the judge we'd just escaped. He apparently didn't know much about family law. I might have just dodged a bullet, a clueless judge making a fateful decision about custody.

Fifteen minutes later, we entered the small room with its paneled walls, with only the judge, a bailiff, and another court person present. Caroline and I took the two seats and table to the left, Sophia and hers went right. The clean-shaven judge had a full head of black hair streaked with grey and appeared distinguished, fit, and no nonsense. After getting settled, he wasted no time.

"We'll take thirty minutes, so I'm giving you each twelve minutes, and the last few minutes I'll wrap it up. Mr. Zinn, you are first."

My attorney did all the talking at the podium, highlighting and reiterating that most evidence was in Maryland, and the issues with key witnesses who could not be subpoenaed. She parroted some of my observations, made to

Michelle, including that the attempt at making Virginia seem like the real jurisdiction was an elaborate sham, and that Sophia should not be rewarded for the manipulations. The characterization of me was a caricature. She backed up everything with what details time afforded us, as we were mostly summarizing our court papers. I thought she did amazingly well considering she was a kind of stand-in.

When Sophia's attorney spoke, she tried to say the relevant witnesses were Sophia's friends in Virginia, but as we'd preemptively observed, none were barred by an employer from testifying in Maryland. They claimed the other witnesses like a pediatrician were there, too, but we'd already pointed out how many more such professionals were in Maryland. We had destroyed their talking points before they raised them in person. When she was done, the judge responded.

"It's been about four months since I handled a jurisdiction case," he admitted, "so I want to take a fifteen-minute recess to review the applicable documentation."

Then he left, as did Sophia and her attorney, who went to the lobby. I stayed in the room with mine.

I'd scrutinized the judge's neutral face during arguments for any sign of his thoughts, but he betrayed nothing. Not a frown. Not a brow raised. Not a pursed lip. He remained unreadable. *I hate this guy*, I'd thought in frustration, not meaning it.

The judge would return with a verdict on jurisdiction, one that would effectively decide custody. The mediator had predicted it. Michelle agreed. So did I and Caroline. This was it. There would be no trial, no accusations, no defending. There would be no three days of witnesses, testimony by us, or evidence. Due to the timing of Dave's fifth birthday in two weeks and subsequent entry to kindergarten in six weeks, it all came down to jurisdiction. Whoever won today got Dave M-F for the coming school year, and control of the situation. The loser would have to move states to ever reach 50-50 with him again; someone was about to lose that by summer's end. And whatever state he went to school in, Anna should, too, once old enough. I felt surprisingly relaxed, given the stakes, but logic strongly suggested I would win. I consciously refused to consider the alternative, not ready for failure.

More was at stake than custody. We had arrived at this place due to constant deceit of every kind from Sophia. There was all the malice, contempt, and cunning. The victimization of both myself and Anna, an infant. The angelification and exoneration of herself. Twisting and slithering logic, lack of accountability, and missing responsibility. The demonization, badmouthing and bullying of me. The gathering of accomplices, each a willing and ignorant toady, amorally supporting her against me while believing themselves to be virtuous heroes. A reversal of abuser and victim. No ethics, morality, or justice. If she won with such tactics, it repudiated all standards of decency. A loss for me would be psychological, philosophical, and spiritual, a world-view shattering trifecta of heart-destroying betrayal of everything that matters to me.

This was no exaggeration. For a year and almost seven full months, this array of evil from Sophia had been my entire world, and this was the moment of literal truth. Did she earn evil things with evil tactics, or did I earn good things with good tactics? Would honor, integrity, and truth matter, or was it all worthless in the face of all that can be wrong with humanity? It was a genuine battle of good versus evil, the fate of two young children at stake even more than my right to see them. If I lost, how could I continue to try being a fair, honest, and decent person, when she destroyed everything I loved this way? I couldn't bear it, in my dark moments, consumed by despair that I faced utter destruction. If she won, every moment in my childless, empty house, their unused toys neatly put away instead of happily discarded wherever they'd left them, would be a reminder that none of my values mattered.

And yet I faced oblivion quietly, patiently. I was experienced now, and had been long before meeting Sophia, this hardly being the first awful situation in a life full of them. I had prevailed over most if not all others. It's not that I was overconfident in the outcome, only that the worst possibility was too awful to consider most of the time, and I wasn't doing it now. I have the ability to block things out and I sat there for fifteen minutes using it more earnestly than ever before.

Suddenly the bailiff announced the judge's return and we all took our places. I reluctantly glanced at Sophia, whose face seemed more mask-like than usual, as if sobered up. We had yet to exchange a word in person about going through a divorce aside from her once yelling without provocation that she didn't want to be married to me anymore. For all her feigned calmness, ferocious anger lurked beneath the surface. I couldn't consider the possibility that the judge was about to make her happy. I waited as he entered and sat, still adjusting his robes and turning his chair into position as he opened his mouth and immediately blurted out the verdict.

CHAPTER TWENTY-THREE

Negotiations

The judge said, "Well, I've had a chance to review the necessary notes and am ready to render a decision." He exchanged a nod with a court reporter. "Based on the 14 years of marriage happening in Maryland..."

And it was all I could do not to leap out of my seat. I knew how this sentence was going to end. It wouldn't make sense to say that and then conclude that Virginia was retaining jurisdiction. Sudden elation soared within me as I listened to the rest of his rational, expecting and finally hearing the most glorious words I'd ever heard in my life.

"...and the first four years of Dave's life happening in Maryland, the divorce happening in Maryland, most of Dave's schooling being in Maryland, and there being a three-day trial scheduled in Maryland next January and we can't even do one day trial here in Virginia until next May, Virginia is declining the jurisdiction on this case on the grounds that it is an inconvenient forum. The Virginia case is hereby dismissed."

He struck the gavel and I gave way to an eye-watering grin.

I won! I fucking won! Yes! You bitch! You and all your lies can go fuck yourselves! Twelve months to plan this shit.

Twelve minutes for me to defeat it! Ha! Fuck you! I fucking won!

The judge said something about the attorneys needing to write up his decision together and then sign it before turning it into the court for him to sign, but I was hardly listening. He finally left the room and my attorney turned to me.

"Congratulations," said Caroline to me, smiling.

I beamed at her. "Thank you. You were wonderful. Great job."

"It was my pleasure. You can step outside if you want. Her attorney and I have to draw up some papers. This will take ten to fifteen minutes."

"Sounds good. I'll come back in a bit."

I now loved the judge. He was awesome.

I left the room, not bothering to look at Sophia or caring if she noticed my grin. Once in the lobby, I started walking away and realized I was strutting. My first instinct was to stop myself, but then I thought, *Fuck it. Let it ride.* I strutted my way all the way back to where Anna sat in her stroller, grinning hugely.

"Guess who's coming to live with daddy!" I said, putting my arms out, but she looked ready to fall asleep. I kissed her forehead and walked away to call my mother, telling her the news, noticing that Sophia sat outside the courtroom texting someone, probably Alexa or Cindy. I wished both had been there so I could tell them to fuck off.

"It was all so well-deserved."

I had virtually guaranteed myself some custody of Anna, and Dave during school. If Sophia didn't agree to school in my state, I'd file an emergency motion in Maryland to let the judge decide, and he'd almost certainly choose my state. To celebrate, I got a massage, used my hot tub, ordered some sushi for dinner, and opened a bottle of wine once home. I had won.

When I was alone, I kept saying "I win!" all the time over the next several months, always with a tone of delighted, smug self-satisfaction. In the shower. "I win!" Driving. "I win!" Shopping. "I win!" Taking a walk. "I win!" Brushing my teeth. "I win!" Cooking. "I win!" Eating. "I win!" Going to the bathroom. "I win!" And every time, I would laugh. The joy and relief were deep.

Two days later, Anna turned one and had not spent a night in my home. It was now six months since she was supposed to be with me 50-50. Since Sophia's legal papers were filed, it had been obvious she withheld medical care for Anna's tongue-tie because it helped her jurisdiction claims. With Anna's tongue fixed, she wouldn't need breastfeeding, I would get overnights, and Sophia's thin jurisdiction case would begin to collapse as Maryland also acquired jurisdiction over Anna. The plan all along had been to deny me the 50-50 custody at six months, and when Sophia learned that Anna choked on bottle milk and that tongue-tie was the cause, she purposely didn't get her tongue fixed last summer, this January when I learned of it, or in the months since. She wouldn't even allow the barium swallow test because it would prove the procedure was needed. And she continued to cancel appointments with Kris and not cooperate with treatment. None of this was a coincidence. She was an evil, unfit mother.

Now that I'd won the jurisdiction fight, it became a moot point. Would she cooperate with Anna's treatment now? Probably not because she could still keep her from me.

Less than a week later, I attended the court appointed parenting class. Both female instructors were custody evaluators, and I was not alone in asking questions about this process. During a break, I approached one for more details. I explained the two locations, two kids, and the jurisdiction fight I had just won. Then I asked, "My attorney said custody evaluations can't cross state lines, so –"

"That's not true anymore," she interrupted. "As long as it's within twenty-five miles."

"Her apartment is in Fairfax."

"That should be within range, but we would double-check."

I would do it the second we stopped talking (it was true). "That's great. That would mean not hiring a private evaluator."

"Oh yeah, that's very expensive and this would be free."

"You're making my day."

She chuckled. "We'd go to both residences for an hour each, to see what they're like, but also to see how that parent's relationship with the children are. We'd also spend an hour with the kids here in a room we have set up, no parents, just one-on-one with us and the child. We'd probably only do your son, due to age."

"Makes sense. Do you also talk to other people like neighbors, pediatricians, teachers at pre-school? His old nanny?"

"All of them, depending on what is being alleged. We try to get as full a picture as possible."

"That's great."

Sophia was going down in flames.

They would catch her lying and might penalize her for that, according to Michelle. Sometimes the penalty was a fine, but sometimes the judge gave less custody and rights. In some cases, the person lied about (that would be me) was awarded damages for the cost of defending against the deceit. I liked that idea very much. It costs far less to make false accusations than it does to prepare to defend yourself against them. I suspected Sophia was trying to make me incur as much legal debt as possible so that the only way I could get out of it was to sell the house for the cash, only to have her suggest with feigned innocence that, since I was moving anyway, that I just move to Virginia.

I asked, "What is the end result of the evaluation?"

"We put everything into a report, which is read to the court at the settlement date."

I knew that was scheduled for October. The likely timeline was that we filed the emergency order in the next week, and the Maryland judge ruled that Dave attended kindergarten with me. Then the evaluation would happen. Then we'd have the settlement date, with the evaluators almost certainly recommending Dave stay with me.

Regarding Anna, Michelle had told me the court cannot order a medical procedure, but they *can* order parents to follow medical recommendations, and that would put Sophia in the hot seat to both get Anna's tongue fixed and cooperate with Kris, who had now agreed to testify.

Sophia was going down in flames.

Even if a judge told her to cooperate, she would not, getting herself into real trouble. I might end up with more custody of both kids. I felt good. The momentum had shifted to me.

"I win!"

I continued separating entanglements from Sophia, removing her from accounts at Netflix, Sam's Club, and more. I got new bank accounts rather than trying to remove her from joint ones I would just close. I moved automatic payments to my accounts and cancelled her access to any credit cards of mine without telling her. Sophia continued refusing to return my car. Michelle said it would make me look good and Sophia bad to a judge amid other examples of me sacrificing and Sophia refusing to.

A week after my victorious court date, Sophia made an offer via her attorney. She agreed to move to Maryland within a year and to equal legal custody with a moderator who would make decisions when we could not agree. Then came the bullshit. She suggested Dave be at school in Virginia so he'd be there weekdays, that Anna be breastfed until two years old so that I had no custody of her for an additional year, and that I not get 50-50 with Anna until she turned four, in another three years, and three-and-a-half years after I was supposed to already have that! I was flabbergasted.

Wait. Didn't I win the jurisdiction fight? How lopsided would this offer be if I had lost?

She had balls.

She also stated that Dave wasn't ready for kindergarten and should go to a Montessori school instead (this lasts for years), and lo and behold, there was one right down the street from her! How fortuitous! A sign from God! It begged the question – if he wasn't ready for kindergarten, then why did she enroll him in one in Virginia behind my back in June? Because she'd adopt any position that might get her what she wanted, even if it contradicted a position she'd just taken. The U.S.S. Intellectual Honesty has sailed, sunk, become a reef, and was now a popular dive location. Sophia knew a Maryland judge was about to force Dave to school with me and this was the latest attempt at getting my agreement with her, using bullshit, as if this had worked even once so far. But that was one of the things about her. She just kept repeating something on the theory that it had to work sooner or later. "Relentless" is my go-to description for her.

I shot this down and she responded by suggesting that Dave not start school at all. I talked to the Kindercastle principle, who said they'd already assessed him, he'd passed, and they would immediately test him again if necessary. I considered this a significant stab at my son, who is intelligent and would go on to do very well in grade school, such as reading *above* grade level. Being left back was considered humiliating when I was growing up and I doubt it has changed. His friends would find out in college due to his age not matching up with theirs. Sooner or later, mockery would come, creating emotions that are...wait for it...negative!

This was a preemptive strike against my son so that she could keep custody at 50-50 or even gain more. Her rationale appeared to be that being exposed to negative emotions (that only I experience) is so damaging that any price my son had to pay to avoid it was worth it (that includes being kidnapped). I intended to use this suggestion against her in court to prove that she was an unfit mother with very serious judgment problems that warranted her having zero legal custody. If it were up to her, Dave would have never seen me again, been left back, and been medicated into a zombie to make his emotions easier to control. She had already withheld medical treatment from Anna. This woman was a danger to the well-being of my children.

Within days of this, we began a text conversation she started.

Sophia: You weren't paid into our joint account?

Randy: No. Moved that and house bills to mine. Trying to pay CC debt due in Jan. 0% APR expires

S: We don't have money.

R: You do.

I knew her direct deposits had dropped by $400 a paycheck for a long time. By my calculations, she'd stolen $7000 while asking me almost every month if she could pay down $3000-$5000 on her cards.

S: I'm paying off my own. And that money is our safety net.

R: It's really yours.

S: Yes but now that you know about it, it's ours.

So I caught her admitting to the theft. It reminded me to be careful. She sent another message.

S: I want to do this without lawyers.
R: Then stop being ridiculous. Just move to MD.
S: I can't. Anna needs to be fed at lunchtime.
R: Then let her tongue be fixed.
S: It's not a tongue issue now but a preference for breastfeeding. The ENT said she'd adjust by two years.

So that explained why she wanted to keep Anna another year. Did she think the ENT's suggestion was a mandate for non-interference?

R: Are you doing the food log?
S: Yes.
R: Good. Because you know it won't look good that you aren't following doctor's orders.
S: No doctor has told me to do either the tongue-tie fix or swallow study, so I'm technically not disobeying.

I shook my head. I wasn't sure what Kris's actual degree was, but she was a professional who, at the least, was licensed to do what she did. And the VA pediatrician said to do what Kris recommended. And Kris said have Anna's tongue fixed. Sophia was saying that, because the pediatrician said, "Do what Kris recommends," instead of "Have Anna's tongue fix," that this somehow wasn't an official recommendation and she was therefore not failing to follow a doctor's orders. I doubted a judge would accept this logic. Sophia had become a certified piece of work.

R: I suggest seeing another ENT now. And you should allow the swallow study.

S: Okay. I can agree to those after Anna's one-year appointment.

That was overdue and I expected her to weasel out of any agreement. She sent another text.

S: If Dave went to school in MD, would you agree to let me nurse Anna until 2?

I could get Dave through a judge. I didn't need her agreement.

R: Maybe. I want nights with Anna.

S: You could do that in MD if I stay overnight.

R: No. It undoes grounds for divorce.

S: We can do a quick uncontested divorce. Or you can just have an affair.

I snorted. Or she could just admit to hers. It's not every day your wife suggests you cheat on her. Was now a bad time to ask where the love had gone? I knew an affair was grounds for divorce if proven, one that eliminates a waiting period. But I decided to dodge the outrageous suggestion.

R: Why would you need to stay overnight?

S: You don't want to deal with a crying baby.

R: Did it before. And don't tell me what I want.

S: You can't handle it.

R: Look, knock that shit off. Lie to your friends all you want, but stop insulting me with that. I'm not stupid and my memory isn't as screwed up as yours apparently is.

S: Well I don't think you can.

R: I wasn't asking your opinion. And you were the biggest source of my upset. Still are BTW. But with you out of my life, I'm way calmer!

S: You're scary when mad. Dave gets scared.

R: Stop projecting your shit onto him. Dave wanting my approval is the reason he gets upset. It doesn't mean I'm doing something wrong.

S: You could be better. The way you act might give him the impression you will abandon him.

Eureka!

I heard her father's abandonment of her in this. Is that what she thought happened? Had her father been a hothead, then left for good? Was this another piece of the puzzle? Maybe his impact on her had left a deep impression internalized by age three when he left. Did she feel responsible? Is that why she couldn't accept that she'd upset me? Because it might mean I would leave, too?

And yet, ironically, by refusing to acknowledge my upset, she just repeated the upsetting behaviors, driving me away, and pulling away herself. She never asked why I was divorcing her. Did she assume my emotions were it, that her long held fears had come true, that another person who had loved her was abandoning her over his emotions? What she could never understand was that it was her behavior – the actions, the words – that ended us for me. She was the one who left the relationship – and over emotions.

She didn't know why I'd filed for divorce. Did she have any idea that her violating the verbal agreement led to me protecting my access to my kids? Probably not. That required accepting that behavior has consequences. There was no point in asking her what she thought. I couldn't trust anything she said. What was the point of interacting with her? And yet here we were, having a text conversation that seemed to be getting somewhere. As if reading my thoughts, she sent me another text.

S: We just weren't meant to work out.

R: Don't agree. You could've fixed a lot by doing your share or accepting that I wanted changes.

S: This is true. But you needed help understanding that your emotions affect me.

Wow, she admitted to something. But I disagreed with her comment about me.

R: You never said this. You attacked me instead.

S: Yes, I handled it poorly. I know that now. It always turned into an argument.

R: Your timing had a lot to do with it. And you were too focused on yourself.

S: I made a mistake in trying to change you, but I felt like you didn't care about my needs or how I felt.

R: You weren't asking me to. You were attacking me. When I'm upset, I'm not going to care about someone else's needs, especially when they aren't brought up.

S: I didn't communicate my needs well. That's my failure.

Hearing her accept some responsibility made me hate her less. It's amazing how a little honesty can heal wounds, and how dishonesty makes them fester until something dies. I'd just heard more admissions and apologies in a few minutes than I had in the fifteen years with her.

Days later, I was at her apartment, the kids asleep, as we briefly talked in person for once, about Kris's recommendations. She made outrageous claims that Kris was biased and wasn't a real doctor, Sophia therefore didn't have to do anything Kris recommended, and this didn't amount to not following a doctor's orders. I didn't respond before leaving. The door had barely shut behind me when I began texting Kris, saying we needed to talk, as we did the next day, when I told her these things.

Kris sounded exasperated as she replied, "That explains a lot."

"Doesn't it? She's claiming that the pediatrician said to follow your recommendations but did not say to have Anna's tongue fixed. *You* said that. This is the dumbest splitting of hairs I've ever heard."

She sighed and I could tell she was trying to be polite and professional. "I honestly don't know what to say about that."

"I'll say it for you. It's bullshit. It would be great if you could explain this stupid distinction to the pediatrician and have her explicitly say to Sophia to have Anna's tongue fixed, and put it in writing."

"Sure. Good idea."

"I think it's time to discharge Anna from you working with her, but it's not because of you."

"Sophia has no confidence in me, I can tell."

"Don't take it personally. It has nothing to do with you. I think you've been great."

"Thank you. To be honest, there's really nothing more I can do because Sophia isn't cooperating, but I feel like I'd be giving up on Anna to not work with her anymore."

"I know, but I have a plan. What I'd like you to do is discharge Anna with your records of what has happened and why she's being discharged. You know, it's not because she's doing fine."

"Right."

"What I'll do next is find another feeding specialist, we'll go to him or her, and Sophia will repeat all the same bullshit. This will establish a pattern that will help ruin her credibility about all of this."

"Ah. I see where you're going with this. I'm so sorry that you have to deal with all of this. I feel really bad for Anna."

"So do I, but this is the best thing you can do for her now. Also, I think it's time to officially ask you if you'd be willing to testify in court, not for me or against Sophia, but just to the truth of what you've seen, including who shows up at appointments and who cancels them."

"I keep detailed records so it's all in there, and I'd be happy to testify. I'm just sorry that it will come to that."

Things were happening quickly now that I'd won jurisdiction. Sophia and I exchanged multiple offers back and forth via attorneys, though some of hers were bullshit and we shot them down. She finally agreed that I would have Dave weekdays and he'd go to school in Maryland, a huge victory. This meant that, if I could afford it, I'd be keeping the house and she'd ultimately be returning to Maryland. The attempt at forcing me to Virginia on her terms had failed. I would drop Dave off at her apartment Friday night or Saturday around lunch, this alternating every week. She would get holidays except for Thanksgiving and Christmas, which we'd alternate every year.

My attorney said her strong opinion from talking with Sophia's lawyer was that the attorney had no idea we were even seeing Kris. This was both startling and not surprising. I had suspected Sophia was feeding a quite warped version of reality to everyone (because she believed it), and this was doing her legal team a disservice. But now she agreed to use a "parent coordinator," which meant that for legal custody, if we couldn't agree on something, this neutral third party would become involved, talk to medical professionals and others involved, and make a decision for us. This person would presumably be immune to Sophia's bullshit and side with me, so this was great. I had no doubt Sophia expected it to work in her favor.

But we were still at an impasse over Anna. Sophia claimed that if I drove our daughter home from her apartment, Anna would be traumatized alone in the back of the car. She was concerned about emotional damage. Sigh.

When we saw the Virginia pediatrician that week, Dr. Hutchens saw firsthand Sophia's obsession with this. She was in her 60s, a bit short, and slender, her long, straight grey hair as un-styled as the rest of her. She came off as utterly devoid of pretension and artifice, perhaps too much so. No makeup, jewelry, or attempt to present herself. I pictured her walking barefoot on a rural farm more than someone with a doctorate degree and working in a major metropolitan area. She seemed a little out of place and you might've been forgiven for being surprised at the mental sharpness that belied her appearance.

We stood in a typical pediatrician's exam room, Nina sitting down with Anna on her lap, me leaning against the exam table with its plush, blue top. Just outside the window, I could see our cars below.

"I think it's important to find out if any aspiration is occurring," Dr. Hutchens said, meaning liquid getting into the lungs.

"So do I," I said.

"I'd rather wait and see," Sophia disagreed.

Dr. Hutchens said, "We need to find out what's going on and not guess. She can develop chronic lung problems that can be very serious. The barium swallow test will clear this up." This test worked by having Anna drink a liquid that would show up on an x-ray so you could see if it went into the lungs or not.

"She won't like the taste of it," Sophia protested.

"So what?" I asked, fed up.

"The x-ray is also harmful."

"X-rays are completely safe," said Dr. Hutchens. "There is no reason to be concerned about this."

"Well, she won't like being in a strange room, with all these strangers there, and having a strange food in her mouth."

"Are you being serious right now?" I asked rhetorically, because I knew she was.

Dr. Hutchens said, "None of that will prevent the test from working. We'll still see where the liquid goes."

Sophia said, "Being under stress is not how she normally is when swallowing so I don't think it would be a valid test."

"Stress does not change the swallow mechanism," said Dr. Hutchens.

"I still don't like it."

Trying to not be snide, I asked, "Well then why don't we just skip the test and go right to having her tongue-tie fixed?"

Dr. Hutchens said, "I do think this needs to be done, but since Sophia is hesitant, the test will prove whether it is needed and is a good next step."

That's exactly why she's refusing it, I thought. I may have been on the verge of getting custody of Dave, but it wouldn't stop Sophia from keeping Anna away from me. "I just want to be clear that you are recommending the tongue-tie procedure occur, right?"

"Yes."

"Can you put that in writing?"

"Of course." Dr. Hutchens smiled slightly. I'd already told her about the divorce and custody issues. I always had to be the one to tell people because Sophia wouldn't, and they needed to know extra elements were at play, namely a divorce, two states, two kids, and a custody dispute that Anna's health was right in the middle of.

"I don't want her going under anesthesia for that," said Sophia.

"It's very safe," said Dr. Hutchens, "and they aren't deeply under anesthesia either, though her tongue-tie is anterior."

"Meaning what?" I asked.

"It's farther back and that does mean it's harder to reach. The local hospital is literally world class at performing this procedure and I have no reservations about it at all. But let's do the swallow study and verify if it's needed." She needed to write up an official recommendation for the hospital so we could schedule an appointment. "Before we finish today, I'd like to do a quick test of her eyes," said Dr. Hutchens, before explaining why and that the test involved a brief flash of light into the eyes. Sophia argued with both of us for five minutes about how traumatizing this would be.

"It's not painful," the pediatrician said. "I promise you. Countless kids have this test and never cry."

"It's not physical pain that I'm worried about," Sophia said.

I rolled my eyes. "Would you stop? This is ridiculous."

"Well, I don't want her to get scared."

"It's not gonna kill her."

"It may traumatize her."

"It's a flash of light! She'll get over it. Doc, I'm authorizing the test, so let's do it."

So we did, and when the light flashed, Anna looked startled for a moment, and that was all. The pediatrician needed to give her two shots and I expected another argument, but Sophia made no objection, despite knowing it would hurt. I later asked about this inconsistency and she admitted that she would've preferred no shots but recognized the importance of immunizations. There were apparently limits to her insanity. I kept thinking there are parents who want to wrap their kids in bubble wrap so they never get physically hurt. Sophia wanted the same for our children's emotions, projecting her fragility onto them. Did she have a phobia?

Dr. Hutchens said that Anna was supposed to be standing unsupported and even walking by now but could not, yet another developmental milestone missed while in Sophia's exclusive care. She recommended we see a physical therapist about this. Naturally, Sophia would not make the appointment and since I had no custody, even if I made one, I couldn't take her without Sophia's cooperation. I suspected much of what Sophia did was about power. I intended to use all of this in court because it seemed negligent at best, maybe even a kind of child abuse.

Negotiations continued. Michelle believed Sophia's attorneys had told her she'd lose the emergency hearing and to get as many concessions as possible now. Sophia started texting me directly to negotiate. I hadn't filed for the hearing due to making progress, but I was threatening to if they didn't budge ASAP. Due to Anna's tongue, months would pass before I could have her anyway, and I did agree that Anna would not instantly go 50-50, but gradually, one night a week for a month, then two nights, and finally to 50-50. Then she said she'd sign the custody agreement that day if I agreed to another condition, which told me how important it was to her, but I told her no.

Randy: I do not like this condition of you moving to MD, and within a 20-minute commute of here, before the transition to 50-50 starts.

Sophia: It's not that bad. I can sign an 8-month lease now and move in April. Anna likely won't be able to take a bottle until nearly then anyway.

I grudgingly admitted to myself that this was true. I was pushing for one overnight with Anna starting in January, but Sophia had pushed it backed in one of our exchanges with attorneys.

R: Is the lease the reason you pushed 1 night back to April?

S: Yes. I can do a 12-month, 8-month, or 1-month, which is what I'm doing now but it's too expensive.

R: I still don't like the condition and see no reason for it.

I said the same to Michelle, who convinced me to take the deal because I was getting most of what I wanted, and a few more months without Anna wasn't worth no deal and an expensive three-day trial in January, with no certainty of the outcome. We were trying to end the whole custody question, not just pressure them to avoid the emergency about where Dave attended school. She had a point and I could end this right now, mostly victorious.

"What I don't like," I began to Michelle on the phone, "is that she can refuse to move, and then I don't get Anna at all."

"Let's put it in there that you get one night each week starting in April, and two nights starting in May, and this happens whether she moves or not."

"Okay. And it stays that way until she moves, and then both go to 50-50."

"Yes. She will move, trust me. If she doesn't, she seldom sees Dave, but that would also mean the kids are separated almost all the time, except the weekends and one visit of Anna at your place midweek. As a mother, I can tell you no mother is going to do that to her kids for long."

"Don't take this the wrong way, but I'm now wondering if you've been paying attention."

CHAPTER TWENTY-FOUR

One Problem Down...

Within days, in August, we had a signed term sheet for physical custody. This specified most of the details on parenting and would be incorporated into the official parenting agreement filed with the court. Several items were cancelled, including a deposition of Kris, the filing for an emergency hearing, the custody evaluation that had been scheduled, another court date in October, and the three-day trial in January. I also emailed the Virginia elementary school and told them Dave wasn't going there after all; I enjoyed that. I really did. I took care of everything he needed for grade school, including supplies, remaining paperwork, and a play date at school to make new friends.

I did some math and learned that the jurisdiction fight alone had cost me at least $10,000, not including several thousand on the fake mediation. Sophia's attorneys had probably told her it was worth a shot. Yeah, when you make a fortune on us, sure.

While all of this was going on, Dave had two birthday parties, one with Sophia's friends and their kids, and which I did not attend, and one at my house with several pre-school friends and their dads. One of them worked at

NASA, where I had just taken a job, having given my two weeks' notice to the employer a few minutes from my house. My salary was corrected and went up by $20,000. I was having a good August, and Dave and I went to the county fair several times. I was thrilled to know he'd be with me weekdays and part of every other Saturday until April, when I would lose time with him but gain time with Anna after Sophia moved to Maryland and both kids went to 50-50.

"I win."

And so did my kids. The first great victory of their lives had just happened and they didn't know it. I took Dave to Kindercastle every morning, and they bussed him over to grade school, then picked him up later, and I got him a few hours later. It worked out well. He got plenty of play time with friends and had adjusted well to everything with my help. Nina still lived with Sophia as a live-in nanny and hadn't seen her husband in a year and a half.

After fifteen months, Sophia finally leased a minivan and returned my SUV. I temporarily kept her sportscar in the driveway until selling it, since the other half of the garage was full of boxes of her crap, and which she refused to take. Her stalling tactics still plagued my life. She had agreed in a signed legal document to immediately choose three parent coordinators, instead of waiting until January like she'd wanted. I was to pick one from that list, but the months dragged on with only excuses because she was, in effect, going for January anyway. This was her style. Push for something, not get it, get a concession out of me in exchange for agreeing to what I wanted, then going for what she wanted anyway so that she got it *and* what I'd conceded. Even legally binding agreements were not to be honored. My attorney implied there wasn't much we could do other than taking her to court, which would be expensive, and so we were letting her get away with it. I was back to loathing Sophia, not that I had ever really stopped.

She had tried to limit the coordinator's ability to resolve conflicts, so that she could create stalemates that defaulted to no action (that would get her what she wanted), but I'd refused until talking with Michelle, who thought I could use it to get sole legal custody.

"What do you mean?" I asked over the phone.

Michelle replied, "We already know she refuses to cooperate with anything, so what I foresee is you bringing an issue to the coordinator, who will make a recommendation, and since it isn't binding and Sophia doesn't want to do it, she won't. Once this happens at least three times, we can then bring this before the judge and lobby for sole legal custody."

"Would it work?"

"Yes, because it shows good faith on our part and bad faith on hers, and that she's just preventing all progress. We'd be showing that it's not working out due to stonewalling."

I sighed. "Part of me doesn't like it, but I see your point."

"Either way, you get what you want. Either she cooperates before the coordinator gets involved, or she doesn't and you get a coordinator's recommendation that will almost certainly align with what you want, because Sophia is consistently ridiculous and her positions are not well-founded. And either Sophia follows that recommendation so that you get what you want. Or she doesn't and fails enough times, and we get you sole custody."

"Can't we use past incidents of non-cooperation?"

"We could, but they don't carry much weight. It would be far better this way because this person will have actual authority that Sophia will defy anyway."

I sighed again, wanting to get on with Anna's improvement. "Okay. I get it. Let's do it."

It seemed like every last stunt Sophia pulled was about control and refusal to be fair, but maybe it was my turn to set a trap. She deserved it.

Sophia finally chose three parent coordinators from which I chose Beth, for the usual reasons I selected someone – her mind was attentive, she didn't need everything spelled out for her, she sensed where I was "going" with something, and she quickly provided insight that was informed, smart, and on point. She appeared to "get it" when I discussed Sophia's emotional issues on a brief call before I decided on her. We'd first meet her in January, just like Sophia had wanted.

The first intended subject was Anna's treatment, but it became a moot point days before meeting Beth. Anna finally drank a 4 oz. bottle from my hand without issue. She had learned to compensate, but I was uncharacteristically shortsighted due to ignorance. Anna had achieved my goal, which meant I would indeed get partial custody starting in April, this no longer threatened. I was thrilled. But compensating is not ideal and could cause other issues with speech, muscle problems, and damage to teeth roots, and so I should have continued my push for intervention. But I did not, unaware. Sophia had so far refused to accept a replacement for Kris, to improve Anna's abilities with food or liquids, but this also appeared to be another agenda item suddenly tabled.

A third issue was Sophia's continued refusal to get physical therapy for Anna so she could learn to walk. The pediatrician had explicitly recommended this and written paperwork referrals, so this time Sophia was indeed refusing the doctor's direct orders, not for the first time. But, around this time, Anna could finally stand on her own and was starting to walk.

Anna's inability there had not impacted my ability to have custody, and yet Sophia had still done nothing. Did she just not care? Was the laziness behind everything, and not, as I had suspected, about keeping Anna to herself? No, I think they mutually reinforced each other. If you had a job where success required someone to do absolutely nothing, Sophia was perfect for it. Sophia took the fact that Anna had eventually reached these milestones as proof that her non-interventionist attitude was the right choice, the fact that they were significantly delayed be damned. Anna also started to talk a little, once again behind schedule. Suddenly there was no urgency to meet Beth.

But we met her anyway to have an initial conversation. I arrived at Beth's Bethesda home very early due to an unexpected lack of traffic, and as I waited in my car, Sophia sent a text telling me she'd been laid off from her job. I started laughing. And laughing. And laughing. That job was the reason for the entire jurisdiction fight and constant bullshit trying to make me move to Virginia. She'd acted like she was so damn important as a Vice President and now they ditched her. I couldn't stop laughing. It seemed like everything was going my way.

But she was nothing if not what Michelle called "a difficult bitch," a startling but accurate comment from a professional family law attorney. Sophia refused to admit when this happened and said she wasn't filing for unemployment benefits because her boss asked her not to and gave her six weeks of severance as incentive. Employers pay unemployment insurance to the state so that, when it's their fault that they let you go, their premiums may rise. Her employer had run out of money, financing her business personally. And her product, that Sophia was partly in charge of, had failed to sell. I enjoyed her being unemployed going into a financial settlement, especially since she'd tried to make me sound in court papers like I was deadbeat. Really, I couldn't stop laughing.

In the week leading up to this, she had refused to provide financial statements when I had, saying she was moving money around. Now I knew why. What was she up to? Trying to hide money? Almost certainly. I suggested she get a job in Maryland, rubbing it in with plausible deniability, but she didn't know where her next job would be and implied it would be farther away in Virginia. If that happened, I would eventually take Anna away from her on the grounds that Dave was fine in school and the kids should be together. I enjoyed my momentum and leverage.

The initial meeting with Beth happened in her home's front living room, its wide windows casting light on typical furniture in a somewhat "busy" room – a plethora of objects gave the eye something to look at besides the conversationalists. Magazines, books, figurines, pictures, keepsakes and more. So far, each therapist's home I'd been to was similar. Was it coincidence or were they purposely helping people evade eye contact?

Beth was an unremarkable middle-aged woman, straight brown hair streaked with grey, average height and build, and dressed in tan slacks and a solid-color turtleneck, a few rings and bracelets visible. She evaluated children as well, but that was done in the basement, which we briefly visited, an array of toys cluttering the room. After introductions and covering Anna's recent changes, the first subject was Sophia's impending move in April 2018. It was now two years after the drama had started with the comment about never kissing me again.

The meeting was uneventful but included an admission that Beth could testify in court. I intended to get Sophia to say stupid things in front of her. We could also meet individually with Beth if desired. The cost was $250 per session, split between us. It was only now that Sophia learned

I'd switched jobs four months earlier; she withheld information so relentlessly that I'd decided to give her a taste of her own medicine. It wasn't important anyway, but she hypocritically acted like I always did this sort of thing and used it as justification to continue refusing to admit when she'd lost her job, framing these as equivalents when I hadn't been unemployed, a key difference.

She repeatedly refused requests to supply a letter from her former employer about termination, making me ask through my attorneys to hers. This cost money, unnecessarily. The letter mattered because the children were on her insurance, which was ending in a week. I needed proof of this "qualifying event" before I could put the kids on my insurance. She was preventing this, risking them having no health insurance.

Sophia also refused to supply discovery documents that had been due a whopping *nine months* earlier, my attorneys now planning to go after her in court to make a judge force her to comply and to also pay my costs of trying to force her. Michelle had asked four times, in writing, and was including these requests in the paperwork. All of it was mounting proof of no cooperation that might get me sole legal custody. But damn it was aggravating. And unnecessarily expensive. Being married to someone financially irresponsible is bad, but divorcing them is far worse.

The threat of additional legal action finally produced ninety pages of documents, plus a demand for me to produce various items. Some were outrageous, like copies of all hard drive contents from all of my computers, which would've included my diary. Michelle told me not to worry because such overreach couldn't be compelled and was standard tactics, though we hadn't employed them.

Of particular offense was my copyrights. While married, I had released multiple albums, all paid for with marital funds. I had also published a handful of fiction and non-fiction books. Michelle said that they could be considered marital property and that Sophia was entitled to perpetual royalties from my work. I was incensed because I was the one who did everything on them, and after a few years, she had refused to even listen to an album or read a book. And now she would profit from my work? It perfectly represented a fact of our marriage, one I felt deep resentment for – I did all the work and she still profited from my labor. In researching this, I learned that she could even be entitled to ownership share of work I created at zero expense and did not release, just because I'd invented it while married. I told Michelle to find a way to kill this. I didn't care how she did it. I didn't want to discuss it, I was so angry.

Fortunately, my lackluster careers as an author and musician finally paid off. Yay for me. I seldom sold a CD anymore, having retired in 2014. Even before that, I never recouped album expenses. With books, I had gotten nowhere with one genre, had only a book I gave away for free in my fantasy career, and had just released two non-fiction books in a series. The frustration with lack of progress was a thorn in my side, but now I laughed that my failure could get Sophia to relinquish the financial claims as not worth it.

With books, I had seldom made $200 a month, before expenses, but I'd just made $700 over the holidays. However, vendors like Amazon pay up to three months late and the deposits weren't on the bank statements I was now required to supply 18 months of. I knew the money was coming but I wasn't required to get a "coming royalties" statement. I was due to get the deposit any day and hurriedly supplied the statements right before the next one would've shown the sudden change in profit. She never found out that I began making more than $1000 a month, which would've seemed more worthwhile to insist on getting half of. She would ultimately relinquish all claims and never get a penny of the tens of thousands I would make.

Buried in her credit card statements were two transactions that startled me. One was for an online dating site for single parents while the other was a more generic dating site. The timing of both charges was the shocker – six months after moving out, giving birth, and stopping her psychotherapy for emotional problems, including diagnosed depression. The charges were early 2017, right when I was supposed to start getting custody of Anna. What made her think she was ready for another relationship? Was her self-denial and lack of awareness really that off-kilter? Even worse, she had still been acting like we were getting back together to my face, though I'd known better. I couldn't help imagining this conversation between her and a dinner date over drinks...

"So what's your situation?" he asked, cutting his steak.

"Well," she began calmly, "I'm still married. Separated, but whatever. I left my husband." She smiled obscenely, a glass of wine in one hand.

"Oh. Uh, how long ago?"

"Six months. Right before giving birth to my daughter."

"Ah. Okay. Really? Wow. That's tough." He stopped cutting.

"Not really. He had it coming. I would've done it sooner, but he wouldn't give up the kids."

"Well, you know, being a parent is important."

"Nah. I mean, my dad abandoned me when I was three, and I turned out fine."

"Okay." He looked at the food, then toward the door.

"It's better if the kids never see their dad again."

"Sure." Eyes darted to his own wine glass.

"I never wanted to have kids, but whatever."

"Oh. Okay. I mean, I like being a parent." He smiled.

"Why? It's all work. No payoff really."

"Okay." The smile fell.

"I mean I was in therapy when all of this happened, but it was fine. I stopped going after giving birth and then my therapist retired. What are ya gonna do?"

"Um. Okay."

"My husband was emotionally abusing me. The kids, too."

"Um." Someone else exited the restaurant and he watched mournfully as they went.

"Yeah, so I had to leave him. But everything is great now."

"So you have the kids?"

"Sort of. But my mom lives with me now, so she can help."

"Oh."

"So, I think I need a refill. Good wine, huh? You're buying, right?"

"Um. Sure." He looked at his watch.

"Waitress!" she bellowed, holding aloft her empty glass. "Fill 'er up!"

I scheduled a one-on-one meeting with Beth and told Sophia about it, as we were supposed to. We were even required to give the other a list of the topics intended to be discussed, and then afterward, what was actually discussed. But to my amazement, Beth informed me that Sophia had met with her the day before and I hadn't known. Sometimes I wondered why I was still shocked, however briefly. As a result, I refused to tell Sophia about my meetings with Beth. Two could play that game.

I gave Beth an earful about Sophia's lack of cooperation, producing documents that backed me up. She agreed with me, not Sophia, about what was best for the kids. But the big revelation was that Sophia's apartment lease was not expiring in April, but in August, meaning she wasn't moving until then, at least. While I would still get Anna one night starting in April, and two nights starting in May,

50-50 custody of both kids had just been postponed. I would still have Dave M-F. At a meeting with all three of us a week later, I brought it up.

"Yes, my lease doesn't expire until August," Sophia admitted when asked.

I said, "You were supposed to sign an eight-month lease that expires in April."

"No, it was August. You must have misheard me."

"Stop gaslighting me. I'm not stupid and I didn't mishear it. You moving in April is the entire reason that I'm getting Anna at one night starting in April and not January like I wanted. Stop lying."

"Well, the months start with the same letter. You must've gotten confused. I never had any intention of moving in April."

Snidely, I snapped, "Finally an honest remark! Should I call the newspapers?"

"I was always going to sign a twelve-month lease. The eight-month one was too expensive."

"Like you've ever cared about money. Now you're going to tell me that I misheard eight for twelve. What's the rationale going to be? That they're both divisible by four and that somehow made me mistake one number for the other?"

Beth failed to suppress a smile.

Sophia said, "You're being rude."

I threw her own favorite response back at her. "Whatever. This was discussed in August. An eight-month lease is April. Why did you sign a twelve-month lease?"

"I didn't. I signed a ten-month lease."

"What? Wait a minute. You told me last year that the only options were one month, eight, and twelve."

"I never said that."

Smoke probably should have come out of my ears. "I'm so *sick* of you lying to me and gaslighting me. And you're not making any sense. A ten-month lease signed in August would expire this June, not August."

"I signed the lease in October, so ten months is August."

I threw up my hands in disbelief. "Why the hell did you wait two months to sign whatever freaking lease term?"

"I didn't get around to it."

"Wow, two honest comments in the same conversation. Why am I only finding out about this, what, five months later?"

"Because I knew you'd react emotionally and cause a scene."

"*I'm* causing a scene? When are you going to get it through your head that lying and gaslighting is upsetting to other people?"

"I'm not lying or gaslighting."

"So then what do you call withholding information?"

"I call it none of your business."

Not getting up and walking out took an effort. Me being deprived of more custody of my daughter was none of my business? Her gall was stunning. "Beth, this is exactly what I'm talking about. She withholds information this important and then acts like I'm unreasonable for being suspicious of her."

Beth nodded. "Let's all take a moment here. Sophia, he is right. You really need to be more forthcoming regardless of what reaction you fear. It has already become apparent to me that what is upsetting to Randy is being kept in the dark."

"*Exactly*," I couldn't help adding. To Sophia, I said, "You know, your instincts are completely backward and you'll never figure it out, even with me telling you. You hide things and I get upset that you did so, but you ignore that and assume I'm upset with the information, rather than the hiding of it, so you just keep hiding the information. We're stuck in this repeating loop because you don't tell me things and can't hear what I tell *you*."

Still not getting it, Sophia said, "I'm telling you about it now."

"It's too late! Five months later is way beyond not good enough. And I found out from *her*, not you. You fessing up when confronted with it doesn't count."

"Well, if it doesn't count, then why admit to it at all? It's not like I'm benefiting from the admission."

"Jesus. You really *don't* get it, do you? You're causing the very negative emotions that you claim to be too sensitive to deal with and want to avoid." I had to stop myself from telling her she was hopeless, which I only restrained myself from saying because Beth was there and could testify about it. Fortunately, she was getting a good look at Sophia's lack of cooperation. Sole legal custody, here I come.

Beth interrupted. "Why don't we talk about the move itself. Sophia has indicated she doesn't want to move twice, first to another apartment, and then to a house."

"Why would she need to?" I asked. "She could just move from the apartment straight to a house."

Beth answered for her, and I was fine with that. There was a reason I avoided talking directly to my wife. "To afford a down payment on a mortgage, she'd need the equity from you selling the house, which must happen sooner than is likely for her to have the money."

I sighed in annoyance. This was probably true. "It's not difficult to move a half empty apartment to another one."

"It's still a lot of work," Sophia said, adding with a smile, "and you know I'm not a fan of that."

An attempt at self-deprecating humor. The miracles would never cease. "The problem here is that I can't refinance until the divorce is final." I suddenly realized I would have to do it immediately to get her to move, whereas I'd been thinking to wait up to the full three years that I could ask a judge to grant me.

"I'm doing you a favor really," Sophia began, "because you can't handle two kids."

I shot her a nasty look. "I would stop right there if I were you. First, you're the one who is so incapable of handling it that you have a 24/7 live-in nanny in the form of your mother. Secondly, stop insulting me. And don't you *dare* act like keeping my daughter from me is you doing me a *favor*." God I hated her. For a woman who claimed she wanted me to never experience a negative emotion again (because I'd express it), she was remarkably good at causing them.

We didn't get much farther, but a week later, we reached several agreements. Sophia decided to move in August when I agreed to let Nina watch Anna for the next two years, even when Anna was in my house. This would mean my soon-to-be ex-mother-in-law living in my home. You can imagine I wasn't thrilled, but it was at least free daycare for Anna aside from room and board, which wasn't much. Nina didn't seem to eat much.

One reason for the sudden progress was that Sophia had two job offers, one at her old employer, further away in Virginia, and another in Silver Spring, Maryland for more money. On learning of this, I said the choice was obvious, and while she agreed, she wouldn't commit until trying to extract some concessions from me, the deal about Nina being one of them.

The more irritating surprise was about Anna. Sophia wanted to move back, by one month, me starting to get custody. Instead of April, she now wanted May.

"What the hell for?" I asked.

"Because it will be harder for me to go back and forth. The agreement says I need to keep bringing Anna Tuesday and Thursday, but if I work in Maryland, then after work I have to cross the bridge to Virginia, get Anna, then bring her back over the bridge to visit, and then go home again later. It's a little much. I'm asking if I can bring Anna up to visit just on Wednesday instead, for now."

Always reasonable, I had to admit she had a point. The traffic in the D.C. area was consistently the second or worst in the nation. But I didn't really care what hardship she endured. Not after everything she put me through. "I might agree if I get an additional visit with Anna on Sunday to compensate, but what does that have to do with pushing back custody a month?"

She responded with a series of comments about a new job being stressful, time consuming, and all of this some-how impacting Anna, who was now able to stay home in-stead of being dragged to work, because Sophia was breast pumping and Nina fed her at home. I was unimpressed with the excuses, especially given that she'd dragged Anna to her job for forty hours a week until she was a year and a half old. Sophia hadn't seemed to think this was stressful to our daughter. As usual, she adopted whatever line of logic which would get her what she wanted, consistency be damned.

Some of this discussion happened on the phone and centered on the idea of her emotionally coddling Anna, which of course led to a conversation about emotions. She admitted to having handled the subject poorly all these years only to do so again, remarking, "I think I learned a lot about emotional abuse over the last 15 years."

"Don't ever say something like that to me again," I snapped. The passive aggressive remark infuriated me. She knew nothing of abuse. She was never letting this attack on my emotions go.

I refused to move back the start of my custody of Anna until I had an idea. Dave was supposed to be 50-50 custody during the summer, unlike his M-F with me during school, but I was looking into summer camps and not liking trying to split him between states. It was too pricey to do a partial week in MD, and another partial week in VA, to which Sophia had suggested we alternate weeks. I didn't like it, partly because Sophia never planned anything and I would have to plan his camps in two states, but get her to agree and cooperate on paperwork and other bullshit.

Instead, I suggested that I keep Dave M-F for the rest of the summer until she moved, in exchange for pushing back Anna's start of custody with me by one month. Besides, she'd be busy packing and apartment shopping and it would be easier without him in the way. She agreed to this and to not tell our lawyers (to save money), but I wrote it up in an email, sent it, and she acknowledged it and returned the email. While I wasn't happy about yet another delay on Anna, I got six more weeks of time with Dave, and he was ultimately more important at that age due to all the things we did together. I was able to schedule his entire summer with no more than agreements from Sophia while I, as always, took care of everything.

Of course, because of this arrangement, Sophia had now agreed to move to Maryland in August. It was still a delay from April, but sometimes you have to let shit go. I was nearing the completion of my victory over her.

Around this time, my cat Minx became terminally ill and I spent weeks trying to give her medicine. Ultimately, I had to put her to sleep and explain to a sad Dave what happened. It was probably for the best, as she had been getting sick in random places in the house, leaving a nasty mess that a toddler could get into. Though I'd had cats most of my life, I decided to go without until Anna was older. The house seemed emptier now. I was truly alone when the kids were their mother.

Figure 10 The Cat

But I enjoyed the solitude. In those quiet moments, I looked forward to a new life without Sophia upsetting me. Her chances to do so in my house were mostly eliminated. Once the divorce was over, the rest would vanish, or so I hoped. But I soon had reason to worry about whether I'd be able to keep the house at all.

CHAPTER TWENTY-FIVE

A Sleep Over

As financial settlement progressed, I became unhappy with the direction it was taking because it seemed like Sophia was getting away with theft. The way she'd reduced her direct deposit amount had stuck me with some payments we were both liable for, and some debt existed before she moved out. To my surprise, even my attorneys were saying to forget about it. Michelle also revealed that she had been forced to repeatedly go after them and issue four different subpoenas (at a cost of $15,000) to get financial records they had refused to give us, despite being legally required to do so; I felt Sophia should reimburse me. Sophia now claimed she had no severance, so we were also tracking down this hidden cash, at more expense to me. I felt certain all of it was Sophia's ploy to force me (and our son) to lose the house by raising my legal fees so high that I couldn't pay my legal debts and the mortgage, and on learning I had to sell the house, she'd sweetly observe that since I had to buy a new house anyway, I might as well do so in Virginia.

Michelle said a judge may refuse to settle the debt, but she had a plan for getting me a lump sum in cash without specifying exactly which outrages it was for. Alimony was out because we'd made too similar a salary for too long, but Sophia would be paying me child support. She also had to give me tens of thousands from her retirement accounts because I had both raided mine for cash and stopped contributing, but she had done neither and they were no longer similar in balance.

By April, we did a financial mediation with a retired judge who wasn't much help, but we made progress, agreeing we'd keep our own cars (and my motorcycle), I'd keep my businesses and copyrights, and we would split childcare costs. We decided on the retirement redistribution amount to me. All house property would be mine except a few items. They refused to pay for the expensive jurisdiction fight, Michelle thinking a judge might side with us about that if we went to trial. They agreed to reveal attorney's fees, so we showed them ours. Then they redacted theirs and gave us pages that were effectively blank.

Sophia pulled another maneuver. I had paid the mortgage for two years, not her. They agreed this part of equity belonged to me. I had also paid the taxes, but Sophia's name was on the mortgage, not mine, and she had the audacity to deduct the taxes I had paid from *her* tax return. I couldn't stop her. She pocketed $5000 of a tax refund that should have gone to me. She eventually agreed to give half of it back, which was still bullshit. They outrageously said I could keep her useless horse as a supposed concession to me. Were they *trying* to piss me off all the time? I suspected I knew why – "He thinks the horse is worth thousands, but it's worth nothing. Let's offer it to him!"

While we'd made progress, we had no agreement, which meant we could not avoid the existing court date the next day, when we learned the date for the divorce trial (as opposed to the custody one we'd avoided) – way out in October. An agreement would result in an uncontested divorce and have us done in weeks like I wanted.

We had Sophia served with a deposition to force the disclosure of financial documents withheld for a year now, again costing me more money. But if they had to do that deposition, it would cost her far more than me, adding pressure.

She and I argued about it all via text as I pointed out the expenses she'd caused, from the crazy apartment to the $12,000 spent on the horse and more. She said all of it was my fault for filing "stupid lawsuits." Were these stunts financial revenge? Did she expect me to stay married to her after everything she'd done? The comment implied she wasn't going to file for divorce or custody, ever.

I increasingly thought I was going to lose the house, a possibility I'd been worried about for years. A common piece of advice is to just sell the family home, use what funds you need to pay attorneys, and start over in a smaller, more modest home. But the idea upset me. A lot of "love" had gone into that house, by me anyway. Dave loved it, too. Both my savings and checking were empty. I could get no more cash from a 401k or in loans against my life insurance policies. And yet I still owed tens of thousands, not to the law firm, but to the credit cards I'd used to pay Michelle. Most debt was on 0% APR balance transfer offers that were expiring soon, so I needed cash.

But Sophia was refusing to let me have the 401k money she owed me in cash, insisting on just rolling it over to my 401k where I wouldn't be able to touch it until I retired. My financial advisor said it was better that way anyway because I could take more equity out of the house to pay my legal bills and the percentage rates made that a better option in the long run. But taking house equity raises your monthly payment because if you used to owe $300k on the house and take $50k out, you now owe $350k. I initially thought it would make me unable to afford the house, but I dodged a bullet. For a 30-year loan, let's say the payment was $2000. Now it would become $2700. But the old payment was actually $2600 because it had been a 20-year loan, not a 30-year. Relief washed over me. My payment would only go up by $100. I was keeping the house and would get out of financial trouble! I was thrilled! In May, Sophia agreed to a substantial cash payment to me that Michelle thought was good, even if less than I wanted, since no one gets that.

"I win!"

A few days before my birthday, Anna was to spend the first night in my house, at twenty-two months old instead of six. Sophia had pushed for twenty-four and virtually gotten it. Letting that go took effort. So did ignoring the digs Sophia made now, as she tried to tell me how to change a diaper (as if I hadn't done it thousands of times), insisted her mother should spend the night on the couch, and that she take Dave because I supposedly couldn't handle both kids (I'd never had the chance). None of these insulting remarks should have caused negative emotions, of course. I only let her take Dave because I felt he'd distract his sister and keep her awake; he'd been sleeping in my room where we would be. I asked Sophia to write down Anna's entire schedule, but she had to ask Nina to do it because she didn't know despite having 100% custody for 22 months. It spoke volumes.

With the house already baby-proofed, my only preparation was an inflatable bed. She wouldn't use a crib, though I had Dave's in my bedroom. I'd brought her to the room many times so it wouldn't be new and exciting the first sleepover night. Nina would take the couch and spare blankets I had. Sophia insisted on remaining in the house until Anna fell asleep.

I took my daughter upstairs and dimmed the lights. We got onto the mattress and for a moment she lay down beside me. I wasn't surprised when she climbed off and tried to walk past me, but I pulled her onto my stomach and rolled her back into place. She did it again, and so did I. She repeated it, but this time she made no attempt to get past. Instead, she looked at me expectantly. I laughed.

"Oh, we're playing a game, huh?" I obliged and it seemed I'd invented my first game with her, just like I'd so often done with my son. This third time, she didn't get off and settled in next to me, drifting off to sleep. I texted this to Sophia, who finally left with Dave.

As I lay there, I remained awake a long time, thinking about everything I'd gone through to reach this. My kids were adorable asleep, and I lay there grinning at Anna. She radiated sweetness that made even strangers smile on seeing her. By now, she had morphed into a cute little girl with full cheeks, warm brown eyes, and Sophia's square jaw. The skin that had seemed so dark at birth was actually white like both of us. She had thin, straight black hair, which Nina routinely butchered, cutting the bangs so high on her forehead that it looked ridiculous and led to arguments. I eventually demanded they never take scissors to her hair again as I took her to a hairstylist.

After I drifted off, she cuddled up beside me. Sometimes she sat up, put her back against me, and flung herself back onto me with arms wide, one hitting me in the crotch and the other my chin, as if luxuriating in laying on her dad. It was funny, sweet, and a relief. I had worried Anna's whole life that Sophia was doing permanent damage to our bond, likely on purpose. Sophia made herself fall out of love with me so she'd wouldn't be bothered by my emotions (didn't work), so it was plausible that if she kept Anna from loving me, Anna would be saved. Now Anna showed just how comfortable she was with me despite spending only 4 hours a week together before this. I'd see her much more now, and sleeping together like that was probably great for our bond. In the morning she was all big smiles, climbing on me. We didn't need the sunrise outside to start filling the room because we grinned like the sun at each other. I could finally be happy to have her with me, and we stayed in my room for a while because Resting Bitch Face Nina was lurking like an ogre downstairs, ready to disapprove of anything I did with my daughter.

As the weeks and sleepovers continued, Nina still on the couch overnight, I tried to create a bedtime routine with Anna to ease her transition to sleep. Since neither Sophia nor her mother would always be present, that routine obviously could not include them. The routine was simple – I would change Anna, bring her a warmed milk bottle upstairs alone, put her in the crib where she stood and drank it while watching a video on an iPad, and once finished, we'd lay down on the mattress. That's it.

Sophia, being psychologically and emotionally clueless, began interfering in this with help from Nina. On multiple occasions, they went upstairs and into my bedroom, causing Anna to cry when they left, which proved to Sophia that her presence was needed for comfort, so she wouldn't leave until I made her, which would cause Anna to cry, and Sophia to try to return, and cue the Chinese water torture. No explaining their mistake registered. Several times, I was warming up milk and suddenly they were taking Anna upstairs without me. They kept trying to give her the bottle instead of me. They also changed her before I could. Interference everywhere. It came to a head one night when Nina got Anna so upset that she puked. I laid into Sophia about it and they finally stopped. Maybe I should've thrown up on Sophia all those years.

Now that I had Anna overnights, a new problem arose the first time I returned her to Sophia's apartment and then tried to leave without her. When I started putting on my shoes, Anna came to put hers on, too, which was cute. I had to explain that she wasn't coming with me. She began to cry and so I took off my shoes and stayed longer. At some point, I tiptoed to the door and quietly left, but when the door shut behind me, I heard her high-pitched scream, which had happened before, so I asked Sophia about this.

"She always cries after you leave," Sophia admitted. "I think you need to sneak out."

"I did."

"I know, but you let the door make a noise."

"Fair enough."

"We need to distract her in another room, I think. She gets really upset and we have trouble calming her."

That's because you suck at comforting people, I thought. While I didn't want my daughter crying, part of me was pleased that she was attached enough to me to do so. "I guess the good part is that she loves me."

Sophia shrugged that off. "No, she just thinks you're fun."

I glared at her for telling me my daughter didn't love me and writing off the sign of that love as something else. "You're a real asshole sometimes, you know that?"

She looked startled. But I didn't see a dawning of realization.

This was how my escape routine began. It lasted from mid-2018 until early 2020. Every time I left Sophia's place, her, Nina, and Dave distracted Anna away from the door, with me present before I softly headed away once Anna wasn't looking. On went the shoes, maybe a jacket, and I left soundlessly, slowly pulling the door closed. Nina or Sophia would come and lock it. Sophia still seemed to think the kids were afraid of me, but if that was true, they would've cried when I showed up, not when I left.

Despite this, it sometimes didn't work and I remember many little scenes of my daughter screaming, tears flowing, as I was leaving. Of particular note was an instance many months later when Nina no longer stayed over and I brought Anna to the apartment alone. Nina met us in the parking garage, and Anna cried as she went away with her 24/5 live-in nanny. You'd expect her to be more attached to Nina than me, but she wasn't. This spoke volumes about the powerful, positive impact I had despite being afforded far less time. The kids could tell who had fantasized about their existence.

They continued doing well. Dave finished kindergarten and sometimes complained about going to his mother's on the weekend. He wanted to play with me and see neighborhood friends. I took the training wheels off his bike as we practiced in the empty tennis court next to the house, an activity I still remembered doing with my dad. Dave got it quickly and we began bike excursions. I did a school field trip for his kindergarten class and volunteered for their field day. I took him to the circus, county fair, a trampoline park, and finally bought a season pass to the nearby amusement park. By mid-June, he started the summer camps I'd arranged, and I had Anna overnight two days a week now, with Sophia initially refusing that this be two days in a row. Did she have to be difficult about everything? We were supposed to work out problems with help from Beth if needed, but we never returned to her.

At the end of June, we had a court date to finalize the divorce, a rubberstamping event, as with multiple agreements signed for custody and finances, this was now uncontested. I was sworn in at the plaintiff's table on the right while Sophia was not on the left because she wouldn't be saying anything. Michelle asked me a series of questions, none of which I was expecting except that I 'd just watched several other couples do this. She started with asking me to confirm where I lived, my age, and whether the signatures on the agreements were mine and Sophia's.

"And you were not coerced into signing this?" she asked.

"Correct."

"And you are waiving alimony and understand that you can never ask for it again?"

"Yes, and I understand."

"You were separated in July of 2016 and have not spent a night under the same roof since?"

"That is correct."

"And there is no hope of reconciliation?"

You could say *that* again. "Correct."

She then read off the names of the kids and asked whether the agreement satisfied everything.

"Yes, it does."

Now the middle-aged, brown-haired, female judge spoke up. "I understand the parties were married on October 12, 2001, that you've been separated more than a year, and the plaintiff has lived in Maryland for more than six months. All custody and financial matters have been resolved to mutual satisfaction. I am therefore approving this motion for an absolute divorce but holding the case open for the retirement account statements to be filed. This is fairly standard practice and does not mean that the divorce is not final."

And that was it. I was no longer married!

Despite the hugeness of this, it was almost a non-event by now, the drama over. I mostly felt relief about legal bills stopping and all the work causing them; this had dominated my life. I looked forward to having control over my finances again. The horse was off my books. There was no retainer going forward and I would just get a final bill. And I already had my plan for getting out of my legal debt and refinancing the house, for which I'd already gotten preapproved for a loan. To my surprise, my credit rating was doing well despite my debt.

I had made mistakes along the way, the biggest being the verbal custody agreement prior to separation. But it might not have mattered given Anna's tongue-tie preventing it anyway. However, legal custody would have been included and might have meant forcing cooperation with Kris and the tongue being fixed. Second guessing gets you nowhere and I was mostly pleased with the outcome.

Sophia's impact on my finances rankled. And I did blame her. The divorce did not have to be so expensive. All it takes is one to do it, and that was her. What I had wanted was fair. What she had wanted was lopsided, wrong, destructive, and based on deceit. Back in 1996, my music degree had caused tendonitis so severe that it disabled me, leaving me unemployed for a year and making $200-600 a *month* for two more years. I had climbed my way out to make six figures, own my consulting company, and live well. It wasn't quite rags to riches, and Sophia's only real contribution was her slightly smaller paycheck. But then she became a financial wrecking ball and I had been at risk of losing everything, including my home.

I had felt ganged up on by her friends, employers, lawyers, and therapists, a mob of enabling women who didn't know what they were helping her do. I'd beaten them all using the truth. Sophia's lies and manipulations had only delayed my inevitable custody of Anna, a goal of hers. My original goal was preserving my rights and I had done it, despite so much.

"I win."

It was "all so well-deserved."

As Michelle and I walked back to the law firm, we talked about how everything worked out.

"I feel like I pulled two come-from-behind victories," I admitted, "on custody and finances."

"I agree, though this is the logical conclusion. She really only had pregnancy going for her on custody and leveraging that into keeping Anna."

"What I don't really understand is why her attorney was willing to pull all this bullshit. I mean Sophia, I understand, because she's nuts, but shouldn't her attorney have put the brakes on it?"

"They may have been feeding off each other, the attorney trying to get the client what she wants, even if unrealistic. I've seen that before. What really bothers me is their lack of cooperation on discovery. I've never seen that. It was unprofessional, and I know her attorneys. They don't act like that."

There wasn't much I could say to that. Part of me hated all of them.

Now the only things left were refinancing the house, and Sophia moving, taking the rest of her stuff from the house and garage, returning some of mine, and the kids both going 50-50. All of this was cued up in August and I was glad that the bullshit was about to be over.

But then Sophia continued refusing to let me have the kids on the same nights, or Anna two nights in a row, meaning I had her an entire day. I had Dave five nights a week and Anna two so that I never had a night off. Every woman I said this to, from neighbors to my mother and friends, immediately said Sophia was trying to prevent me from dating. By contrast, Sophia had a live-in nanny she could leave Anna with while she went out. The biggest problem, to me, was that my kids were perpetually separated, and when I pointed this out, Sophia's blunt response angered me.

Sophia: So what?
Randy: Nice attitude. There is no justification for this, so we're switching so that I have them together.
S: You've never put Anna down for a nap and would need to if she's there all day.

R: Seriously? You think there's a difference between putting her to bed at night and in the afternoon? And I put Dave down for hundreds of naps. Knock it off.

S: You've never changed a poopy diaper with her, only one with pee.

R: Bullshit. And I have years of experience doing it with Dave.

S: Girls are different. You have to wipe away from the vagina.

R: Oh I see. It is true that I'm only capable of wiping in one direction. Something wrong with my arm. Might have to get it looked at by some doctors, maybe physical therapists. Maybe I'll get a bionic replacement and pay extra for the "wipes asses both directions" feature.

S: When you can change a diaper with poop in it, then we'll talk.

R: Who the hell do you think you are? You do not dictate to me when and if we'll discuss a subject about my kids. You do not make policy. You do not state conditions I must meet before you consent to a change. I agreed to start with them separate as a favor to you. Favor revoked. Another favor gone now is that your mother is now banned from my house. Fuck you. And get your shit out of MY house or I will put it on the curb for bulk pickup. You not having a place to put it is not my problem.

Her Majesty's attempt to unilaterally dismiss me like I was an annoying fly infuriated me.

My mother and neighbors thought I was being far too nice in allowing my ex-mother-in-law to stay over in my house while I had Anna, and I had agreed but hadn't seen much harm. But I was done. And while Sophia didn't respond to my outburst, I started having the kids together within days, and without Nina. Anna was now two, Dave six, and this was the first time. I enjoyed not having someone hovering and being judgmental about my parenting. That first night with both kids in my house overnight was something I'd waited a long time for, and I was supremely happy to do it, especially without my ex mother-in-law around. Sophia and her mother left, and for the first time, I had both of my children, unsupervised.

We played with blocks, making towers. We used giant Lego pieces to build other structures. We rolled around on the floor, laughing and tickling each other. We played "cars on the road," as Dave called it, pulling out a big mat with roads and buildings depicted on it, and driving various size cars around on it. I used a hand puppet to make them giggle as I pretended to take bites of their hands and feet. We went upstairs to my music studio and then banged around on the keyboard, making a racket. Anna played with my shakers, tambourine, and other noise makers. They took turns hitting my electronic drum set with sticks and sitting on the drum stool, both trying in vain to reach the foot pedals. I'd done all of this with Dave before, and some of it with Anna, but never together. It was time to ensure they knew how to play with each other, to form the bond that was us.

Dave wanted to sleep in my bed, like he did when it was just the two of us. He had mostly abandoned his room, possibly due to it being half furnished, since his mother had the rest of his bedroom set. But he also just loved to be with me. Now he lay there snoring quietly, Anna doing the same on the inflatable mattress by the window. I pulled up a chair, put my feet up on the bed's corner, and sipped a glass of wine in the dark, watching them, smiling, and thinking for an hour or two.

Figure 11 Anna's Sleeping Arrangement with Me

This was my family, the three of us. Sophia had always been the odd one out. Me and my kids would live our lives how we wanted. When telling Dave he'd get a sister, I had said this meant there would be another like him and I, and now we could finally be together, more than two years later. We would have fun together, laugh, cry, the whole bit, because we were whole human beings, not stunted, damaged people who needed therapy or medication. Now that Sophia wasn't breastfeeding, she had both.

"You guys will have the best life I can give you," I whispered to my sleeping kids. "We will have fun together, being silly, playing games, and goofing around. I will answer any question you have, teach you everything you want, make you glad to be alive and have someone who always listens to you. You deserve at least one parent like this and have one in me. I will see to it that you never forget it. We'll argue sometimes, get in a fight, be upset with each other, but we'll say we're sorry, we'll mean it, we'll make up, and we'll go back to having fun. You both already know what it is to be loved. You don't have to think about it. You just know it, take it for granted, and I wouldn't have it any other way. I promise you a lifetime of more of the same."

I drained my glass and joined Anna, grinning long after I fell asleep beside her, I'm sure.

For her second birthday, we didn't do much, but Dave had a party that included Sophia's friends Amanda and Kate. I reminded Sophia she was free to not invite Alexa because I never wanted to see her again, and she understood why because I told her I knew about the kidnapping suggestion. Let her wonder how I knew, but I knew. And Alexa didn't show. I haven't seen her since Anna was born. I no longer cared what her friends thought but didn't enjoy seeing them.

Just when it looked like everything with the divorce was wrapping up, Sophia refused to move.

CHAPTER TWENTY-SIX

What It's All About

Sophia's reason (this time) for not moving was that I hadn't refinanced the house and given her equity to use as a down payment. I reluctantly conceded that this was true and was working on it. I had told my loan officer, Kent, that I was going on vacation that August and would love to "close" on the refinance before I did. In one act, I would secure the house and get the money to pay all credit card debt, having only the loans against life insurance to worry about, but those were at 1%, effectively, and a low priority. I wanted it all behind me, turning vacation into a post-divorce relax-a-thon. He agreed.

Despite how it may seem, Sophia and I got along provided divorce and custody were not the subjects. This was true enough that we all went to Myrtle Beach for vacation the same week, staying in the same complex of hotels in a resort, swapping the kids as needed. The financial notary came to my house early on a Thursday morning to sign the papers, and my packed suitcases were right there beside us. After two and a half years of worrying about losing the house, I officially secured it. No sooner did the notary walk out than I threw my suitcases in the car and left for the beach. Sophia and the kids were already there a few days ahead of me.

I was elated and ready to have fun.

I hung out with the kids at the pool, sometimes on the beach. They reacted with excitement as I expected, because neither Nina or Sophia did much with them. I was definitely the fun parent. Sophia and I had been going there since before Dave was born and the hotel complex had changed a little, adding a splash park, where I now took Anna, who held onto my hand as I showed her ways to make it more fun, such as plugging a water hole and then letting go so it sprayed all over her. I took her into the lazy river, having her on my back or an inflatable tube as I pushed us around.

Dave joined us, pretending to race. He and I sometimes played alone if Sophia took our daughter back to her rooms, giving me and him some time to toss balls around while he jumped into the pool and tried to catch one before plunging in. He sometimes played with other kids, giving me time to enjoy a hot tub. When I was on my own, I played golf and otherwise relaxed. Dave had taken up golf with me and proven pretty good for a six-year-old, so we went golfing together, too. By agreement, Sophia went home before I did, leaving Dave with me for a few more days of guy time, golfing, putt-putt, a nearby amusement park, a boating trip, and general goofing around. By now I'd decided to grow a beard and liked the change.

Since Sophia hadn't moved by September, Dave remained with me weekdays for first grade and my time with Anna stayed at two overnights a week. This became status quo. Not having Anna more frustrated me, but our bond was strong. I privately conceded that life would've been harder and required expensive day care if I had her more. Dave greatly benefitted from doing things with me that might not have worked with Anna along, like golfing, biking, or amusement park visits. From birth, Anna had worn a serious expression, worrying me that she'd be as muted and expressionless as her mother or grandmother. But Dave and I now slowly got her to be like us, smiling, cheerful, and silly, traits that continued to grow more pronounced until taking over completely. I had saved Anna!

Figure 12 Scrunched Together

When I had them at my house, she insisted on squeezing herself between Dave and I on the couch so that we were shoulder-to-shoulder. I was on one end, Dave was in the middle, and Anna could've taken the far side next to Dave, but did this instead, always grinning up at me as if to say, "Ah. I'm right where I want to be!" After the fighting between my older brother and sister, I loved how well my kids got along, often hugging each other, Anna constantly imitating and following him. This was no coincidence.

Dave deserved some credit for being a wonderful brother, but I manipulated this with the love of forethought.

Anna's two-year checkup was two months behind. Only now did I learn she had been referred to a speech pathologist for significant speech delays two months earlier, but Sophia hadn't told me or made an appointment. I had thought divorce would free me from the staggering sloth. Sophia did finally get Anna speech help through the county, but only limited progress occurred.

The following June, Dave finished first grade and was still with me weekdays through the summers. And I still only had Anna two nights a week. Sophia's excuses for not moving were always bullshit, but there was nothing I could do. Arguments were short partly because Dave's time with me benefitted him and I wasn't looking forward to the loss of time together. My other objection was that I could not finish redoing some of the house until Sophia removed some furniture during her move.

But in October of 2019, Sophia put an offer on a house near me. Part of me didn't believe her and I remained suspicious until a moving truck showed up at my house. But she finally did it in January of 2020. I had ordered furniture for upstairs. Dave needed a new bedroom set once she took the rest of his old one. I gave the "white cherry" master bedroom set to Anna, so I ordered an all-black one for myself. I converted my music studio to Anna's room, moving studio gear to the master bedroom sitting area. I painted all three rooms and redid the curtains and hardware. Anna immediately loved her room. Dave hadn't slept in his in years but loved it and happily moved in (a miracle!). At long last, my house changes were done and every last piece of Sophia's stuff was gone.

In retrospect, Sophia's plan all along had been to keep Anna from me this long. At that failed mediation in 2017, she had offered me zero custody of Anna for two years and succeeded in getting to 22 months through lies. She had offered me 50-50 on Anna when she turned four, and now Anna was three years and nine months old and about to start 50-50. How had Sophia stolen the victory from me? The answer was Michelle, who as a mother had persuaded me that Sophia would not refuse to move because it would keep the kids apart, and no mother would do that to her kids, and I should therefore accept their addition of a condition – that 50-50 didn't happen until Sophia moved. Sophia had said she'd move in April 2018 but this wasn't in the agreement, and she never had any intention of doing it, and the condition was technically being satisfied. Michelle was a fool, and so was I.

Sophia had no honor and was far and away the most deceitful, manipulative person I had ever known. She was a relentless mover of the goal posts with a Chinese water torture-like drip of lies and empty promises meant to manipulate my expectations, emotions, and reactions, trying to wear me down into submission to her screwed up desires, illogical and ever-changing rationalizations, and hidden plans. Outright lies, sins of omissions, and gross mischaracterizations of the truth. Misdirection. Bait and switch. Empty promises. A storm of lies, all centered on the Original Lie – negative emotions aren't real. She was evil. And devious. Brilliant in her own disturbed way. The volume, depth, and breadth of deceit employed were no accident despite her lie that she hadn't told any lies. This was literally not believable. It is the equivalent of being a fish and somehow not knowing you live in water.

I let it go due to the benefits to my time with Dave, and the certainty that my daughter adored me. That March, both kids finally went to 50-50, me losing some time with Dave but gaining more with Anna. They were always together now, except when he was in school. They were closer than ever, following each other around, Anna imitating her older brother all the time. And I was finally able to say goodbye to my daughter instead of sneaking out; she stopped bursting into tears when I left. I surmised that she was finally getting enough of me.

The entire divorce was now over. Nothing remained pending. I was happy. So were the kids. Exchanging them was easier, just ten minutes one way. And I could use Sophia's driveway instead of hunt for parking. No more waiting in the heat or cold with a kid or two until she eventually let us in. So many irritating things ended.

Just when things were looking great, the coronavirus pandemic struck, causing widespread economic devastation starting in March 2020. I lost my job immediately and remained out of work up to the publication of this book. I had just climbed out of financial debt and began sinking into it again with no end in sight. Dave began virtual school through the rest of the year, all with me at first, but it otherwise didn't impact the kids or custody much.

Anna had received free speech therapy for a year in Virginia via the county but was still hard to understand due to the tongue-tie. She mostly said one or two words at a time, neither clearly. She struggled producing many sounds and was doing substitutions, like saying "bo" instead of "no" because the n sound was too hard. Some of this appeared to be related to the unfixed tongue-tie. I had told Sophia last October to begin arranging for county-led therapy in Maryland, as we'd stop qualifying in Virginia once she moved. She agreed, then didn't do it, lying repeatedly that she had and was waiting for a reply. Finally, in May, she confessed to never doing it. Incensed, I badgered her into telling me the name of the Maryland and Virginia locations, and within two hours, I had downloaded all the forms, filled them out, and returned them, sending one request for records to Anna's old VA pediatrician for needed records. While I was at it, I had her records transferred from there to the MD pediatrician, ending that era.

Dave hadn't learned a word of Russian in all this time, incidentally. This did not surprise me in the least.

By the time the Maryland location was ready to begin services for Anna, it was too late. It took weeks for them to get the records, virtually meet with us, and do their own IEP (Individualized Education Plan), and review it with us on the second to last day of school. While they sometimes did speech therapy over the summer, Anna was just advanced enough to not qualify and couldn't start until September. Sophia had cost Anna 6 months of speech therapy and she was now more than 25% behind where she was supposed to be.

In the wake of the delays on speech therapy, I called Kris, the old SLP. I wanted tips on helping Anna over the summer. As I worked on getting Anna to make certain sounds, I didn't know which would be easy or hard, or what milestones she needed to reach. Kris did a virtual evaluation, instantly picking up on Anna's issues and giving me ideas. Anna had a phonological process disorder where she substituted sounds she could make for ones she couldn't. Kris did this for free, partly because I'd lost my job, but she also wanted to help Anna and felt sympathy born of upset with Sophia's mothering, or lack thereof. At some point, talk turned to Sophia.

"Please don't tell her you're talking to me," pleaded Kris. I realized that she was afraid of Sophia, an ironic turnaround, as Sophia had said the kids were afraid of me.

"I wasn't going to," I said.

"She said the nastiest things to me. I was so upset. I've never had anyone do what she was doing. Some of it was said to me and the rest was said to Dr. Hutchens about me. We were both shocked. It was awful."

This didn't surprise me. Saying cruel things without conscience came with ignoring the negative emotions they cause. I wondered how many people were afraid of Sophia because she ignored the reactions she caused in them, meaning she'd just do it again, oblivious and unapologetic about her impact.

"I'm so sorry. Please know none of it was personal, even though it probably sounded that way. She was just trying to find excuses not to help Anna so I couldn't have custody."

"I know, I know. She admitted it at the first visit."

Shock. "She actually said it?"

"Yeah. I couldn't believe it. She said as long as Anna's tongue wasn't fixed, you couldn't have her."

"Wow." Now I wondered what would have happened if we'd gone to trial for custody. Kris almost certainly should have admitted to this if called as a witness.

In the fall when Anna started virtual pre-school and some speech therapy from the county, I felt it was inadequate and asked Kris to refer me to someone in my state. Instead, she helped us for free, evaluating Anna again and giving me a curriculum of sorts. I had always liked her and felt grateful for the help. Sophia continued to know nothing about it, by mutual agreement. I wanted Anna to communicate better than her mother, but it wasn't looking good for entirely different reasons.

Then in November I took the kids to a routine dentist appointment, Anna's first. The dentist saw Anna's severe tongue-tie and an upper lip-tie no one had mentioned but which I had wondered about. We discussed concerns, which he had about Dave, too, as he exhibited "tongue thrust" when swallowing and the pressure against his teeth was destroying the roots on the bottom front. The snipping of Dave's frenulum at birth had been with scissors, which offered a less deep and precise fix than the laser that was now an option for both kids without anesthesia, one of Sophia's big objections for Anna having the tongue fixed.

He referred me to a nearby SLP who evaluated both kids, strongly recommending Anna's tongue be fixed and that no amount of speech therapy would help until it was done. At long last, Sophia agreed to let it happen, but due to Covid-19, she wanted to delay until June when the world's population might have enough vaccinations to reduce the risk of catching the deadly coronavirus. Part of me agreed, but we had a tense negotiation and consultation with the dentist before she finally agreed to March at the latest. This was still in play as I finished writing this book.

With my increased time with Anna, I understood her better, though sometimes I honestly had no idea what she was saying. A sound like "cak co" turned out to be "popcorn," which I only learned when she took my hand and led me to it in the pantry. I immediately worked on getting her to first say "pa," then "pop," and finally "popco," but I couldn't get the "rn" sound at the end from her. She was consistently doing "consonant deletion," where the final sound is omitted. Usually she was closer, but she had developed her own way of saying many words. "Day" instead of "Dave," "yet" instead of "yes," and so on. She'd say "pay" instead of "play," so I realized the L sound was hard and began getting her to say "la," then "lay," then "low." After weeks of this, one day she just walked up to me and announced, "La!"

Anna cooperated well with these drills, for five minutes each time anyway, and I made her watch my mouth to see how I was making a sound. When I watched her attempt it, she really struggled to move any part of her mouth into the right position. Sometimes five seconds passed before she could do it, and the SLP said Anna's compensations for the tongue-tie and lip-tie were leading to muscle control problems in her mouth so that she would eventually have to relearn how to talk. It broke my heart. For entirely different reasons, I'd had speech problems for twenty years, starting when I was eight, and I didn't want my sweet daughter suffering the ridicule and isolation that I had endured. The thought destroyed me. I was determined to help her.

The V sound was another she couldn't make. One day, I sat on the floor beside her as she stood next to me. I went through the L sounds only to move on to "va," which she got after several tries, always grinning when she got it, partly because I was genuinely excited when she did and we'd high five or exchange a hug. I then attempted getting her to put "luh" and "va" together, only realizing as I did so that it was the word "love." I started to laugh.

"Hey, it's the word love! That's an important one."

She smiled and gave me a hug. "La you, daddy!"

And that's what it was all about.

About the Author

Randy Zinn is a proud father to a son (b. 2012) and daughter (b. 2016) and loves spending time with them when not writing memoirs, making music, playing golf, or lap swimming. Under another name, he's published non-fiction and fantasy stories with a literary bent, and released several albums of his music (hard rock and acoustic guitar). He holds a Bachelor of Music in classical guitar, Magna cum Laude, and has worked as a software developer/architect in the Washington D.C. area for over 20 years as an employee, contractor, or consultant through his own company.

He's also faced a variety of personal issues, including Attention Deficit Disorder, speech problems, sexual assaults, depression, suicide, bullying, being Learning Disabled, and a devastating injury, all of which he overcame. The tales in his memoirs cover them all and his dramatic, life-changing transformation.

Connect with me online

http://www.Randy-Zinn.com
https://www.facebook.com/pg/randyzinnauthor
http://bit.ly/ZinnAmazon

If you like this book, please help others enjoy it.

Lend it. Please share this book with others.

Recommend it. Please recommend it to friends, family, reader groups, and discussion boards

Review it. Please review the book at Goodreads and the vendor where you bought it.

JOIN THE RANDY ZINN NEWSLETTER!

Subscribers receive the latest updates, the chance to join the ARC Team, and bonus content like deleted scenes, short stories, private/color photos, and priority access to learn more from Rand about what interest you.

http://www.randy-zinn.com/newsletter

Randy Zinn Books

CPSIA information can be obtained
at www.ICGtesting.com
Printed in the USA
LVHW092048170321
681766LV00005B/91